DO YOU REMEMBER . . .

1. The series that ran for twenty years with the same dialogue in every episode: "ARF ARF ARF!" "WHAT IS IT, GIRL?"?
2. The '70s adventure series that defined its era with a T&A jiggle, prime time sex . . . and feminism?
3. The show that gave Johnny Carson his second biggest rating and 58 million viewers?
4. The STAR TREK episode where the crew beams down to a planet inhabited by obnoxious children who taunt them by chanting "BONK, BONK, ON THE HEAD"?
5. The soap opera where a character vanishes from the show while on a trip to the attic to bring down his skis . . . and this plot oversight isn't "corrected" for *20 years*!?
6. The show that accidently exposed the hilarious quirks of a highly esteemed chef?
7. The cult classic movie starring a half Apache, half Japanese heroine and her dragster driving, go-go dancing, karate-chopping sociopath girlfriends, Rosie and Boom-Boom?

DON'T MISS A SINGLE EPISODE OF . . .
BAD TV

1. *Lassie*, of course.
2. *Charlie's Angels*
3. Tiny Tim marrying Miss Vicki
4. "Miri," 1966
5. *All My Children* (the character is Bobby Martin)
6. *Cooking in America* featuring *New York Times* columnist Pierre Franey
7. *Faster, Pussycat! Kill, Kill!*, 1965

BAD TV

The Very Best of the Very Worst

craig nelson

Delta
Trade Paperbacks

A DELTA BOOK

Published by
Dell Publishing
a division of
Bantam Doubleday Dell Publishing Group, Inc.
1540 Broadway
New York, New York 10036

Copyright © 1995 by Craig Nelson
Designed by GDS/Jeffrey L. Ward

Library of Congress Cataloging in Publication Data
Nelson, Craig (Craig D.)
    Bad TV : the very best of the very worst / by Craig Nelson.
      p.   cm.
    ISBN 0-385-31359-4
    1. Television programs—United States.   2.   Television programs—United
States—Miscellanea.   3. Television broadcasting—United States—Anecdotes.
I. Title.
PN1992.3.U5N45 1995
791.45'75'0973—dc20   94-14967
                                                                        CIP

Manufactured in the United States of America
Published simultaneously in Canada

January 1995

10   9   8   7   6   5   4   3   2   1

BVG

Man . . .
Woman . . .
Birth . . .
Death . . .
Infinity!

—*Ben Casey*

Contents

INTRODUCTION:

The Bad vs. The BAD

My dream is to have someday a bank of TVs where all the different channels could be on and I could be monitoring them. . . . I love the tabloid stuff. The trashier the program is, the more I feel it's TV.

—Camille Paglia, *Wired*

Each of us, at one time or another, has a terrible idea that, for a moment, we think is a burst of genius. But how many of us have been able to get network execs, studio chiefs, and Hollywood producers to invest millions of dollars in our crazy schemes? How many of us have gotten hundreds of people—writers, directors, editors, actors—working their hardest to complete our insane visions? All in the name of infecting millions of American homes with such remarkable moments as *My Mother the Car* . . . *Pink Lady & Jeff* . . . *Manimal* . . . *The Hathaways* . . . *The Pruitts of Southampton* . . . *Cop Rock* . . . and *Poochinski!*

Every time something amazingly bad gets on TV, it's a miracle. Millions of dollars were spent, hundreds of people were involved, and no one put on the brakes; nobody said, "Uh, wait a minute, maybe we should think this one over. . . ." While there may be many TV productions that are merely dumb or boring, truly awful television—creations that stupefied a nation—are in a class all their own. You'll remember your favorites, as well as learn all about the classics you missed, with *BAD TV*.

Every year the networks and the various television production companies spend over $300 million to produce around 120 pilots for approximately twenty available prime-time slots. With that much going on you'd think that everyone in America was creating television pilots, and with those kind of ratios, you'd think that everything on TV would turn out to be a masterpiece. But as all our tube experience has shown, the airwaves are filled with product so determinedly awful, it defies comprehension—exactly the motto and battle cry of this book.

Created through hours of painstaking research in consultation with a

3

nominating committee of television professionals across the United States, *BAD TV* brings back all those horrifying memories, those instances of utter hilarity, and those magical times when you stared at your TV in complete, shell-shocked disbelief. *BAD TV* is an indispensable reference for too-bad-to-be-true videos that you'll want to rent ASAP, and a book filled with hours of memories and plain nastiness—all of which are well deserved. And what's more, every show in this book was actually aired.

The last rule had to be strictly enforced since, as you'll remember from that 120-made/20-aired ratio, we'd otherwise have to create something the size of the *Encyclopaedia Britannica.* So you'll be missing such never-aired wonders as *Ghostbreakers* (1965, Margaret "Wicked Witch of the West" Hamilton is a hypnotist in combat with otherworldly powers); *Baffled* (1972, Leonard "Mr. Spock" Nimoy is a crime-fighting race-car driver); *Scamps* (1982, Bob "Gilligan" Denver is a would-be novelist who gets a part-time job in a day-care center); and *Pests* (1992, from the makers of *Dinosaurs:* a guy gets fed up with the roach infestation, and makes his own super bug bomb. The results? Three giant, animated, talking roaches, of course).

There's bad TV, and then there's BAD TV. Bad TV is just boring and amateurish; something you banish with a quick flick of that remote control. BAD TV, however, is something truly amazing, enriching, and compelling; TV so bad, it's in a class all by itself. You won't find here shows that are merely dull, meretricious, sickening, and poorly done; *BAD TV* only showcases amazingly, stupefyingly, remarkably "I can't believe they did this!" television. While bad TV is to be avoided, BAD TV should be watched as often as possible.

BAD television completely entertains, but not in any way intended by the producers, writers, or actors; it provides great psychological benefits; it shows us the way we really are, warts and all; and it uncovers a number of mysteries of the universe.

Who, when driving past a terrible car wreck, can't help but slow down to get a closer look at the carnage? Even the most squeamish rubberneck with passion, and BAD TV provides incomparable rubbernecking pleasures. What a great feeling it is, as a remote controller, to stumble upon a broadcast horror; to watch in amazement that something so dreadful ever made it on the air; to be filled with the awe that only comes at trying to comprehend what kind of human being would produce and distribute such dreck; to fall into a stupefied, comatose state of half-living at the shock of what you're seeing right in front of your very eyes. With *BAD TV* you'll stumble no longer, and be able to immediately dial up a fright or two when the spirit moves.

Both people who hate TV and those who love it claim it's a drug, and apparently they're not so far off. Television is the only form of entertainment where the medium's light is pointed directly at your retinas; all the others—from books to film—are reflected light. Those light patterns, from the TV's cathode ray tube scans, produce alpha, beta, and delta waves in the brain—a mild, meditative state that is in fact profound enough to lower metabolism. If regular television can produce such effects, just think of what trancelike states you'll obtain in the realms of the BAD.

As will be seen time and again here, we see nothing wrong or immoral about wallowing like a pig in cheap nostalgia; it is, in fact, an area where BAD TV shines like the Milky Way. Since none of these programs is in any way "timeless," they're all the more pleasurable as pure nostalgic trash. If you don't get a warm, gooey, retro sixties buzz from *That Girl*'s go-go boots, wait till you see *My Living Doll*'s robot couture and frug lessons, or *Hullabaloo*'s Paul Revere in his tricorn hat and Nancy Sinatra surrounded by thirty-foot-high Victorian boots. If you think the Beave lived an idyllic, problem-free 1950s American dream life, just wait till you see the prelapsarian existence of the *Hathaways* chimpanzee family!

Tatty nostalgia doesn't hurt anyone; it provides gainful employment for many who otherwise would be forgotten has-beens; and it's no more of a waste of time than trying to sell your screenplay to Hollywood. But c'mon, networks; enough with the classics! USA, haven't we all seen enough *Miami Vice* and *MacGyver*? Where's *Love That Bob* and *The Pruitts of Southampton*? Nick at Nite, *The Lucy Show* is wearing thin; bring back *The Girl with Something Extra*!

A great mystery of these shows is: *Where did they go?* Considering how much viewers will put up with when it comes to TV inanity, it's remarkable how quickly we can get the truly terrible sent into cancellation heaven. While many ghastly movies are available today at your video store or through a mail-order service, much of TV seems to have just vanished. If you think it was easy to find this stuff (that the denizens of Hollywood would be generously forthcoming with examples of their worst mistakes), think again. While the Museum of Television and Radio is an excellent facility, for example, their mandate is to preserve the best of broadcast, and not to try and hold on to everything that ever got on the air—especially not the highlights of this book. If you're even slightly interested in American culture, I urge you to write or call your cable service, your local syndie station, or your favorite channel (such as Nick at Nite or

HBO) and demand they put all this great stuff on the air—you'll find the addresses at the back of this book. I know that someone, somewhere, has a copy of *Poochinski*—please contact me and name your price! It's now my only reason for living.

Bad television is not just a pleasure to watch; it also provides immense psychological benefits. There is, for example, one tiny problem that all of Hollywood (movies, videos, even little TV) can produce. If, deep in the dark recesses of your mind, there's even a passing thought that what Hollywood makes has any connection to reality, you can end up feeling . . . totally inadequate. You could, in fact, end up just like Gloria Steinem (who curiously has never gone public with the TV roots of this condition) and suffer from massively low self-esteem.

Are your parents as wonderful and understanding as the Cleavers? Are your brothers and sisters as great as the Bradys? Do you have sincere, sexy friends, like on *90210*? Do you live as well as the Cosbys? Do your grandparents have a house like the *Golden Girls'*? In every way Hollywood portrays a life that is relentlessly far superior to your own—except when it comes to BAD TV.

Watching BAD TV is rejuvenating and therapeutic, as it immediately rights those feelings of insecurity. Even your family can tell better jokes than *Big Brother Jake;* even your friends aren't as insipid as Mayim *Molloy* Bialik; even your boyfriend isn't as creepy as the guys on *Studs;* and even your lawyer wouldn't make an idiot of herself suddenly singing and dancing (for no reason) like the lawyers on *Cop Rock.* You can think up a better idea for a sitcom than *Great Day,* and, if you were a network executive, you'd have the sense not to put *Mixed Nuts* on the air.

Television . . . The Mysteries of the Universe . . . and the Secret of Life

Many have asked: "Sure, BAD TV is fun and all, but how can it make me a better person? How will it improve my life?" The new science of "garbology" says we can understand a great deal about a culture by studying its trash—and we couldn't agree more. BAD is wonderful as an educational device. If you want to learn about something, and you try to study its best moments, there are lots of problems because you get distracted by what makes it good. The writing, the acting, the imagination, the good camerawork, the dramatic power, the funny jokes, all detract from serious analysis. The BAD, however, strips everything naked, since it makes you incapable of suspending disbelief, as if a veil were dropped from your eyes. All the fakery and fraudulence of Hollywood smacks you right in the face, and the artificiality of all popular culture is embarrassingly revealed. On a great sitcom, for example, the laugh track is background noise, but on a BAD sitcom it's an earsplitting sonic nightmare of nonsensically forced gaiety that makes you squirm with cognitive dissonance.

BAD television should be explored in great depth because its very existence raises such profound philosophical questions, and the shows themselves frequently explore deep mysteries—of both the human spirit, and the universe. Watching these programs with the right attitude can lead you to the very precipice of the unfathomable: Why do we love things that are beyond terrible? Why will people publicly humiliate themselves in front of the entire nation, as they do every night on *Love Connection*? Why does Patty Duke insist on starring in a sitcom?

The people who make TV really only want one thing in all the world: your happiness. To that end they are constantly trying to create programming that piques your interest, embodies your dreams, and shares your concerns. When they succeed in doing so, the programs explicitly reveal America's hidden and not-so-hidden needs and desires (such as the schadenfreude of game shows or the hidden desire of owning an animal that's a cross between Superman and Jeeves). When they fail, they instead create a reality that exists only in the land of television (such as the demonism of Shelley Winters or the seventies idea that, in the very near future, the world will be filled with clones). Sometimes, if the TV reality is seductive enough, it becomes part of our beliefs and desires, creating a Moebius loop between reality and television. While regular television must be deeply analyzed to uncover these underlying moments, on BAD TV those hidden daydreams, longings, themes, and philosophies rise to the surface like grease on a pizza.

What television answers for us better than anything else is this: Who are we, as Americans?—whether it's the past's whiter-than-white, or today's Hispanic woman lawyer with her notebook computer. TV also shows us what we'd like to be, featuring the families, the jobs, or the loved ones we wish we had. *Star Trek: The Next Generation,* for example, isn't just sci-fi; it's the greatest job anybody could ever get. Captain Picard is the universe's best boss; his crew are the best employees and co-workers that anyone could ever want, and the United Federation of Planets even provides employment opportunities for psychics.

Many of our chapter introductions include "sneak preview" revelations of America's secret longings, our own idea of who we are and what we'd like to be, as well as the wacky beliefs that only exist in TV-World. Of course, our greatest hope is that you'll make your own findings, and thereby learn the special joys of floating on the American *zeitgeist*—a state of being that previously was only available through deep TV study and analysis, but is now instantly accessible for you in the pages of this book.

ⅠⅠ

Our journey begins with *It's a BAD, BAD, BAD, BAD World*—a section that prepares you, dear reader, to enter this awesome and mysterious universe, much as a diver must be prepped for deep-sea exploration. First off is THE BAD CLASSICS (THAT'S WHY WE LOVED THEM) HALL OF FAME, which reviews the great shows everyone was crazy about because they were so empty headed—*The Brady Bunch, Green Acres, Dark Shadows* and *Lost in Space,* for example.

You'll then remember the unimaginably low points of broadcast history in HOW COULD YOU? (WHEN BAD THINGS HAPPEN TO GOOD PEOPLE), which includes *Dallas*'s "It was all a dream" episode, the *Dynasty* Moldavian massacre, *The Beverly Hillbillies Solve the Energy Crisis,* and *The Harlem Globetrotters on Gilligan's Island.* This chapter also details the tragedies of the once-greats who have fallen into the clutches of the BAD, such as *Life with Lucy* and *Still the Beaver.*

CURSES! will reveal those certain cursed actors (including Nancy Walker, Jodie Foster, and Jack Scalia) who never have a hit series, no matter how hard they try, and fully explore Bette Davis's TV career (you'll see why you can't remember her many, many appearances). There are also thematic curses that appear throughout the history of television—f'rinstance, Sam Donaldson's cursed tongue, the PBS How-To Superstars' cursed work schedules, and of course the dreaded curse of being short, cute, black, and adopted—which you'll find covered in depth.

Part II is *The Tammi Awards;* a ratings guide and awards presentation for the all-time worst shows ever on television. Since these amazing flops represent such an incredible waste of talent, time, and money, it took many hours of careful thinking to devise an appropriate token of appreciation. What is the ultimate symbol of waste? Could it be anything but TMI (Three Mile Island)? Thus, THE TAMMI AWARDS were born—for waste so great, it's nuclear:

ⅠⅠ

Just like Emmies, Tammies are given to worst in genre: sitcoms, game shows, sports, variety shows, drama, and kids' programs. Each entry is rated with 1 to 6 Tammies, and The Golden Tammi will go to the worst show ever made in the history of television. Prepare now to relive or discover such remarkable fare as *She's the Sheriff, The Gong Show, Amerika, Thicke of the Night, Studs, Co-ed Fever, My Mother the Car, Turn-On, Love That Bob,* and *It Pays to Be Stupid.*

Tammies are also awarded for BASTARDS! (MY PARENTS WERE MOVIES), which shows very simply why television should stop trying to turn feature films into TV, with such memorable series as *Baby Boom, Down and Out in Beverly Hills,* and *Bob & Carol & Ted & Alice,* and a special bonus section, REMARKABLY BAD MOVIES, which picks the most outstandingly bad features that are on television practically every night which you've probably avoided . . . but shouldn't.

Like television itself *BAD TV* toes the very thin line between sincerity and artifice, adoration and hatred, stardom and obscurity, sanity and derangement. It used to be that, when we said "TV," we meant a very specific kind of material: the shows produced by the networks. Today, though, with cable's multitude of channels, TV has become a superhighway into our homes, requiring a whole new definition of the medium, and making programming departments everywhere completely desperate. Today, anything can—and does—get on television. With five hundred channels coming in the near future, what new beasts are slouching towards Hollywood, waiting to be broadcast?

We are, right this very instant, living in the Golden Age of BAD TV.

> The good old days of the network monopolies begin to look like the good old days of the Cold War. Everybody knew who was who and what was what, and the truths told by Walter Cronkite or Johnny Carson were as certain as the border crossings between the capitalist paradise and the communist inferno. But now that the world has slipped the bonds of military empire, it is besieged by the fevers of nationalism. . . .
>
> Transposed into the idiom of American television, the parallel expressions of anarchy and irredentism take the form of Rush Limbaugh or Howard Stern, and the facade of cultural imperialism crumbles into the separatist states of moral feeling elected to office by a hand-held camera, a 900 telephone number, and a rented studio on Santa Monica Boulevard. The

season's political candidates travel the pilgrim road of the tabloid talk shows, making confession to Larry or Barbara or Phil, and in the distant reaches of the cable system, once-upon-a-time celebrities drift like dead moons. . . .

—Lewis Lapham

⚠

A note on credits and dates

This is a book that is meant to be read and enjoyed, and including lots of reference materials would detract from your pleasure. If you need to know details on cast, credits, producers, networks, and airdates, there are plenty of references (such as *Total Television*) in the Sources section of this book where you can find everything you need to know.

A good example of why all this information was deleted is the case of airdates. It used to be that all major network series began in the fall and ran for at least a full season (sixteen weeks) before being canceled. Now, television seasons have been reduced, and a full year of shows is now only twenty-two to twenty-six episodes; series can start and be canceled at any time; they're frequently preempted; and airdates are whimsically moved around on the schedules, always in search of the Nielsen families' elusive happiness. What this means is that, if you wanted to be absolutely accurate in defining, say, the airdates for *The Pinky Lee Show,* you'd have to say "April 19, 1950–November 9, 1950, and January 4, 1954–May 11, 1956, in prime time and March 5, 1955–June 9, 1956, on Saturday morning."

It's a dreary situation, and if you feel the need to know this much detail on dating, you're probably watching too much television. Our dates here refer to when a series started, when an episode aired, or when a movie was released, and detailed dates are given only for special circumstances.

Acknowledgments

There were so many people deeply involved in the creation of this book that the author throughout is usually referred to as "we." I'm especially grateful to have the guidance of an outstanding agent and human being, Helen Rees, as well as one of the publishing industry's most creative editors, Jeanne Cavelos. Nicole Aron, Steve Cox, David Feldman, Amy Krakow, Chris Kreski, and Liz Perl provided invaluable assistance, as did the Museum of Television and Radio, fellow travelers on the America Online and CompuServe information networks, the remarkable staff of the

New York Public Library system, and Sal Mauriello, who runs the *real* Museum of Television, all by himself, in Wayne, New Jersey.

While the "Nominating Committee" provides credit to those who came up with specific ideas, many of them were far more helpful in the writing of this book than these single mentions can possibly convey—for everything else, thank you all so much. Of course, none of those mentioned here is at all responsible for any errors or omissions that may exist; those are solely due to the author's own laziness, incompetence, and profound character flaws.

The Nominating Committee

Nicole Aron: *Amazing Discoveries; The Survivors; Star Games; Worst Moments: The Soaps*
Léon Bing: *Cocaine: One Man's Seduction; I Want to Live!; Johnny Belinda; Mafia Princess; Paper Dolls; Rainbow; Someone I Touched*
Denis Boyles: *The Curse of Sam Donaldson's Tongue*
Gloria Brame: *We've Got Each Other*
Alan Carter, *Entertainment Weekly: The Curse of Soap Sex*
Jeanne Cavelos: *Born Innocent; The Cash Flow System; Focus on Beauty; Sneak Previews*
Glen Cason: *Condo*
Donna Chernoff: *Strays*
Frank Coleman: *Bigfoot and Wildboy*
Grayson Covil: *Svengali*
Aaron Dickey: *The Girl Most Likely To . . .*
James Duke: *The Occasional Wife*
Todd Erichsen: *When Things Were Rotten*
Mary Evans: *The Chevy Chase Show; The Girl with Something Extra*
Dave Feldman: *Holmes and Yoyo; Meeting of Minds; Thicke of the Night; That's Incredible; Treasure Hunt; Treasure Isle; Turn-On; Waverly Wonders*
Paul Harris: *Occasional Wife*
Ed Hooks: *Crime Time*
Robert Jones: *Lace*
Kim Kaufman: *McLaughlin*
Bill Knoedelseder: *Rollergirls; Twin Peaks*
Rick Kot: *The Pruitts of Southampton*
Amy Krakow: *Never Too Young; Jalopy Races from Hollywood*

Gary Krakow: *Andy's Gang; The Hathaways*

Larry Kraman: *You're in the Picture*

Chris Kreski: *Bad Ronald; Dirty Sally; Keeping Secrets; Pray for the Wildcats*

Arnie Levin: *Fantastic Television; Saturday Morning TV; TV Turkeys*

Ruth Locke: *The Lawrence Welk Show*

Jennifer Mendoza: *Out of This World*

Edward Moran: *NBC News Update, with Jessica Savitch*

Jim Morrison: *Automan*

Michael Musto, *The Village Voice:* "Infantilism" on *Donahue*

Liz Perl: *Kimba the White Lion; Lidsville; Run, Joe, Run; Sigmund and the Sea Monsters*

Mary Ann Petyak: *The Thing with Two Heads*

David Rakoff: *Shop Till You Drop*

Stephen Robb: *The Facts of Life*

Melissa Rogers: *Vinny and Bobby*

Stephen Roney: *Easy Street; The Peaceful Kingdom; The People Next Door*

Jeff Rovin: *A Man Called Shenandoah*

Andrew Ruthven: *Swann's Crossing*

Jerry Slaff: *The Curse of Tex Antoine's Tongue*

Ronni Stolzenberg: *Love, Sidney; Rude Dog*

Laurie Stone, *The Village Voice: Gourmet Cooking*

Sharon Ullman: *How Could You: The Soaps*

Vincent Virga: *Night of the Lepus*

Richard Zacks: *Chained for Life; The Conqueror*

> When I lie in the sack and flick on the remote switch and look at the box, I see things like *Let's Make a Deal*—a clinical study in avarice and greed where perspiring yo-yos go into convulsions trying to latch on to a warehouse full of free acquisitions while the studio audience screams and gurgles.
>
> I see *The Dating Game,* where a vapid, miniskirted beauty throws out well-rehearsed, thinly veiled sexual asides to a trio who are obviously lusting for her body.
>
> I see the dregs of television, *Gilligan's Island* and *Hee Haw,* and all the havoc and damage that man can wreak on his fellow man.
>
> —Rod Serling, 1973

PART 1
• • • • • • • • • • •

It's a BAD, BAD, BAD, BAD World

The BAD Classics
(That's Why We Loved Them)
Hall of Fame

Television is chewing gum for the eyes.
—Frank Lloyd Wright

Television is cotton candy for the eyes.
—Aaron Spelling

THROUGHOUT THE HISTORY OF TV THERE'S ALWAYS BEEN A BUNCH of collegiate eggheads on the sidelines, whining and moaning that all television is utterly worthless and has terrible effects on the people who watch it. Just this once, give their opinion much more than it deserves—some thought:

What would it be like if all of TV was completely great?

What if every sitcom was as terrific and not to be missed as *I Love Lucy*?

What if every adventure show was as engrossing as *Mission: Impossible*?

What if every drama was as magnificently done as *Hill Street Blues*?

It'd be a catastrophe, that's what. Why would we ever leave the house and go to work? Why would we bother cooking meals, spending time with our friends and family, doing anything but watching television? Wouldn't a nonstop diet of excellence make us all perpetually exhausted?

When taking a critical look at TV it's good to remember that most people's jobs are emotionally, mentally, and/or physically demanding—not exactly the light and breezy life led by your typical tubephobe (a tenured university prof who has to teach *at least* two classes a week). When Americans come home at night—especially if they've had a particularly bad day—something that's a little bit engaging, a little bit on the light side, and a little bit mindless is frequently just what the doctor ordered.

Part of what keeps TV in the less-than-utterly-compelling realm is its very nature. You watch a show, and every twelve minutes there's a commercial, so you run to the bathroom or turn over the steak or check how little Ernie's doing with his homework, and then go back to the show. If you miss a few minutes, so what? In any other medium these constant interruptions would be considered staggering; say you were reading a Stephen King novel and, just as our heroes were entering the sewer system to go into battle against pure evil, you turn the page and the novel's become a car-repair manual—you'd be outraged. But such interruptions on television are completely normal and, overall, they just add to the lite persona of TV we've all come to love.

Truly perfect TV, from *The Beverly Hillbillies* to *Beverly Hills 90210,* is in fact commonly a mix of the engaging and the stupid, the weighty and the lite, the charming and the idiotic. For example, we viewers think pathetic or ridiculous TV characters are that much more likable, and we want them to be regular Joes and Janes as well. Famous movie stars can be exotic, but television stars should be the kind of people we might bump into at the Laundromat. That's why it's so common for TV stars to bomb in movies (it's like having to pay to go see something starring your in-laws, who should've got you in for free)—while movie stars on TV look like they're from Mars. The lite feelings we all have for television can even be seen with the reviews; while practically every movie released is extensively reviewed in all the press, on radio, on the news, and on shows like *Sneak Previews* and *Siskel & Ebert,* new TV shows receive a small *People* mention here and a *TV Guide* blip there and that's about it.

Academics also like to complain that TV is mired in itself, using the same plots and the same character types and the same format over and over again throughout its history—and then putting it all in reruns! It's this very repetition, though, that makes series regulars become familiar people who engage our interests and make us want to watch them over and over again. Practically all children, for instance, love to impose order on their lives, whether it's the same bedtime story that they want to hear every single night or meals being served at the exact same time every day or that the furniture in their room has to be just so; this kind of order and repetition is exactly what generic TV provides. As much as adults complain about "the grind" of their lives, how many of us would want it completely otherwise—for example, having to think about going to work at a different time and in a different location every single day?

There's something very comforting in watching a show so predictable, you know what's going to happen next, starring actors who are only a little better looking and a little more interesting than the people you meet in day-to-day life. If part of the enjoyment of great television is its soothing mindlessness, its familiar comfort, and its lack of surprise, just think how much you'll enjoy the Olympian empty-headedness, the dramatic incompetence, and the outright plagiarism of the BAD!

▲▲

We now honor the great shows that went more than a little bit over the top in the mindless, the ridiculous, and the predictable departments—the whole reason we loved them in the first place. Some may wonder: "How dare you include the masterpiece [*your favorite show name here*]!" In fact, the greatness of pure entertainment often lies in the balance between sincerity and froth, between the light and the gripping. A close look at these shows reveals that much of our best TV has profound elements of the BAD in it—as well as the following truths about American longings, and the laws of TV-World:

- The perfect pet would be a cross between Superman and Jeeves.
- When wealthy people move to a new neighborhood, it's a laugh riot.
- There's nothing as much fun as watching people reveal some deep, horrible secret.
- Well-to-do country people compulsively spend their money on junk and schemes.
- There's nothing as much fun as watching people dress up as fruits and vegetables and become drunk with greed.
- Well-to-do Hungarians compulsively spend their money on junk and schemes.

The Adventures of Ozzie and Harriet, 1952. The show with one of the funniest titles ever, since "adventure" is far from what happened here. Were Ozzie and Harriet Nelson agoraphobes? She never got out of the kitchen and he barely got as far as the front yard. In fact, if Ozzie ever worked for a living, it was a secret kept from the audience.

When son Ricky became a rock star, surely the show would develop lots of dramatic twists: drugs, groupies, and the perils of touring. Instead, Ozzie made sure to keep rock 'n' roll a mere hobby, and have poor Rick be a lawyer with his brother, Dave.

Why oh why did this fifties icon keep us enthralled for fourteen long years? Was this the beginning of the terror that is The Family Channel?

ALF, 1986. Would you ever have believed that one of the most popular sit-coms in American history would be about a family whose life revolves around a furry, smart-mouthed puppet? That the puppet would look like a beady-eyed cross between an anteater and an orangutan, and that it would ceaselessly entertain the family and help them with their personal prob-lems? That you could have a hit show by making it primarily for kids, but with some of the same self-indulgent humor as *Garfield*? Now, the 229-year-old cat-eating Alien Life Form named Gordon Shumway is a car-toon, a plush toy, and lives on forever in syndication.

All nasty innuendo aside, one thing ALF's writers did especially well was in the surrealist, *Far Side*–type humor department. ALF's parents were Biff, Bob, and Flo, for example; he worshiped the god Barry, chewed tabby-flavored gum and, like all Melmacians, had a heartfelt motto: "Are you going to finish that sandwich?"

The Andy Griffith Show, 1960; *Gomer Pyle, U.S.M.C.,* 1964; *Mayberry, R.F.D.,* 1968; *The New Andy Griffith Show,* 1971; *Return to Mayberry,* 1986. Do you ever wish you could just get away from it all; away from homelessness, crime, poverty, AIDS, racial conflict, and all the other is-sues of today's frenetic American urban life? *The Andy Griffith Show,* et seq., completely fulfills the promise of escapist television with its all-white cast living in a quiet rural setting and no problem bigger than an Opie-fired baseball through Aunt Bea's window—Sheriff Andy never even carried a gun. Though the *Beverly Hillbillies* family of shows may be always remembered as the ruralization of national television, *Griffith* and its entourage were the only ones to successfully bring Norman Rock-well paintings to life (or at least to TV life).

The A Team, 1983. Simultaneously an action/adventure show and a par-ody of action/adventure shows, The *A Team* took what was formerly an all-male audience-pleaser and cartooned it into family fare. With the relentlessly charming Mr. T, the certifiably insane "Howlin' Mad" Murdock, the he-got-this-job-so-girls-will-watch "Face" Peck, ex–movie star George Peppard, and the violent destruction of cars, trucks, vans, and other Matchbox items instead of people, the show beautifully slapped Robin Hood ethics onto a-night-out-with-the-guys mayhem. Why run away with the circus when you could run away with the *Team*?

Batman, 1966. "I don't know who he is behind that mask of his, but I know when we need him. And we need him now!" Commissioner Gordon said it for all of us when this knowingly BAD show was the megahit of its day. One of the few successful transfers of a cartoon to live action (just think of the movie *Dick Tracy*), *Batman* took the very serious world of the comic strip and blew it up with wacky psychedelic graphics, camera angles tilting in all directions, stomach-churning puns, and the most accessorized heroes in TV history (taking the batpole to the batcave and into the batmobile or the batboat or the batcopter and using the batarang, batcuffs, bathook, batphone, batsignal, or batostat—to name a few).

A brilliant paean to the style of the sixties, *Batman* was too much for its own good, and sadly petered out after four seasons. Now, almost thirty years later, the show holds up remarkably well; its villains (Burgess Meredith as the Penguin, Cesar Romero as the Joker, Frank Gorshin as The Riddler, Julie Newmar, Lee Meriwether, and Eartha Kitt as Catwoman, Liberace as Chandell, Ethel Merman as Lola Lasagne, Zsa Zsa Gabor as Minerva, Shelley Winters as Ma Parker, Tallulah Bankhead as Black Widow, Vincent Price as Egghead, Joan Collins as the Siren, and Milton Berle as Louie the Lilac) make it a must for catching repeats on— eek!—The Family Channel. Commie rag *Pravda* warned: "[Batman] is nothing more than a glorified FBI agent, a capitalist murderer who kills his enemies beautifully, effectively, and with taste, so that shoulder blades crack loudly and scalps break like cantaloupes."

The Beverly Hillbillies, 1962; *Petticoat Junction*, 1963; *Green Acres*, 1965. These three great BAD classics are actually one giant show; in *Beverly* rich people move from the country to the city, in *Green* rich people move from the city to the country, and *Petticoat* is where they all intersect. The central predicament in each comes from the main characters being "fish out of water"—a TV sitcom genre all its own—and one pioneered by Paul Henning, producer of all three.

Beverly is, to date, the most popular sitcom ever produced in the history of television; the eight most watched half-hour programs of all time, according to Nielsen, are all *Beverly*s. Though you'd think Jed, Granny, Elly May, Jethro Bodine, and Cousin Bessie were a normal American family, in fact Granny is Jed's mother-in-law, Jethro is his nephew, Jed and Granny's spouses are "dead" (which, as we all know, is sitcom code for divorced), and Bessie is a chimpanzee.

One tubeaholic loves *Beverly* for its parody cameo names, like Crunch Hardtack and Dash Riprock, and is surprised that having a pickup truck with a sofa for the backseat never became a trend. *The Beverly Hillbillies* is simultaneously utterly nutty, inane, and the greatest TV series of all time.

Petticoat Junction, on the other hand, is probably the slowest-moving sitcom in the history of television, with the narcoleptic pacing of a great dream (no wonder the major set is the Shady Rest Hotel). Save for Sam at his general store and Floyd and Charlie on the chugalug Cannonball, *Petticoat* residents work about as hard as Ozzie and Harriet, and spend their endless free time doing even less (at least Ozzie and Harriet had to help their kids with their personal problems). When someone suggests that fire chief and hotel comanager Edgar Buchanan do some work, he claims lumbago and hits the porch rocker. The three water-tank skinny-dipping gals, Billie Jo, Bobbie Jo, and Betty Jo, lounge around, waiting for husbands, their roles so dull it required six actresses to play them (with only Linda Kaye "Betty Jo" Henning, the producer's daughter, able to hold down the job for the full eight-year run).

Producer Henning is a television genius for three reasons. He insisted on having great theme songs for all his shows; he got the word *Hooterville* on network television; and he perfectly understood the importance of casting secondary roles with great B stars. The latter really rings out in the case of *Green Acres;* star Eddie Albert is not interesting; costar Eva Gabor is just interesting; but the show's real draw is its fantastic supporting cast: Pat Buttram's Mr. Haney, Hank Patterson's Fred Ziffel, Grace Canfield's female Monroe, and Arnold, the smartest pig in the universe. In fact, probably the most memorable character on *Green Acres* is the pig; he drinks lime soda, plays cricket, watches Walter Cronkite, and paints his room orange. Memorable cast members on *Beverly* and *Petticoat,* meanwhile, included Nancy Kulp, Sharon Tate, Bea Benaderet, Edgar Buchanan, Meredith MacRae, and June Lockhart.

Beverly Hills, 90210, 1988. Most mindless television is terrific because you can watch, talk on the phone, or read *People* magazine, all at the same time. *90210,* though, is so light, so airy, so mildly engaging that you can talk on the phone *and* read *People* magazine at the same time—a real TV breakthrough.

This 1950s throwback, where all the kids are cute but good, all the parents are firm but understanding, and all the skin is really, really white, is *The Brady Bunch* of a whole new era; a fantasy nostalgia of kiddom. If only we could all have lived this way: if only real teen emotions were this interesting . . . if only high-school life was this tranquil . . . if only your kids' biggest drug problem was like Republican egomaniac Shannen Doherty being caught with a cigarette . . . how great things would be! Just as it's about to fall over the cliff of unbelievability, though, *90210* flirts with realness via its one real Beverly Hills denizen, the gawky, tumultuous, body-perfect Tori (daughter of producer Aaron) Spelling, in whose disturbed visage one can instantly view the turmoil and drama of the true-life Beverly Hills High.

The Brady Bunch, 1969. In the 1970s, while everyone else was watching socially relevant sitcoms like *All in the Family* and *Maude,* a group of kids was enthralled with one 1950s holdover. These kids wanted a little more Hugh Beaumont and a little less Carroll O'Connor, and they turned *The Brady Bunch* into one of America's cultural sensations. However, the ever-growing popularity of this show (which, at least in New York City, can now be seen on *three* different channels in syndication) should be alarming for anyone who preaches "family values," since *The Brady Bunch* has immense appeal for any child whose home life is turbulent, who feels ignored, and who wants to commit incest—obviously a much bigger niche audience than anyone ever imagined.

First off, anyone who's ever been in contact with a family the size of the Bradys understands both the reason for birth control and the fear of real violence: screaming fits, tears, punches thrown, flying toys and furniture, even broken limbs are everyday occurrences in a big family. Unlike real siblings, however, the Brady kids don't hate each other's guts. They merely have (on rare occasions) mild spats. Some (including the actress who played her) believe that "the youngest one in curls" is the stupidest child in the history of television—yet no Brady *ever* tried to slap some sense into her.

Secondly, the Brady adults never seem to ever work, or have any kind of life of their own. They're parenting twenty-four hours a day, seven days a week. This means that, if you're a Brady child, there are mobs of siblings, parents, and a maid just waiting to help you with your incredibly trivial problems. As a Brady you'll never walk alone.

Finally, the show's only real tension (since even the Beaver got into more trouble than these kids) is sex. The Brady creators brilliantly divvied up the half-siblings along gender lines, and evenly paired them off. For every brunette Brady boy there's an equivalent, not-related-by-blood, blond Brady girl. It's an entire family of couples (even the seemingly sex-free Alice got her plumber), and the kids' pairings practically hit you over the head with an undertone of illicit sex.

Every fan knows the greatest benefit of being a Brady: never going dateless on a Saturday night.

Charlie's Angels, 1976. One of the many perks of being the ultimate sixties hero, Mr. James Bond, was the endless parade of ornamental beauties who always knew both how to get into trouble and how to properly reward their savior. Though these girls could on occasion knock out a villain with a well-placed vase to the head, their real job was bikini or evening-gown modeling and knowing just how to say "Oh . . . James!" as the end credits rolled. A mere ten years later and "You've come a long way, baby!" with *Charlie's Angels:* the show that defined its era by introducing a rash of T&A "jiggle" clones and bringing sex back to prime time (an episode where "Jill" accidentally revealed a smidgen of her nipple for a fraction of a second received immense ratings).

Oft derided by the forward-thinking, the three Angels were of the same supermodel ilk as the Bond girls, but they did just as much Holmesian deduction and gunslinging as Bond himself ever did. Played over the years by six different actresses (but always including an athletic blonde, an intelligent brunette, and "Tressie" descendant Jaclyn Smith), the Angels did everything completely by themselves and never needed the aid of men; their boss wasn't even allowed to have a body, but was a mere voice on the phone, setting up the plot and congratulating the women when they got their man (villain).

It's nitpicking to notice that an eternal wind machine is always ruffling Farrah Fawcett-Majors's style-setting layered mane, that the plot's implausibilities always pile up to mountainous heights, that the requisite car chases are downright snoozy, or that the main suspense point of each episode was in waiting to see which Angel would go bra free. *Charlie's Angels* remains great TV to this very day.

Dark Shadows, 1966. "My name is Victoria Winters . . ." began every episode of this daytime soap which, long before Anne Rice, put the sex and religion back into bloodsucking where it belongs—and had America's

**Jonathan Frid reveals one of the Collins family's many, many
secrets in this early moment from _Dark Shadows_** (Photofest)

preteens racing home from school to catch every breathless minute. With
fall-wearing, abandoned orphan Victoria (portrayed by Claus Von Bulow
mistress Alexandra Isles), murderous diva Joan Bennett, immortal
phoenix Laura, helpful ghost Josette, nasty witch Angelique, gravedigging
drifter Willie, and the courtly, debonair, skirt-chasing vampire Barnabas
Collins, _Dark Shadows_ mixed the immense family trees of Europeans
with a big old haunted house, a moody overlay of Gothic decor, and
glacially hypnotic soap pacing—as if the whole thing were taking place
underwater—to create something completely new. Everyone (accompanied by a spine-tingling slide whistle) is always teetering on the brink of
discovering a horrible secret, just like in _Peyton Place_—but while a _Pey-
ton Place_ secret is that your school principal is boffing the lonely divorcée next door, a _Dark Shadows_ secret is that your cousin is two thousand
years old and sucking blood out of the handyman.

   In 1991 an attempt was made to resurrect the series in prime time with
Ben Cross as Barnabas, but the originality of twenty-five years earlier was

missing and the magic was gone. Be sure, though, to catch the original when it's aired, or rent the videos tonight. You have to see them to believe what manic plotting, hambone acting, overabundance of relatives, and ten-cent special effects captivated the nation a mere two decades ago—and that, even with all its BADness, *Dark Shadows* retains its own peculiar charm.

Divorce Court, 1957. This great, epochal drama of justice, which spawned a host of imitators (*The People's Court, The Judge, Superior Court,* etc.) and even an entire channel (Court TV), began life when *divorce* was a dirty word—and the show played it up to the hilt, claiming its raison d'etre was to "help stem the rising tide of divorces." In those early days *DC* was as much of a hankie-wringing soap opera as *Queen for a Day,* with pathetic, maudlin love-gone-wrong stories and an emphasis on the tragedy of its subject.

Today, all the original elements are intact: the whispering narrator that implies we're watching a real case broadcast live; the extreme pleasure of seeing couples bitterly fight it out; the time given to each party to air their side of the story (allowing us to judge their relative merits); the game-show suspense of "who will win?"; the hostile, aggressive lawyers, digging at the truth; the artifice that "none of the participants knows the outcome of the case until Judge Keene [just like *People's Court* Wapner, a real retired California jurist!] delivers his decision," and that very decision, which is always a philosophic soliloquy on the nature of love, delivered as if from the Book of Solomon.

Since divorce has become just another everyday occurrence, though, today's *Divorce Court* has turned into a living tabloid to compensate, featuring cases like a man suing for divorce because when he got married, he was suffering from amnesia, and lines like "She's a dyke and a criminal and I don't want her near my son!" It's all in the passion, the drama, the revenge, epitomized by the show's new logo: A pulsating heart in the word *Court* where the *o* ought to be—and it's all just as great as the original.

The Facts of Life, 1979. An eternal mystery: why was this show so popular? Perhaps it's the *Gilligan's Island* of its era; something kids love that drives adults insane. Every week beautiful Blair (winner of the "Most Naturally Blond" contest at school) and her plump teen friends would find themselves with personal problems emblematic of society at large (usually involving a special guest-star relative), and address themselves to "big questions." What will Tootie do when she finds out her dad's an alcoholic? What will Jo do when she finds out her dad's a convict? What will Blair do when she finds out her cousin is a stand-up comic with multiple sclerosis? What you'll do is be amazed at the low-rent jejune nature of the whole enterprise, which is a lot more entertaining than the jokes. While the writers and actors try to be *All in the Family,* they can't even hit the standards of *90210.*

Just like its leads *The Facts of Life* was willing to do anything to be popular, even letting go half the cast (including Molly Ringwald) after season one, adding Australian exchange student Pippa in the wake of *Crocodile Dundee,* and keeping the cast together after graduation by having them open a bakery and live above the store. It's a show that brings new meaning to the word *silly,* and for its endless run, we couldn't get enough.

The Flying Nun, 1967. America is obsessed with nuns, and pretending to be one has done wonders for the careers of so many (just ask Julie Andrews, Whoopi Goldberg, and Mary Tyler Moore). But before the constantly irrepressible Sally Field launched herself into fame (and a role her career would barely survive) as the way we'd always remember her—Sister Bertrille of Puerto Rico's Convent San Tanco—no one had thought: *Why not have a nun who can fly?*

Sister Sally is unique: though almost all TV leads spend their airtime helping people with their personal problems, only she can offer instantaneous service (if the wind is right). Like all great BAD TV *The Flying Nun* revolves around a core mystery: Does our Sister spurn billionaire Alejandro Rey's amorous intentions because she's so devoted to her calling—or because it would mean giving up her hat?

Geraldo, 1987. The whole world likes to pick on Geraldo Rivera (aka Jerry Rivers), and most of the time he deserves it. Neck and neck with Robin Leach, Jerry is the ultimate in TV trash; this is, after all, the reporter who, in an interview with Charles Manson, turned to Manson and blurted, "You're a mass-murderin' dog, Charlie!"

Once a serious journalist on ABC's *20/20,* Rivera hit the jackpot in 1986 when he opened, to massive hype and publicity, Al Capone's never-before-seen safe. Inside was nothing of interest, but outside was the biggest rating a syndicated special ever got, and Rivera got his daytime chance. Instantly becoming the show you love to hate, *Geraldo* was unique at the time; in a TV world of smoothie news anchors and feel-good

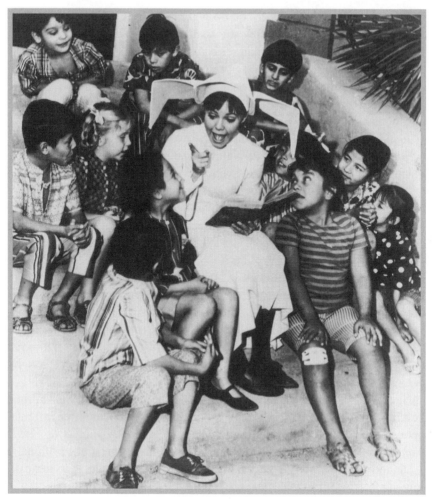

Sally Field performs one of her few nunly duties that doesn't require an altimeter in *The Flying Nun* (Stephen Cox)

chat-show hosts, Rivera's brainstorm was abrasively hard edged (with every story pitched at fever pitch) and had a remarkable knack for lurid shock. Guests commonly stormed off the air, and there was frequently a screaming match avidly encouraged by our seamy host. When *Donahue* is so cute you're going to hurl, a little *Geraldo* will get you right back on your feet. The show has, in fact (with *A Current Affair*) gone on to spawn the entire genre of tabloid TV.

After a few years of trying to outtrash the *National Enquirer,* even Rivera publicly admitted that he was getting embarrassed by his own show, and tried to revitalize his serious-journalist persona with a new program—only to crash and burn into cancellation (see below).

Geraldo Rivera's
Top Ten Favorite Guests of All Time:

- The bravest kid in the world
- A woman who was a Mafia mistress
- A man with over 1,001 tattoos
- America's busiest groupie
- A real-life *Rain Man*
- A man obsessed by the number 1
- A transsexual who can't make up his/her mind
- A levitating yogi
- A Cher look-alike drag queen
- A couple who weighs 1,200 pounds

Our Favorite Geraldo Rivera Guest:

- Geraldo himself, on the operating table, having fat from his butt injected into his forehead. Said *People:* "Talk about carrying coals to Newcastle. . . ."

Get Christie Love!, 1974. While there are many, many shows about cops who can't stand the system and must be adorable renegades following their own rules, few of them are as wildly demented as *Get Christie Love!* When Teresa Graves graduated out of her *Laugh-In* bikini and into the LAPD, she became a beautiful black undercover female detective who wears lots of miniskirts as part of her disguises. The title refers to the criminals not liking her because she arrests too many of them, and the police executives not liking her because she's such a wild rebellious soul, and all of them out to get her in what's really a female TV version of *Shaft.* Christie Love was not only a great looker who really knew how to dress, she was one of the few African-Americans starring in a TV show at the time, so all of us who wanted to be black (a majority of American teens) made sure to catch all the Black Panther TV trials, as well as every episode of *Get Christie Love!*

Gilligan's Island, 1964; *The New Adventures of Gilligan,* 1974; *Rescue from Gilligan's Island,* 1978; *The Castaways on Gilligan's Island,* 1979; *The Harlem Globetrotters on Gilligan's Island,* 1981; *Gilligan's Planet,* 1982. Like *The Brady Bunch* this is one of those classics that kids love and adults find utterly inane. A trifle, a whimsy, the ultimate television bibelot, *Gilligan* is probably the trashiest long-running show ever, since the writers never cared about such inconstancies as having a "three-hour cruise" end up in the middle of nowhere or allowing the Thurston Howells trunkfuls of clothing or having this uncharted isle filled with visitors: pilot, painter, dictator, mafioso, entomologist, robot, surfer, sailor, even a couple of cosmonauts drop by. But if you stop quibbling over details and let *Gilligan* do what it does best—gently wash over you like a warm mist—this show is a paean to empty-headed Grade B-ness: B slapstick from Bob Denver and Alan Hale, B intellectuality from Russell Johnson, B-girl-next-door from Dawn Wells, and B sex from Tina Louise. Kids know what adults seem to forget: that when B's try as hard as they can, they can be just as entertaining as any A on earth.

Hee Haw, 1969. On the air for over twenty-two years with over five hundred episodes and still going strong, *Hee Haw* proves the rule of ingenious counterprogramming. What began as a twangy imitation *Laugh-In* eventually became the only national variety hour (when everyone else had given up variety), the only national country show (when everyone else had gone urban/suburban), and the only reveler in all-out cornpone (when everyone else was trying to see how far they could get past Standards and Practices). Against all expectations Roy Clark, Buck Owens, Barbi Benton, and that cartoon donkey are beyond mere TV stars . . . they have become infinite.

Honey West, 1965. Like Christie Love, Honey West is a spiritual descendant of Diana Rigg's tough-but-pretty Emma Peel (pre-Emma, you'll remember, the tough gals were Stanwyck, Crawford, Russell, and the like—not exactly makeup queens). In fact, Honey's an American Peel remake, being a karate and judo expert (as well as a whiz with a gun) who uses Bond-like futuristic gadgets and a black jumpsuit to always get her evil man. Both Emma and Honey were free-lance PIs who flirted like crazy with the villains before moving in for the kill; when you wondered, *Will they go all the way?* it meant, will they have to shoot the bad guy themselves?

Honey, however, did have a few things Emma never had: the nicotined

**That mole . . . that ocelot . . .
it could only be Honey West** (Photofest)

voice, the Marilyn mole, the Jackie O! sunglasses, the tiger coat, the martini olive radio transmitter, and the defining element that so deeply impressed her legions of *Honey* home viewers: a pet ocelot.

Incredible Inventions, 1992. Ron Popeil is back! The creator of infomercials in general and Ronco in particular deserves some kind of homage from all us BAD TV lovers. Just think back on these magic moments: the Veg-O-Matic ("It slices it dices it chops it juliennes!" and it sold nine million); Seal-A-Meal, the Pocket Fisherman, London Aire hose (which never run, even when rubbed with Brillo pads), Steam-A-Way, Record Vacuum, Glass Froster (for instantly frosting your favorite drinks), Hula Hoe (weeder), the Buttoneer, the Spatter Screen, Mr. Dentist, and Mr. Microphone! How can we ever thank him?

Today, Ron's the guest star on two infomercials; one for a remarkable electric food dehydrator that can shave hundreds of dollars from your fruit leather expenses, and *Incredible Inventions*—already a BAD classic. The pitch here is GLH (Great Looking Hair) Formula Number Nine—"a powder in an aerosol form which actually thickens hair many times over!" It's spray paint for bald men, and it requires one of nine lifelike colors, a finishing "shield," a special spray if you want to wash out the stuff—and it's all only $39.92! So if you or someone you love are trying to get by with a comb-over, why not paint your pate with Popeil—and give something back to a man who's given us all so much?

The Joe Franklin Show, 1950. On the air for forty-three years and 21,425 broadcasts, this amazing program can still be caught in late-night reruns on cable superstation WWOR-TV (as well as on radio with *Joe Franklin's Memory Lane*). Franklin began his show-business career by hosting the radio sensation *Vaudeville Isn't Dead* and went on to marry his current wife on TV's *Bride and Groom,* two peak experiences that obviously established his own broadcast aesthetic. With *The Joe Franklin Show* Franklin has simultaneously performed two great public services: he kept the Borscht Belt alive for a nationwide audience long after its appeal had vanished, and he allowed his guests airtime when no one else on television would touch them.

If your favorite show is "Public Access," then Joe is your god; who can ever forget such Franklin regulars as the singing funeral director, the spoon-playing maestro, the nose-whistling postal worker, the world's fastest painter, the dancing dentist, or the world's tallest belly dancer, each intro'd by Joe as "a legend," "the greatest of the great," or "a thing of beauty and charm is a joy forever." Though his schmaltz was mercilessly parodied on *Saturday Night Live* by Billy Crystal, Joe's long-lasting success may give him the last laugh. "You want to know the real magic formula for a successful talk show host? Sincerity," says Joe. "When you've learned how to fake that, you've got it made."

Knots Landing, 1979. As of its final season in 1992 this was the only soap still hitting the boards in prime time, with thirteen years and more than three hundred episodes in the can, and graduates like Alec Baldwin, Julie

Harris, Lisa Hartman, and Donna Mills. Why has it endured far beyond *Dynasty, Falcon Crest,* and even its parent, *Dallas*? A true knack for the BAD! In 1991 alone, for example, Michelle Phillips had to impersonate a dead woman and dig through canine feces in search of a significant microfiche, Claudia stole someone's liver, and Joan Van Ark's head trauma led her to hair experiments. In a mere twelve years Michele Lee has been a widow, a single mother, a talk-show hostess, a drug addict, a kidnapping victim, a shooting victim, and the victim of a psychotic fan, while Joan Van Ark has been a novelist, a waitress, a wife (four times), an insatiable adulteress, and a head case. This nuttiness makes *Knots Landing* utterly addictive once you've seen a few shows, and its cancellation is much more of a loss than *Brooklyn Bridge, I'll Fly Away,* or any of those other snooty, unpopular series.

Lassie, 1954–1974; *Lassie's Rescue Rangers,* 1973; *The New Lassie,* 1989. Over the years Lassie has been portrayed by eight different dogs (all males) and a cartoon; she's lived on a farm, with forest rangers, on a ranch, and all alone; and she's survived two much-beloved mothers, June Lockhart and Cloris Leachman.

Why should the wonderful Lassie be included in BAD TV? Well, if you've been living in a cave for thirty years, the big dramatic moment of every episode goes something like this:

"Arf Arf Arf!"
"What's that, Lassie? What is it, girl?"
"Arf Arf Arf!"
"You say that there's a man trapped in the old Sutter mine up on Highhill Road next to the Hopewell place?"
"Arf Arf Arf!"
"You say that there's been a cave-in and he's got a broken leg and only fifteen minutes of air left?"
"Arf Arf Arf!"
"You say that Timmy tried to help him but got caught in the falling rock and can't get away and there's a giant puma about to tear him limb from limb?"
"Arf Arf Arf!"
"Well, girl, let's go, then!"

As onetime mom Cloris Leachman noted, "They had to find reasons for us to be morons so the dog could outsmart us."

Let's Make a Deal, 1963. As Vanna White ancestor Carol Merrill lovingly traces the outline of every refrigerator, stereo, cookware set, and giant rocking chair "zonk," rapid-fire carney barker host Monty Hall moves through his studio audience like a buttered-up Santa Claus, perhaps throwing instant cash and prizes your way. While other game shows make winning as difficult as possible (just think what an egghead you've got to be to take home some cash from *Jeopardy!*), once Monty picks you on *Deal,* it's hard not to win something. *Deal* throws out the loot like there's no tomorrow, with a couple hundred bucks going if you've got some odd thing in your purse, or a trip to Hawaii if you can make a good, quick guess. The pacing of this free-for-all (and the contestants' epic of debasement in their loony costumes and hysterics of joy) make *Deal* the most compellingly watchable BAD game show of them all.

Lifestyles of the Rich and Famous, 1983. The line "Greed is good!" from the movie *Wall Street* seemed to sum up much of the eighties, but nowhere was greed so lionized, shopping so mythicized, and the eighties so perfectly captured as on *Lifestyles of the Rich and Famous.* Sycophantic brownnoser Robin Leach (with his relentlessly aggrandizing narration) is the perfect host, giving a play-by-play any sportscaster would envy as the camera swoops and pans across acres of excessive real estate and ludicrous piles of merchandise; Rodeo Drive, according to Robin, is not just a strip of pricey stores; it's where "THE WORLD'S MOST EXPENSIVE BOUTIQUES LINE THE EXCLUSIVE BLOCKS OF A BILLION-AIRE'S BAZAAR WHERE STARS AND MOGULS, MOVIE PRODUCERS AND PRINCES, COME TO BE SEEN AND PAY THE PREMIUM PRICES FOR PRESTIGE DESIGNER LABELS!" The interviews with the rich and famous reveal nothing, but who cares? We only wanna see the stuff! Tragically, the decade turned, the eighties ethos fell into disfavor, and now Robin's doing muffler commercials. In another few years when it's time for eighties nostalgia, *Lifestyles* will be the ultimate way to recapture an era.

Lost in Space, 1965. "Space Family Robinson" gets their mission thrown off-kilter and wanders aimlessly through the universe, confronting danger and cheap special effects. We loved *Lassie*'s Mom June Lockhart still making lunch—but now in a silver Lycra jumpsuit. We loved *Make Room for Daddy*'s daughter, Angela Cartwright—now all grown up and conducting incomprehensible scientific experiments. We loved the "will they or won't they?" continuing drama of Judy Robinson and Major West. But what we waited for every night at the edge of our seats was the Robot's "Danger! Danger! Mr. Smith! Danger!" and Jonathan Harris's eternal reply: "Somebody help me, *please!*"

Love That Bob, 1955. You can read as much of "The Playboy Philosophy" as you want without getting a *real* picture of this long-lost art form. To see and understand completely what it was really like to be a fifties sex maniac (and be totally within societal norms at the same time), just catch an episode or so of *Love That Bob.* With "master thespian" Bob Cummings (in the eponymous role of a fashion photographer surrounded by nubile young models), his live-in nephew (the pre-*Dobie* Dwayne Hickman), and his infatuated secretary (the pre-*Brady* Ann B. Davis), *Love That Bob* has become one of the great camp classics of our time.

Every episode revolves around the middle-aged, staggeringly square and less-than-virile Bob trying to capture a beauty (with the girls all thinking he's the cat's meow), replete with "family-viewing" innuendoes and euphemisms. At the time, Bob Cummings was thought an urbane, sophisticated, swanky kind of guy (when *swanky* was meant as a compliment); to our eyes today he looks like an out-of-control old letch whose job has driven him insane.

Not to be missed.

Married . . . with Children, 1987. One of the extremely rare deliberately BAD (and great for it) shows, *Married* will live on in history as the first prime-time outing to successfully merge sitcom style with bleak, black, vicious humor. Just as we were getting completely sick of the incredibly perky, incredibly loving, incredibly sincere Cosby family (and their luxurious, sweater-filled life-style), the end-of-their-rope, "has it really all come down to this?" *Married* saved the family sitcom from doom. Featuring the regular lineup of mom, dad, bro, and sis, but all with the original attitude of "we're miserable but we must go on" (as if Sam Beckett had decided to go Hollywood), *Married* celebrates the "dysfunctional" family as being the norm, and being able to find humor in a desperate situation as heroic—and perhaps they're right on both counts. While the humor may be a new low for prime time (with whole episodes on such yukfests as menstruation, bra buying, impotence, and the joys of trampdom), and the "how much can we get away with?" stance sometimes going over the top, *Married . . . with Children* is easily the strongest sitcom reflection of real life since *All in the Family.*

The Dean Martin Show, 1965. Though Perry Como's been lampooned (notably by SCTV) for being the most laid-back performer in the history of show business, Dino always had him beat by a mile. "If Dean Martin were any more relaxed," said *The Christian Science Monitor,* "he'd fall on his face," and the *Los Angeles Times* called him "the world's laziest superstar." By contract not showing up for *The Dean Martin Show* until the very day of taping, Dino'd slide down his fireman's pole (not spilling a drop of bourbon), tell a few jokes your grandfather told when he was your age, cast an appreciative eye on his gaggle of showgirls ("The Golddiggers"), croon a few tunes, make a crack about getting soused, introduce the guest stars like Bill Dana, Liberace, and Joey Heatherton, and barely seem to be working. On the premiere Dino opened, like always, with "Everybody Loves Somebody," but never made it past a few bars: "No point in singing the whole song," he slurred, "you might not buy the record." That's just why we loved him, and the *Dean Martin Show,* for nine boozy years.

Mister Ed, 1961. BAD TV has a long and noble history of series with humanoid mammals in the lead roles, such as *Run, Joe, Run; The Hathaways;* and *Mr. Smith.* Americans love animal shows; even PBS gets its highest ratings from nature programming. But when it comes to nationally successful TV animals, something really disturbing is going on. All of the big growling stars are alike in a number of ways, and what this has to say about Americans' unconscious wishes is really bizarre.

Apparently, we all share a secret daydream to own an animal that can talk, do lots of fun tricks, and help us with our personal problems. The creature must have all the things we love about our pets, and none of the things we don't like about other people. Finally, they must provide what (judging from these shows) is obviously the ultimate American fantasy: an animal that combines the traits of both Superman . . . and Jeeves.

See Flipper save a little boy from drowning . . . and then bring Bud a Coke. Watch Lassie rescue orphans from a burning building . . . and then dig holes for fence posts. Enjoy Gentle Ben single-pawedly frightening away the bad guys . . . and then carry supplies like a pack mule.

Mister Ed is a handsome palomino who's much more competent and attractive in every way than his creepy owner, Wilbur. So just ignore the disturbing truths about TV animal stars . . . the fact that Mister Ed was forced to do the twist with Clint Eastwood . . . the creepy information that the producers stuck something funny in Ed's mouth to make him move his lips like that, trying to get it out . . . and enjoy the show!

**Humiliating innocent mammals has a long and happy
TV history as shown in this utterly hilarious moment from
Mister Ed (Photofest)**

P.S.: A Tennessee minister once claimed that, when you play the *Mister
Ed* theme song backward, you can hear a voice promoting the worship of
Satan. Try it sometime.

The Mod Squad, 1968. There's nothing quite as funny as when network
television tries to get hip; beyond the first few seasons of *Saturday Night
Live* or *Late Night with David Letterman,* practically every attempt has
been a disaster. Aaron Spelling's *The Mod Squad* was a success in that it
had a five-year run with great appeal to preteens who didn't know any better, but just try to watch it now. Starring handsome, clean-cut, Sphinx-like
black hippie Linc, handsome, clean-cut disinherited hippie Pete, and
beautiful, wholesome whore child/runaway hippie Julie as undercover
cops and antiestablishment icons, *The Mod Squad* plays every side of the

fence it can find. You can, however, drown yourself in nostalgia with the renegades' wash-and-wear all-polyester suits, velour sportswear, mutton-chop sideburns, Linc's crash pad (featuring Peter Max curtains and love beads), and such special guest stars as Sammy Davis, Jr. (radical priest and "controversial figure like Martin King and Malcolm X"), Robert Duvall (Catholic murderer), and Sugar Ray Robinson (single-parent boxer). And just try to see how many of your friends can recall the now-classic promo line: "One black . . . one white . . . one blonde . . ."

Peyton Place, 1964. Genius scribbler Grace Metalious revealed that, in 1956, the perfect New England village was a cauldron of suicide, abortion, brutality, alcoholism, and incest; a repressed place where the pants and skirts are dropping like flies but, pre-*Oprah,* everyone's afraid to talk. As she told AP, "To a tourist these towns look as peaceful as a postcard. But if you go beneath that picture, it's like turning over a rock with your foot—all kind of strange things crawl out." This combo of loose morals, tight lips, and strange things was such a sensation that *Peyton Place* became the biggest selling novel of all time, even beating out *Gone with the Wind* (and reigning as #1 until being pushed aside by the mighty *Valley of the Dolls*).

The *Peyton Place* movie, TV series, and endless progeny of made-fors *(Return to Peyton Place; Murder in Peyton Place; Peyton Place: The Next Generation)* were all massive hits, but, oddly, the TV series was the real dream come true, even greater to watch now than when it first appeared (isn't it incredible how we were all so obsessed with Mia Farrow and Ryan O'Neal?). Seeing Dorothy Malone, Ed Nelson, Barbara Parkins, Mia, Ryan, and the rest of the huge cast constantly having illicit sex with each other and then terrified, *terrified* that everyone else will find out, is one of those compelling hoots that only BAD TV can provide.

Police Squad!, 1982. The failure of *Police Squad!* to find its Nielsens is a mystery. Made by the same people who created the massive hit *Airplane!,* it served as the basis for the equally successful *The Naked Gun!* and its sequels, and most of the *Squad* episodes were just as good as any of the *Nakeds* (it even stars the perfect Leslie Nielsen).

A deliberately BAD series, spoofs such as this, and the equally deliberate *Sledge Hammer!* (see below) must violate some secret, mysterious, but cardinal rule of TV success. Is it that the central character in a spoof is too unreal to anchor a show and create repeat business? That we always have to have someone on a TV series we can think of as a friend deserving a visit every week? And if that's so, why can we identify with Jethro Bodine, but not Sergeant Nielsen?

Sing Along with Mitch, 1961. Just before the dawn of the Beatles a generation of Americans was decrying that noise called rock 'n' roll and making immense hits out of Lawrence Welk and Mitch Miller. His goatee may look beatnik, but *Mitch* was really straight out of the golden American past—a show any magnificent Amberson might enjoy. Where families once gathered around the piano to croon a few tunes, now they followed the bouncing ball (as the lyrics scrolled across the bottom of the screen), Mitch's trusty baton, the Sing-Along Gang, the Sing-Along Kids, and Leslie Uggams performing such great hits as "Toot Toot Tootsie" and "I've been Working on the Railroad."

Seeing the show now (and you can, on video), it's hard to believe that *Sing Along with Mitch* was such a huge hit a mere thirty years ago; it seems like something from when dinosaurs ruled the earth, and more fun than ever to watch.

Sledge Hammer!, 1986. The show that answers the question: What if *Dirty Harry, Rambo,* and *Get Smart* had a child who grew up to be a cop? *Sledge Hammer!* is so beyond macho that his female partner barely gets a nod, while his Magnum .44 gets talked to (it's Sledge's closest confidant) and taken to bed (its very own satin pillow). In the pilot the mayor's daughter is kidnapped and Sledge vows to bring her back "dead or alive"; other highlights include an episode where he encourages hoodlums to continue their life of violence by becoming cops, gives jaywalkers warning shots, and takes out a sniper by demolishing the building he's shooting from.

At season one's conclusion the ratings were so poor and the producers so sure they were going to be canceled that they blew up the hero in an atomic explosion. But *Sledge Hammer!* was renewed—so an announcement was made that season two would be a five-year prequel. In all the series was strong enough to warrant forty-one episodes making it out of the can, even though it suffers from the same spoof curse that doomed *Police Squad!, Mary Hartman, Mary Hartman,* and *Twin Peaks.*

That Girl, 1966. The epitome of a "perky" girl, Danny Thomas's daughter stars in this update of *I Love Lucy,* with almost identical schemes, pratfalls, and battles-of-the-sexes, but none of Lucy's talent or a great ensemble cast's chemistry. In one classic episode (costarring another child of TV royalty, Rob Reiner), Marlo reads about toe bowling, decides to give it a try, and of course gets her toe stuck in the bowling ball, having to wear it to an awards ceremony.

When originally aired *That Girl* seemed mod and feminist; today, it's charming, but only must-viewing for women determined to follow the sixties revolution in clothes, makeup (with Ann Marie's hairflip being so extreme that it became a logo), and perkydom. It also makes you wonder: did New York City ever before or since look so cozy? Are Donald and Dobie Gillis the same person?

Sadly, starring in *That Girl* so traumatized Marlo Thomas that she felt compelled to marry Phil Donahue.

V, 1983. A wonderfully imaginative and terrifically produced effort that became a movie of the week (MOW), miniseries, and weekly series, *V* is the story of wonderful aliens who appear to be people like us and who convince the world that they're here because they need some cheap chemicals; in exchange they'll give us a big step up into the future. Who doesn't love the Visitors? It's only when TV reporter Marc Singer gets aboard one of the many "mother" ships hovering over every major city and discovers the alien plans to take over the world that an underground resistance is born and a civil war is launched, with the whole thing echoing the Nazi occupation of France—but with a twist.

Turns out those aliens are really reptiles, who snack on live white mice and other appetizing treats. In preparation for her wedding, lizard leader Diana (Jane Badler, who gives Joan Collins and Stephanie Beacham a run for the money as bitch-of-all-time) takes a bath of live eels. A woman who's been having intimate relations with an alien (the pre–Freddy Krueger Robert Englund) finally gives birth; she picks up her beautiful, completely human-looking baby, cooing with relief—until it sticks out its very long forked tongue! She goes into labor again . . . and produces a lizard twin! The creators of *V* seemed to have taken a how-far-can-we-go, how-much-can-we-get-away-with stance, and that's exactly what made it so BAD, and so perfect.

There's a lot of underlying philosophy to the characters on *Gilligan's Island*. They're really a metaphor for the nations of the world, and their purpose was to show how nations have to get along together . . . or cease to exist.

—Sherwood Schwartz, producer

Two vicious alien mouse-eaters plot the destruction of the Earth in *V* (Photofest)

How Could You?
(When BAD Things Happen to Good People)

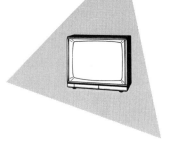

Hollywood is a dreary industrial town controlled by hoodlums of enormous wealth, the ethical sense of a pack of jackals, and taste so degraded that it befouls everything it touches.
—S. J. Perelman

Hollywood is where they put you under contract instead of under observation.
—Walter Winchell

SINCE ITS VERY BIRTH THE EFFECTS OF TV ON VIEWERS HAS BEEN hotly and continuously debated by psychiatrists, educators, social scientists, and other publicity-seeking academics. Does watching violent cop shows make you violent? Do sitcoms' twenty-two-minute happy endings to everyone's life problems make you frustrated that your own problems aren't so easily solved? Does so much sex in advertising debase sexual desire? Different studies have produced wildly different results, and this debate is as raucous among professionals today as when it began forty years ago.

The argument is so powerful because television itself is so two sided. Snooty French eggheads of a certain age, for example, came up with the idea that each person's personal view of the world is created from the library of visual memories he or she has acquired in living—an idea they've pretentiously named "the image-repertoire" If this is even remotely true, for Americans born after 1950, the greatest image provider by far—and the whole cornerstone for a system of beliefs—is TV.

Child psychiatrist (and author of *The Uses of Enchantment*) Bruno Bettelheim, for example, believes that TV has an immense influence. Though he's often too Freudian for his own good, his anti-TV thinking is unusually thought provoking: "Children who have been taught, or conditioned, to listen passively most of the day to the warm verbal communication coming from the TV screen, to the deep emotional appeal of the so-called TV personality, are often unable to respond to real persons because they arouse so much less feeling than the skilled actor. Worse, they lose the ability to learn from reality because life experiences are more complicated than the ones they see on the screen, and there is no one who comes in at the end to explain it all."

Just as you're ready to follow this line and wholly believe that TV has this immense influence, however, you're reminded of how utterly ordinary it is. How many times is the TV left on when no one's watching; how frequently do you find yourself barely paying attention to what's on the air; how often are you stuck flipping the channels and not landing on anything in particular, or flipping channels between two, three, even more shows because one by itself isn't interesting enough to wholly engage your attention?

Television is so pervasive, so constant, so everywhere, it's nowhere. Even people who say they never watch television usually have at least one set, and many have TVs all over the house—making it just another appliance, like a toaster. However, now that you've convinced yourself that TV's nothing, you remember that television reaches such a huge audience it's impossible to believe there's no impact. If a hardcover book sells 50,000 copies, it's a bestseller; if a record sells 500,000 copies, it's a hit; if an average Hollywood movie draws 10 million to the box office, it's a success—but if a network show can't attract more than *20 million* viewers, it's a bomb.

In Hollywood, people who work in features like to sneer constantly about how much more beautiful film is than TV. There's nothing remotely like television, however, for making the viewer believe, "This is real. This is the truth." The bright lighting, saturated colors, and focus on normal people living their daily lives constantly reinforces TV's blood ties with its big-time cousin: the surveillance camera. The very fact that television is so ubiquitous and so mundane makes it seem all the more honest, all the more believable, but at the same time, all the more ordinary and dismissable. TV is so vast that it's the one thing that really unites us, coast to coast, as a nation. You and your parents and your ex-boyfriend and your best friend from high school may not agree on much these days—but you can all enjoy *Murphy Brown* or *Roseanne* or *Nature,* even if you no longer live anywhere near each other. It's TV's very vastness, though, that makes debating the effects of television sometimes seem like debating the philosophical issues of the toothbrush.

The most promising finding today on television's effects is that it has a very big influence, but it's a very light touch—something like when you're riding on a plane, and sitting next to you is a big fat guy, and he's humming to himself: "Tuh la-la-la, Dee da doo da, Tuh la-la-la . . ." and you're trying to concentrate on something important and he's really bugging you, but it's a five-hour flight and you don't want to say anything, but he keeps it up and he's driving you crazy, and finally maybe you do say something, and maybe he stops for a little bit, and then starts up again, and you get off the plane really annoyed.

So you're waiting for your luggage and what do you hear in your mind? None other than "Tuh la-la-la, Dee da doo da, Tuh la-la-la . . ." and for the rest of the day and maybe the rest of the week this tune you didn't even want to hear in the first place keeps going off in your brain.

That's what many now think is the influence of TV; it's nothing more serious than a little ditty, but maybe for the rest of your life these ideas you didn't even want to hear in the first place keep going off in your brain.

ⅱ

Though TV history is filled with schlockmeister producers and stars who appear in one broadcast horror after another, it's also filled with major stumbles by those who should know better. While the *Tammi Awards,* the second part of this book, is a festival of television programs that were utterly without merit, this chapter highlights the disasters of your favorite TV producers, writers, and actors—the people we usually think of as possessed by genius. The greatest TV creators, the very best TV shows, and the biggest TV stars have all had utterly BAD moments. They tried hard, but the pull of the awful was just too strong, and they succumbed. Luckily, most of us forget these ludicrous moments immediately, which kept them from adulterating the reputations of their stars and creators. With "How Could You? (When BAD Things Happen to Good People)," however, *BAD TV* now brings it all back home.

Comedy

The Beverly Hillbillies Solve the Energy Crisis, 1981. As will be seen time and again, padding a fun half hour into a two-hour "special" is almost always a terrible idea; the visible strain to keep it snappy and keep those jokes coming rings louder than the plot. In this made-for-TV movie Jane Hathaway now works for Washington's Energy Department and hilarious misadventures ensue when she thinks Granny's moonshine works as well as the source of the Clampett fortune. The only original Hillbillies coming back for this belabored two-hour special are Jed and Elly Mae; joining them are Imogene Coca as Granny's ancient mother, producer's daughter Linda Henning as "Linda," and Heather Locklear as "Heather."

Bring Me the Head of Dobie Gillis, 1988. Dobie and wife Zelda have problems with son Georgie (who's too Dobie-like for his own good) as well as with Connie Stevens (subbing for Tuesday Weld) who, in the wake of Warren Beatty's death, realizes that she was really in love with Dobie after all. When he turns down her proposal to run away and be rich together, Connie offers everyone in town big bucks if they'll kill him.

Diana, 1973. Popping out of her Lotus Élan in a black leather jumpsuit and kicking the bad guys with her kung fu fighting (while always speaking in those beautiful ultra-Brit tones), Diana Rigg as Mrs. Emma Peel became one of the immortals. So of course NBC thought we'd love her just as much as a humdrum divorcée working in a New York City department store but, oddly, not kicking anyone in the head. Shades of *Sister Kate* (see page 299).

The Harlem Globetrotters on Gilligan's Island, 1981. Scatman Crothers, Barbara Bain, Martin Landau (as an evil scientist), and an army of basketball-playing robots (trying to take over the island for its important mineral rights) cross paths with Gilligan, the Skipper, a millionaire, and his wife, a movie star, the Professor, Mary Ann, and the notoriously fun-loving basketball team. This two-hour special wasn't merely padded to obesity; it wasn't even originally meant for the Globetrotters, but instead as a vehicle for the Dallas Cowboy Cheerleaders, who couldn't fit the shooting into their hectic schedule. So even though this made-for-TV movie is one of the lowest of the low . . . it could have been even worse.

Life with Lucy, 1986. America was thrilled to learn that the Empress of Television, Lucille Ball, was coming back to do a weekly series. All the

The Skipper and Gilligan meet two of the many, many people who just happen to land on their island—but this time it's the Harlem Globetrotters! (Photofest)

elements seemed propitious; the producers included Lucy's real-life husband and two writers from the original *I Love Lucy,* and the show would return Ms. Ball to her signature comedy style of zany schemes and physical slapstick.

Watching a not-so-nimble, seventy-five-year-old *grande dame* and the eighty-year-old Gale Gordon trying to clown their way through this terribly written show with its cardboard characters and rigorous, demanding slapstick was, instead, agonizing; of the twenty-two episodes produced, only eight were aired.

Love, Sidney, 1981. This series began with something brand new to prime time: a sitcom about the relationship between a gay man, Sidney Shorr (well played by the heterosexual Tony Randall) and a straight woman, Laurie Morgan (Swoosie Kurtz). The two struggle with their friendship,

**Mary Tyler Moore finds she can't go home again as a
semiretired-but-perky ingenue called *Mary* (Stephen Cox)**

and on issues such as abortion, child custody, and what really constitutes a family in today's society. Heralded at the time for Sidney being the first out-front leading gay character on TV, the series suddenly decided to drop Sidney's carnal desires (his preferences were no longer discussed); Randall tried to use his star power to keep the series at the same level of gayness as its pilot, but to no avail, and *Love, Sidney* devolved into a poor *Odd Couple* remake.

Mary, 1985. An attempt to exactly recreate the success of the original, seven-year-running *Mary Tyler Moore Show,* with James Farentino, Katey Sagal, bad writing, poorly developed characters, and a hopelessly miscast (as a fifty-year-old ingenue) Mary Tyler Moore.

The New Odd Couple, 1982. Felix Unger, Oscar Madison, Cecily and Gwendolyn Pigeon are back—and they're black! A BAD TV highlight, since most of this series' scripts were virtually the same as the first *Odd Couple.*

Ozzie's Girls, 1973. Ozzie and Harriet's constant unemployment force them to take in boarders when sons Rick and Dave (who produced this spin-off) blow town. The new renters are, of course, comely coeds (one black, one white), whose mischievous antics wreak havoc (but a very *mild* havoc) on the Nelson seniors' golden years.

Partridge Family: 2200 A.D., 1974. In this *Jetsons* hybrid the strangely popular rock-band family turns into a cartoon and moves to outer space.

Still the Beaver, 1983. Featuring the entire original cast save the deceased Hugh Beaumont, this utterly depressing series' central theme was to illustrate how pathetic the lives of all the *Leave It to Beaver*s stars had become. The Beave is now a sloppy, clueless, oafish, and divorced (no surprise) father, who moves back home to Mom with his two sons. June has become a widow who can't wait to forgo her golden years for the chance to raise Beaver's waiflike, motherless children. Wally has grown up to be a creep—just like we always expected—and a lawyer to boot. The only good news is Eddie Haskell's son, a genius mimic of his dad.

Leave It to Beaver was one of the best-written shows on television; *Still the Beaver* seemed like it wasn't written at all, though it did limp on as a series for a few years on the obviously desperate Disney Channel and TBS (where it was called, of course, *The New Leave It to Beaver*).

Tabitha, 1977. Dreary, unimaginative sequel to the wonderful *Bewitched* focusing on the teen trials of the eponymous half-breed and costarring BAD legend Robert Urich.

Topper, 1973; *Topper,* 1979. In the 1953 series (based on the 1952 Cary Grant/Constance Bennett feature), the story of devil-may-care, married ghosts (Anne Jeffreys and Robert Sterling) haunting a stodgy banker (Leo G. Carroll), was elegant and charming. It was eroded to forgettable in '73 by *Girl from U.N.C.L.E.* Stefanie Powers, and degraded even further in '79 by Kate Jackson and her husband (at the time) Andrew Stevens.

The Van Dyke Show, 1988. Dick Van Dyke plays a grade-B actor who retires to live with his son Barry Van Dyke in a small Pennsylvania town. He hangs around the local bijou telling warhorse show-biz tales, has a few misunderstandings with his son and family, does a little slapstick in his spare time, and is so relentlessly dull, you start praying for a club-wield-ing serial killer to show up.

A perfect programming opportunity for The Family Channel.

Drama

After M*A*S*H, 1983. Harry Morgan, Jamie Farr, and William Christo-pher finally return to the U.S.—*M*A*S*H* having lasted longer than the Korean War—and continue their medical careers at an uneventful Missouri hospital. The series began with excellent Nielsens from viewer curiosity; as it devolved into just another "we've seen this before" doctor show with-out the black humor or ensemble style of the original, we vanished.

Cheyenne, 1955; *Sugarfoot,* 1957; *Bronco,* 1959. Starring sexy loners who wandered around, finding adventure, these three Westerns introduced the concept of utterly confusing us viewers with programming incest (see also *The New Odd Couple*). Ready? In its second season (1956) *Cheyenne* alternated on ABC's schedule with an anthology series, *Conflict;* in its third (1957), *Sugarfoot* was introduced, and *Cheyenne* alternated with it. In '58 *Cheyenne* star Clint Walker walked out in a contract dispute; Warner aired *Bronco* as a replacement, but called it *Cheyenne,* and still al-ternated it with *Sugarfoot.* In '59 Walker returned, *Cheyenne* got to run by itself, *Bronco* was spun off as its own series, and alternated with *Sugar-foot.* In 1960 *Cheyenne, Bronco,* and *Sugarfoot* all alternated together, but all of them were called *Cheyenne.* In '61 *Cheyenne* and *Bronco* alternated, and both were called *Cheyenne.* In '62 the "real" *Cheyenne* rode alone for one year, until being canceled, finally, in 1963.

The Colbys, 1987. This spin-off of *Dynasty* did many wonderful things. It brought Charlton Heston and Barbara Stanwyck back to television; it brought Fallon Carrington (killed on *Dynasty*) back to life without both-ering with any silly reincarnation theories; it introduced America to the idea that people could actually be named "Sable" and "Bliss." But the greatest thing *The Colbys* ever did—and one of the greatest moments ever in the history of BAD TV—was to finish itself by having Fallon abducted by a UFO.

Dallas, 1986. Patrick Duffy decided he was sick of playing J.R.'s decent brother Bobby Ewing, and left to "pursue other interests." The producers ac-commodated his career wishes by having Bobby run over by a car, and dutifully buried at Southfork. After a year, however, Duffy decided that the grass wasn't so green after all—and told *Dallas* he'd be glad to come back. Their solution? To have the 1986 season opener, "The Resurrection of Bobby," have wife Pam find Duffy happily in the shower, and realize that she'd dreamed the entire previous six months' worth of shows. All the many nefarious plots and counterschemes that *Dallas* fans had spent so long enjoying (and trying to keep straight) were but Pam's *very long* nightmare.

The scales of TV justice have weighed against Duffy, however. His only other big roles to date have been to costar with BAD Queen Suzanne Somers in the too-dull-to-be-included-here *Step by Step,* and to don green contact lenses and latex-webbed hands and feet (as well as have his acting judged solely in terms of his swimming skills) as *The Man from Atlantis.* Oddly, *Man from Atlantis* was the first American TV show sold to the People's Republic of China.

David Cassidy—Man Undercover, 1978. He wowed us as the teen dream on *The Partridge Family,* singing such megahits as "I Think I Love You." But instead of being happy David Cassidy had to prove himself as a serious actor . . . with this act of TV terrorism. Trying to be a one-man *Mod Squad* Dave hits every cliché as a "youth" detective with a family so schmaltzy, they'll give you heartburn. Why do actors think they can do everything . . . and why do television execs let them try?

The Fifteen Years Later Affair, 1983. Quite a bit past their prime, computer company exec Robert Vaughn and fashion designer Ilya Kuryakin come out of retirement to once again aid U.N.C.L.E. against T.H.R.U.S.H. If you thought the elderly Roger Moore was less than believable in his later *Bond* epics, wait'll you see a portly Napoleon Solo and a haggard David McCallum (along with their athletic doubles) perform remarkable feats of derring-do.

The Jacksons: An American Dream, 1992. The most revealing moment in this much-watched miniseries was the discovery that child star Michael Jackson had a rat for a pet. When Michael finished a performance and learned of its untimely death in a mousetrap, he screamed, "My rat! My rat! My rat! My rat!"

The Scarlet Letter, 1979. This PBS production was not only a dreary adaptation of the racy Nathaniel Hawthorne novel, but Meg Foster's *A* wasn't even scarlet, but gold.

———

Stone Pillow, 1984. Lucille Ball was seventy-four years old when she decided to follow Farrah Fawcett's career strategy and try a dramatic turn while looking as wrecked as possible. The problem is, Lucy's such an indelible clown in our memories that when she first appears as the homeless Florabelle in *Stone Pillow,* with stocking cap, rat's nest hair, and raw eggs for breakfast, it looks like the start of a great comic skit. Compounding the problem is her acting, which is the same big gestures and popping bug-eyes she'd always used as a comedienne. The only true feelings of tragedy this show evoked was that Lucy really looked her age, and the whole thing made us wish she'd done a Garbo, vanishing at the peak of her career and leaving behind only the greatness of *I Love Lucy.*

Filmed on location in New York City during a ninety-degree heat wave, *Stone Pillow* not only tarnished Lucy's reputation; it gave her dehydration, and a two-week hospital stay.

Twin Peaks, 1990. Once upon a time there was a thirteen-year-old boy who saw the premiere of *Twin Peaks* and thought it was the most excellent thing in the history of TV. He made sure to watch every show, had pictures of all the stars on the walls of his room, bought the show's spin-off books, the soundtrack CD, everything he could get his hands on.

He loved how the whole thing was so nutty and so different from regular TV. He read all the press, and was thrilled to find that the actors shared his feelings; Log Lady Catherine Coulson, for example, saying, "The log is a character, or at least it has certain characteristics which can be channeled through the Log Lady. The log is a log. . . . I know this log now. It has a certain kind of centered thing around it. It feels pretty natural. Though it's not a baby, it is a log." And Sheryl "Laura Palmer" Lee explaining her own love of the show with "It helped me learn to accept my own dark side. We're all bombarded with 'what we're supposed to be.' Anytime we've done anything where there's shame and guilt we tend to want to hide it—it helped me let go of some of that. I realize now that I don't always have to be the perfect daughter. I spent many years saying 'I'm fine.' With that attitude, we end up with unhealthy, angry people."

Even though each episode had worse ratings than the one before, and even though his other friends got bored with it, he just kept on loving *Twin Peaks.* He loved the dwarf in the dreams who talked backward, the clairvoyant FBI agent looking for letters under people's fingernails, the middle-aged woman who thought she was a high-school cheerleader, the love

**Farrah Fawcett deliberately looking bedraggled in _The
Burning Bed_ had nothing on the homeless Lucille Ball from
Stone Pillow** (Photofest)

affair at the police department, the startling appearance of the llama at the
veterinarian's, the cryptic clue "Fire walk with me," even the donuts and
"the damn fine cup of coffee."

At the season finale, with its "ironic" collection of cliffhanger clichés, he started having doubts. Watching the final episode of the series, with its endless scenes of characters being chased around in a valance factory (and a tone that made it seem the producers were saying: "We know you loved this, but to us, it's just a joke"), he turned to his dad and said, "This is *bull-shit!*"

Kids' Shows

The Howdy Doody Show, 1947. The *Doody* producers made Clarabell the clown mute so they could pay the actors portraying him (including Bob Keeshan, later to become Captain Kangaroo) reduced rates.

The Pinky Lee Show, September 20, 1955. Hyperactive bow-tie wearing kids' show host Pinky Lee had his eponymous program broadcast live every afternoon, five days a week. One day Pinky collapsed of a heart attack while doing a billy-goat dance in front of his audience of children, and NBC strangely cut the video but left the audio on, so all the kids at home could stare at a blank screen while listening to his writhings and the audience screaming in turmoil.

Lee (whose signature lisp was insured by Lloyd's of London) survived, living for another thirty-eight years.

The Soupy Sales Show, 1965. Notorious pie-thrower Soupy told his audience of children to go get their parents' wallets and purses and send him "those little green pieces of paper." He was fired, but his popularity was so great that an outpouring of viewer mail and phone calls brought him back.

Winky-Dink and You, 1953. By purchasing the Winky Dink Magic TV Kit for fifty cents, a kid could put a sheet of acetate on the TV and, by drawing boats, harps, fire engines, and the like, help the animated Dink with his various adventures. The BAD: Many children weren't allowed to buy the magic kit, so they drew, with crayons and laundry pens, on the TV screen itself.

News and Pseudonews

The Assassination of Marion Barry, 1980. A prankster called local Washington, D.C. TV newsrooms with the startling news that their mayor had been murdered. Rushing to beat each other in being first with their reports, none of the stations bothered checking with City Hall, and the news of Barry's death was reported around the world. He was, of course, perfectly fine at the time, though he would later go to prison for crack possession.

The CBS Evening News with Dan Rather, 1980. Dan, disguised in an old blanket and five-o'clock shadow, goes undercover to share with us his personal and utterly superficial feelings about the Afghanistan civil war.

Eyewitness News, KABC (Los Angeles), 1975. A native Californian stewardess just returned from three months in war-torn Laos was interviewed:

> **Reporter:** What did you learn about the Laotian people? Or, more important, I suppose, what did you learn about yourself?
> **Stewardess:** For myself, I learned I can get along without hamburgers and ice cream.
> **Reporter:** Thank you. I guess we can see that idealism is alive and flourishing among young California people!

The Nightly News, KNBC (Los Angeles), 1976. The very popular anchor Kelly Lange hosted a series of special celebrity interviews during sweeps week in October, and the final interview was with a "mystery guest," an event that the show promoed endlessly. The mystery was solved when it turned out the guest was Ms. Lange interviewing herself. "Look," said she. "You've got your misery. You've got your tragedy. You've got to have your laughs too. You've got to have your chuckles. Otherwise you're just asking too much of viewers who've been hassled all day long."

NBC News Update, early 1980s. Dethroned from her preeminent anchor spot, Jessica Savitch was reduced to reading these brief promo pieces—which on occasion she seemed to be doing drunk and/or stoned.

Oral Roberts, 1987. Oral told his followers that God was going to kill him ("call him back to heaven") if he didn't get $8 million in donations. He didn't get the sum (though a dogtrack owner did contribute $1.3 mil), backpedaled like mad, and is still alive today.

Plimpton! The Great Quarterback Sneak; Plimpton! At the Wheel; Plimpton! Adventures in Africa; Plimpton! Shoot-Out at Rio Lobo, 1971–1973.

David Wolper and self-styled Renaissance man George Plimpton produced and starred in this series about a "regular guy" playing football, driving race cars, hunting elephants, and acting in Westerns with John Wayne. Wolper would go on to produce *Roots;* Plimpton would go on to shill the low-grade children's computer Intellivision.

The Today Show, 1992. Filipino Edwin Bayron appears to explain how he was born as a hermaphrodite, had surgery to complete his female side, and has now become the first pregnant man—but sadly, the *Today* producers had been hoodwinked and this riveting story turned out not to be true.

Sci Fi

Most TV shows are what I call Donna Reed's living room. Donna goes to the door, opens the door, and there's the milkman. "Oh, hello, John," she says. "Two light cream, three heavy cream." But John's got a problem, so they go into the living room, sit on the couch, and talk for seven pages. "Oh, John, you found out your wife is giving you a surprise birthday party and you don't want her to know you know." They shoot the seven pages and then they go home for the day.

Me, if I can't blow up the world in the first ten seconds, then the show's a flop.

—Irwin Allen, producer of *Voyage to the Bottom of the Sea, Land of the Giants,* et cetera

For some reason, when the normally great science fiction TV series go astray, they *really* miss the mark, with episodes that are bombs beyond belief. Why these otherwise decent shows suddenly turn out-and-out BAD is a mystery. Are successful sci-fi writers, producers, and directors just this side of insane? Does working too hard on these kinds of programs drive them over the edge?

Lost in Space:
"The Attack of the Monster Plants," 1965. Giant flowers create an evil Judy twin.
"The Space Croppers," 1966. Devil-voiced Mercedes McCambridge

and her family of outer-space hillbillies imperil the Robinsons with their ravenous crop.

"The Promised Planet," 1967. After landing on a planet of wild youths Will turns into a hippie and Penny becomes a go-go dancer.

"The Great Vegetable Rebellion," 1967. The Robinsons are turned into plant people by a nasty carrot-headed alien.

The Outer Limits:

"The Zanti Misfits," 1964. An alien planet exiles its criminals to earth, where they turn out to be ants with sneering human faces.

"Corpus Earthling," 1963. Because he's got a metal plate in his head, Robert Culp can overhear alien rocks and their plans to invade our bodies and control our minds.

"It Crawled Out of the Woodwork," 1964. A dustball feeds on a vacuum cleaner's electricity and grows to monstrous proportions.

Star Trek (The Original Series):

"Miri," 1966. Get ready for white-hot excitement as the *Enterprise* crew beams down to a planet inhabited only by a few obnoxious children, who taunt them by chanting, "Bonk, bonk on the head" and call them "grups."

"Spock's Brain," 1968. A simpleminded, large-breasted alien woman steals Leonard Nimoy's brain out of his head (replacing it with a metal hat) so said brain can run the environmental machinery of her subterranean, all-female society. Fortunately, the men of the Federation steal it back, forcing the women to again cohabitate with the oafish male lunkheads living on the planet's harsh surface.

"And the Children Shall Lead," 1968. Once again the *Enterprise* beams down to a planet inhabited only by obnoxious children; this time it's because the adults all committed suicide. With special guest star, attorney Melvin Belli, as the "friendly angel."

"Turnabout Intruder," 1968. An ex-love of Kirk's (and who isn't?), rejected as unsuited to command, makes use of alien machinery to beam her psyche into Kirk's body (and vice versa) so she can sit in the big easy chair on the bridge. William Shatner, performing the role of a woman in a man's body, is not to be missed.

"The Way to Eden," 1969. Intergalactic alien hippies, searching for a new Eden, drop by to check out the *Enterprise*'s cool quotient. Kirk proves to be hopelessly unhip, but Spock gets to groove in a way-out jam session.

———

Superman:

"The Brainy Burro," 1957. Two thieves in Mexico commit the perfect crime via a clairvoyant donkey.

"Through the Time Barrier," 1954. A time machine accident sends Jimmy Olsen, Perry White, Lois Lane, Superman, and a gangster back to the caveman era.

"Great Caesar's Ghost," 1954. Perry White goes insane, tormented by Julius Caesar's ghost.

Thriller:

"Terror in Teakwood," 1960. An ambitious pianist digs up the corpse of his greatest rival, using the cadaver's hands to achieve new greatness in pianism.

"The Remarkable Mrs. Hawks," 1961. Farmgal Jo Van Fleet, the embodiment of the goddess Circe, raises the best pigs in town.

Musical Interlude: ABC execs loved *The Outer Limits* theme music so much they used it again on both *The Invaders* and *The Fugitive.*

Voyage to the Bottom of the Sea: Where else can you meet fishmen, heatmen, rockmen, frostmen, snowmen, beastmen, giant jellyfish, vicious puppets, cryonic Nazis, evil robots, and the Loch Ness monster—all in one series?

"The Shape of Doom," 1966. The *Seaview* is terrorized by a giant whale who's swallowed an atom bomb.

"Werewolf," 1966. The entire crew is turned into a pack of werewolves.

"The Day the World Ended," 1966. A senator/hypnotist makes the entire crew believe that everyone in the world but them has mysteriously disappeared.

"The Plant Man," 1967. A vile twin uses mind control to force his brother to make evil plants.

The Soaps

Since the very beginnings of radio (TV's mother), there've been soap operas, named for their most significant sponsors ("brought to you by *Diz*") and instantly inherited by television at the moment of its noble birth. Soaps are afflicted with all the elements of BAD TV that the discerning

viewer demands: on-the-cheap production values, mind-boggling plot in-
consistencies, outrageous miscasting, and acting that often refuses to as-
sist the viewer in the suspension of disbelief—yet none of this has af-
fected the shows' enormous and enduring popularity.

Daytime fans have come to accept, nay, expect and demand, such not-
of-our-world plot devices as long-lost parents, siblings, and offspring; periodic bouts of amnesia or schizophrenia accompanied by psychomatic
blindness, deafness, and paralysis; and popular characters commonly
making return trips from the Great Beyond. A big rule of soap physics is,
if you haven't seen the body, don't count on the character being dead—
and even if you have seen the corpse, it could easily have been a long-for-
gotten twin or a surgically altered substitute who went down in that
sweeps-week plane crash. In a world where children routinely age from
six months to sixteen years over a weekend, how can it possibly matter
that it's biologically inconceivable for the forty-something-year-old actress now playing the town matriarch to have borne the thirty-something-
year-old starlet recently cast as her daughter?

Soaps are so beyond the wacky that it's impossible to nominate any particular series as wholly BAD. For example, during what many fans considered to be a so-so run of episodes on the wildly popular *All My Children:*

- Natalie gets stuck down a well.
- Janet, Natalie's look-alike sister who stuck her in the well, clubs Hayley on the head.
- Natalie develops post-traumatic stress disorder.
- Brian starts to talk like Yogi Bear.
- Janet commits murder.
- Janet has Natalie's husband's baby.

And about the same time, also considered utterly mundane, on *The
Young and the Restless:*

- David is squashed in a trash compactor.
- Sheila fakes her pregnancy and switches Lauren's baby with one she bought from a black-market ring. Sheila's mother figures it all out, but just as she's about to tell someone, she's paralyzed by a stroke.
- Sheila is trapped in a fire and presumed dead. The rescued body, however, turns out to be the meter man.

■ Sheila revives on *The Young and the Restless*'s sister show, *The Bold and the Beautiful,* where she snares leading man Eric Forrester.

■ Sheila returns to *The Young and the Restless* to blackmail Lauren so she won't reveal Sheila's past to the upstanding Eric.

Soaps do, however, have their BAD moments; what follows is a highly arbitrary listing of some of the most famous and infamous of them. But first, what important sociological themes do we learn from this genre? What are the startling revelations of Soap World?

■ Death is about as scary as Hawaii.

■ Hospital cafeterias rival the finest restaurants as places to meet, greet, and eat. Given the slightest provocation even busy CEOs will drop by the hospital cafeteria—a simple phone call will never do the trick.

■ There is no such thing as a secret or a past that stays that way. Illegitimate children given up at birth will always find their way home to mother and a near-consumated affair with a sibling.

■ Despite the apparent failure of Communism, class struggle is alive and well in the USA. Wealthy matriarchs continue to block attempts by the deserving poor to marry above their class, while the machinations of the undeserving poor continue to justify the prejudices of the upper classes.

■ Minorities need not worry about their romantic prospects in communities with negligible ethnic populations. If a town has only one African-American male and one African-American female, they will find each other and fall deeply in love.

■ Any midsized American city can be a hotbed of spies and international intrigue—no military presence or even a defense-related industry is required.

■ No deed goes unpunished. Post-abortion trauma (a scientific phenomenon recognized almost solely by the Reagan and Bush administrations) will befall any otherwise stable heroine should she have the misfortune not to conveniently miscarry an unwanted child.

All My Children, 1970. Twenty-odd years ago Bobby Martin (son of the family-values Martin clan) vanished while on a trip to the attic to bring down his skis. In 1991 the *AMC* powers-that-be acknowledged their unfortunate memory lapse by having bride-to-be Opal spot a skeleton with skis while trapped in that same attic moments before her nuptials.

Throughout the eighties Pine Valley (the fictional setting of *All My Children*) had its own resident psychic and visionary, Jeremy Hunter. Although this monk turned mercenary turned artist and teacher was able to engineer the rescue of numerous damsels in distress, he never did sense the unfortunate Bobby up in the attic. Finally, having run out of victims/love interests in Pine Valley, ABC moved Jeremy to another community desperately in need of something to shore up its sagging ratings—Corinth, site of one of the lowest-rated of soaps, *Loving*. God knows what disasters are sure to befall that show's leading ladies now that Jeremy's in town to save them.

Since Pine Valley's sex goddess, Susan Lucci, has never to date won an Emmy (though she's been nominated fourteen times), we'd like now to give her a special award; she wins for TV's All-Time, Most Cursed Name: Erica Kane Martin Brent Cudahy Chandler Montgomery Montgomery.

Another World, 1980s. When Brittany Peterson went on trial for the murder of her husband, Peter Love, the jury was composed of home viewers who'd responded to a special promotion by the show—and the writers (along with poor Brittany) were required to stick with whatever the fans decided.

During the seventies *AW* consistently placed in the top five for daytime dramas; the early eighties, though, found the *World* fallen from grace, and getting only mediocre Nielsens. The producers madly tried to compensate by bringing in one batch of new writers after another, the writers in turn bringing in one batch of new *AW* characters after another. Entire families were carefully introduced and thrown into the program's soapy stew—only to vanish entirely a few months later. This chaos baffled viewers and drove the ratings even lower; finally, order has been restored, and *AW* is now inching back up in popularity.

As the World Turns, 1956. Only in Soap World could the venerable couple of Bob and Kim Hughes be thought of as pillars of the community. The two have racked up several marriages and innumerable affairs between them, not to mention an illegitimate, long-thought-dead child, the product of an affair carried on while Dr. Bob was married to Kim's sister. In spite of all this sin the two remain bastions of good taste in this daytime version of WASP heaven; when Grandma Nancy makes an appearance, replete with a simple strand of pearls, the decades just fade away—if you close your eyes you can even pretend the *Father Knows Best*s live just down the street.

The Bold and the Beautiful, 1987. This glitzy show, set in the fashion industry of Los Angeles (not a city known for its garment district), features many name-cursed characters such as Ridge, Thorne, and Storm. Despite the enormous wealth of *B & B*'s leading family, the Forresters, all their adult children remained at home with the folks—until a complicated dance of wife-swapping and divorce forced the producers to construct additional sets.

Shouldn't there be at least one episode of *B & B* where a member of this gorgeous cast *doesn't* take a shower? And if *B & B* takes place in the fashion world, how come all the male leads are straight?

Days of Our Lives, 1965. All soaps rely on the common amnesia and plastic surgery ploy; the *Days of Our Lives'* Horton family spiced up the mix by adding incest when sister (later Sister) Marie fell in love with a doctor who turned out to be her brother Tommy (thought to be missing in action in Korea), a victim of torture, amnesia, and intensive reconstructive surgery.

DOL tried the torture, amnesia, and plastic surgery route again in the eighties, using it to explain the presence of a new actor in the role of "even though he fell off a cliff he's not really dead" policeman Roman Brady. But when the original Roman (with his original face) returned to the show in the nineties, *Days* didn't dare risk fan displeasure by killing off the very popular new Roman. Instead, Roman II was revealed to be the amnesia-afflicted plastic-surgery victim John Black, whose implanted memories of life as Roman Brady were part of an elaborate conspiracy too complicated to explain here.

This caused a crisis not only for poor John, but for his "we thought she was dead when we saw the plane blow up but she was really only in a drug-induced coma for five years" wife Marlena, who now had two husbands—and, of course, was madly in love with both (especially after Roman II's second great love, Isabella, died of pancreatic cancer).

If you're a big *DOL* fan, surely in 1992 you would've called that 900 number (and paid for the privilege) to vote on Baby Devereaux's name—and probably you wouldn't even know that the episode where that name would be broadcast had already been taped.

The Edge of Night, 1956. This strangely accented serial was set in Monticello, a city acknowledged by no less an authority than *The Soap Opera Encyclopedia* as having one of the highest crime and mortality rates in the U.S. Local happenings included an attempt by an evil genius to take the town over by mass hypnosis. In 1961 viewers were so upset by the death of character Sarah Lane that Teal Ames, the actress who portrayed her, appeared at the end of a following show to prove that she herself was still alive.

General Hospital, 1973. In 1979 antihero and perm pioneer Luke Spencer raped sweet young Laura Baldwin in his deserted disco; the two went on to become the most popular couple in daytime history, landing on the cover of *Newsweek* in 1981. Following this feminist nightmare Luke and Laura (along with James Bond stand-in Robert Scorpio) saved the world from the evil Cassadine family, whose attempt to control the weather via "carbonic snow" put Port Charles in the deep freeze. Through Luke, Laura, and Scorpio's brave interventions, the evil Cassadines ended up being frozen themselves.

This plot line, commonly known as the "Ice Princess" story (for the secret computer password that averts the Apocalypse), drove the show's ratings so high that Elizabeth Taylor deigned to make a guest appearance as the Widow Cassadine, gifting Luke and Laura on their wedding day with both a curse and a haunted yacht. Post-Ice Princess, Port Charles has been the site of extraterrestrial visits and numerous threats to global security, while Luke and Laura have moved to a Texas steer ranch.

Loving, 1991. One character experiences the horror of cough-syrup addiction.

One Life to Live, 1968. Beloved wife, mother, and daughter Vicki Lord has been a pillar of Llanview society since 1968 when *One Life to Live* made its debut. Despite suffering recurring bouts of schizophrenia Vicki continues to stand for all that is good in the world—so it's unclear whether it was Vicki or her wicked alter-ego Nikki whose secret adolescence in the secret, underground city of Eterna was uncovered in a late-eighties plot twist. And, while it was certainly Vicki who made a two-week trip to heaven (which looked strangely like a spaceship), maybe it was Nikki who gave birth to long-lost daughter Megan, who surfaced right about the same time as the underground city was found and destroyed.

During the 1980s on *One Life to Live*, Vicki has out-of-the-body experiences while undergoing a life-threatening operation; a Christmas Eve ball lasts for two very long weeks; Clint Buchanan, Vicki's husband goes blind, travels back in time to the Wild West, and regains his sight; and Senator Gary Hart's playmate Donna Rice guest-stars—but nothing is as dramatic as the life of one Tina Clayton, Vicki's half-sister. Tina has two weddings halted just as she's about to say "I do"; gets pregnant and then plunges to her supposed death over an Argentine waterfall; and reappears alive at Cord Robert's wedding, destroying the ceremony by claiming he's the father of the baby she's brought with her. It turns out she's lying, but, happily, she and Cord get married later on anyway.

Ryan's Hope, 1979. Although this late soap was generally applauded for its realism (it was set in New York, not a fictional Midwest city featuring a world-class hospital, university, and one or two multinational corporations), *Ryan's Hope* did make periodic forays into the purely ridiculous. Notable examples were the much-married Delia's kidnapping by Prince Albert (a gorilla), and the good Dr. Faith Coleridge's bizarre romantic adventures with archaeologist/mummy fetishist Aristotle Benedict White.

Santa Barbara, 1984. In the world of soaps, popular characters are often killed or sent off to oblivion because the actors playing them are anxious to move on to prime time or the movies. While a few succeed, more typically the actor graduates to a guest spot as Jessica's niece or nephew on *Murder, She Wrote,* makes a brief appearance in a straight-to-video feature, and returns to the security of daytime and the resurrection of his or her beloved character in yet another plot twist.

As part of *Santa Barbara*'s efforts to prepare for Marcy Walker's departure (she was then poised for prime-time stardom in Stephen J. Cannell's *Palace Guard*), the show's writers transformed her character, Eden, from all-purpose heroine (loving wife/caring mother/crack reporter/sharp business exec) into a multiple-personality psycho with endlessly emerging secret histories. Fortunately for the forces of logic and consistency *Santa Barbara*'s cancellation precluded any possibility of Walker's returning to her Emmy-winning role.

In *Santa Barbara*'s 1991 season plucky Gina stole her ex-husband's semen from a sperm bank, only to give birth in an animal hospital.

The Secret Storm, 1954. In a well-publicized 1968 incident (chronicled in the beloved BAD classic, *Mommie Dearest*), sixty-four-year-old Joan

Crawford stood in for daughter Christina, playing the role of twenty-four-year-old housewife Joan Borman Kane.

The Young and the Restless, 1973. Noted for its "high" production values, this ratings winner features lots of hair, numerous occasions for sparkles and sequins, and the too-good-to-be-true twosome of Danny and Cricket. The unnaturally dimpled Danny is easily the first rock star to have been falsely accused of both cocaine abuse and marital infidelity, crimes otherwise unheard of in the music industry. His virtue, however, is matched only by wife Cricket, a teen model turned lawyer. When not crusading against alcoholism, drug abuse, or sex discrimination, Cricket keeps busy by rescuing the less fortunate, including best friend Nina, who repaid our heroine's generosity by sleeping with and marrying Cricket's then-fiancé, the now-deceased millionaire Phillip. In the shifting sands of Soap World, how does this one modern-day saint stay so pure? Perhaps it's because she's played by Lauralee Bell, daughter of the show's head writer and chief honcho.

(researcher and cowriter: Nicole Aron)

Variety

The Hee Haw Honeys, 1978. If you think *Hee Haw* is hard to take, *Honeys* is a torture test. A sitcom spinoff set in a typical Nashville family diner with attached nightclub (offering lots of opportunities for country-singing guest stars) and starring "I'm not really a waitress I'm really a singer with a tight blouse" Hollywood staples, *Honeys* has all the ripsnorting humor of *Hee Haw* but with half the fun or musical talent.

In Living Color, 1990. How would African-Americans like it if two white guys on a current, nationally broadcast show covered their faces and hands with blackened cork and recreated the stereotypes of *Amos 'n' Andy*?
  Enjoy "Men on Film."

Mary, 1978. All-singing, all-dancing Mary Tyler Moore (accompanied by Dick Shawn, Michael Keaton, and David Letterman) hosts a variety hour. Even with a lead-in from *60 Minutes* this show was so terrible, you never saw it; of sixteen shows produced only three were aired, the whole fiasco costing CBS around $5 million.

The Miss America Pageant, 1992. *Miss America* is always a must-watch. The 1950s sexism is hilarious, and the show is filled with magical mo-

With David Letterman and Michael Keaton (top and top left), MTM tries another *Mary* (Stephen Cox)

ments, such as the time when 1992's Kandace "Miss Mississippi" Williams described herself as a "descendant of Julius Caesar . . . second cousin to Kenny Rogers . . . with a rare magnetic electrolytic body chemistry [that makes me] a human magnet."

The Richard Pryor Show, 1977. What should have become a legendary series from the man who is arguably the world's greatest comedian is one of the few out-and-out sad notes of this book. Why did it all go wrong? Pryor's deal with NBC included two unusual but sensible points: *The Richard Pryor Show* wouldn't be scheduled during the "family hour," and his adult humor could flourish, since the censors would keep a loose hand. NBC changed its mind, and scheduled him in early prime time (at 8:00 P.M. EST), when network self-censorship was toughest; in fact, he appeared opposite the hugely popular *Happy Days* and *Laverne & Shirley.*

On his premiere Pryor tried to make light of the whole matter by doing a monologue on how he hadn't given up anything to be on network TV. As the camera pulled back, Pryor appeared in a body suit—as though he were naked and castrated. Though no viewer could possibly believe he was actually naked and castrated, timid NBC censored the bit anyway, and Pryor understandably went ballistic. The furor caused the castration piece to be shown, over and over again, on local and network news shows worldwide—giving it a much bigger audience than it would have ever had on *The Richard Pryor Show.*

Pryor's commitment was for five shows, and only five shows were ever aired.

Saturday Night Live, April 1982. When the Not-Ready-for-Prime-Time Players threatened to boil "Larry the Lobster" live on the air, over 500,000 viewers dialed a you-pay-for-it 900 number to plead for his life.

The Sonny and Cher Comedy Hour; The Sonny Comedy Revue; Cher, The Sonny and Cher Show, 1971, 1974, 1974, 1976. Onetime counterculture teddy bears (whose original *noms de chant* were Caesar and Cleo), Sonny Bono and Cherilyn LaPiere Sarkisian retooled their personas perfectly for prime time: he became befuddled and clownish, she curvaceous and cutting. Their *Comedy Hour*'s shining moments were strong duets alternating with put-down contests, but through all the barbs we knew they really loved each other very, very much (with many appearances by pouting daughter Chastity to prove it). Behind the scenes, though, Cher thought Sonny was an overcontrolling Svengali, and finally separated from him; CBS made them finish out their last *Comedy Hour* season together anyway. She filed for divorce, and CBS then tried two separate shows; both were dismal flops. The network then made it very much worth everyone's while to reunite—creating one of the most bizarre programs of all time.

In the middle of endless television and press coverage over their divorce, *The Sonny and Cher Show* premiered with Sonny announcing "Well, folks, I don't know if any of you heard about it, but Cher and I aren't married anymore." The audience responded with dead silence—a response that would greet most of this show's brief life. The duets were now loveless; the put-down contests vicious; what was once light banter seemed heartlessly contrived; and the regular guests now included notorious mimes Shields and Yarnell. Even if you try to ignore the behind-the-scenes story, watching *The Sonny and Cher Show* is a deadening experience; every comedy skit and musical bit seems to scream: "We're only in it for the *money!*"

Tom Smothers' Organic Prime Time Space Ride, 1971. Tom and his brother Dick spent four years expanding the boundaries of TV variety shows on *The Smothers Brothers Comedy Hour.* With psychedelic graphics (such as the split-second editing and sixty-mph zooms now attributed to MTV) as well as provocative political commentary on such things as Middle America, the Vietnam War, and the Johnson Administration, *The Smothers Brothers Comedy Hour* brought a whole audience back to Sunday night television (giving *Bonanza* some ratings competition for the first time in many years) and immediately vaulted into the top ten for eight seasons. The show's politics, dished out by the brothers and guests like Joan Baez, Pete Seeger, Harry Belafonte, and Dr. Spock (who'd aided draft evaders), also confronted the CBS censors nonstop. Fed up, the network finally canceled the show, even though it was a huge hit and a big money-maker (a move applauded by *TV Guide),* and replaced it with *Hee Haw.*

Tom, obviously exhausted by controversy, went on to star in *Tom Smothers' Organic Prime Time Space Ride*—a variety show exactly as bad as it sounds.

The Tonight Show, December 17, 1969. Falsetto auteur and bathing enthusiast Tiny Tim marries his even more effeminate Miss Vicki before fifty-eight million viewers—and gives Johnny Carson his second-biggest Nielsens in thirty years (surpassed only by his final broadcast).

The Lawrence Welk Show, 1955. Besides foisting the Lennon Sisters, Joe Feeney, Ralna English, and the concept of "champagne music" on the American public, Welk put a shocking spin on *American Bandstand* by having otherwise respectable senior citizens dress up in lurid green-and-orange suits, dance to his orchestra, and viciously elbow each other, madly jockeying for good camera positions, so their children could watch at home.

Watching television is a private act, an act that we perform by ourselves and with ourselves. What it resembles most, I think, is masturbation.

—Michael Arlen

Curses!

Television is democracy at its ugliest.

—Paddy Chayevsky

ONE OF TV'S MANY PLEASURES IS WHEN IT FORCES US TO CONSIDER the deepest mysteries of the universe; those philosophical issues that radiate to the core of our earthly existence. For your consideration: why is television stardom such an utterly incomprehensible enterprise—a twilight zone of the chosen and the ignored, following a logic far beyond the minds of mere human beings?

Why so much success for Valerie Bertinelli, Jane Seymour, and Priscilla Presley . . . but not Bette Davis or Jodie Foster?

Why can't the adult Patty Duke have a successful sitcom?

Why does the public never enjoy the crime-fighting Jack Scalia?

Why is Nancy Walker popular with *Rhoda* and paper towels, and nothing else?

Why do so many series make their stars work overtime?

Why aren't we allowed to see what rich people are really like on TV?

Ponder these mighty questions, dear reader, and remember the anointed—as you study the cursed.

The Curse of Tim Conway

Tim Conway was a great second banana (on *McHale's Navy* and *The Carol Burnett Show*) whose outings as a lead didn't work, even though he received many, many opportunities. First, he tried an *F-Troop* imitation with *Rango* (1967), portraying a Texas Ranger having trouble with Indian schemer Pink Cloud. Next, Tim was joined by pre–screechy child sponsor and pre–*All in the Family* Sally Struthers, as well as the post–*M*A*S*H* McLean Stevenson, for a less-than-rollicking *Tim Conway Comedy Hour* (1970). In the impressively terrible *Tim Conway Show* (1970) Tim and Joe Flynn (Captain Binghamton on *McHale's Navy)* reenact their very special on-screen chemistry as employees of a small airline.

We thought Tim had reached his nadir when the producers of *Laugh-In* tried to clone their hit show for ABC and instead ended up producing one of the industry's most infamous failures, *Turn-On* (1979). Hosted by a riposte-flashing computer and featuring MTV-like zippy editing and electronic music, the promos for *Turn-On* made it look like the most tastelessly sex-ridden show ever on TV (but a tasteless, sex-ridden show featuring Tim Conway), and even before the first broadcast the phone lines at ABC's local stations were jammed with complaints. Within days of the pilot's airing seventy-five affiliates had canceled the show, and the network was forced to cease and desist. At the time, with only one broadcast, *Turn-On* was the shortest-lived series in television history.

But Mr. Conway's lowest moment was to come with *Ace Crawford, Private Eye* (1983), a pathetic sitcom about a pathetic gumshoe (Tim) who wants to be Bogart, with midget Billy Barty (as Inch the barkeep) helping him with his personal problems.

The Curse of Being a TV Cop

Future Cop, 1977. You're Ernest Borgnine, and you have to train a cop robot.

Mann and Machine, 1992. Your partner's a beautiful girl robot (something like a female version of *Star Trek*'s Data) who can't understand your natural human feelings.

Holmes and Yoyo, 1976. Your partner's a robot who is stupid, can eat anything, has a photographic memory, breaks down constantly, and can develop film.

Tequila & Bonetti, 1991. You're Jack Scalia doing a Tom Hanks imitation, and your partner is a pit bull who talks black jive and, when he gets mad, pees on things—*your* things.

The Curse of the Top Five Annual Christmas Specials:

Smurfs! A Christmas Special
The Poky Little Puppy's First Christmas
The Care Bears Nutcracker Suite
Emmet Otter's Jug-Band Christmas
He-Man and She-Ra—A Christmas Special

The Curse of Bette Davis

Bette Davis's television career spans a grand twenty-six years; her biggest successes—two brief, shining moments—came at the very beginning and the very end, with one-night-only star turns on *General Electric Theater* (a 1957 half-hour drama anthology hosted by Ronald Reagan) and the premiere of *Hotel* (1983). Her other starring roles are all in staggeringly ludicrous pilots that, predictably, never became series.

Did Bette know these things would never turn into real work, so she could take the money and run? Or, did she not know how to read?

The Elizabeth McQueeny Story, 1959. Bette leads an all-woman pre–June Taylor dance ensemble through the Old West, entertaining lonely prospectors and cowboys, and helping the stars of *Wagon Train* with their personal problems.

The Bette Davis Show, 1965. Interior decorator Bette graciously moves in with her clients to learn of their special home-design needs and—instead of acidly cutting them and their tasteless ways down to size and berating them for not living up to her high standards—helps them with their personal problems.

Madame Sin, 1972. Bette Davis *is* Madame Sin—a powerful, evil woman who is part mad scientist and part covert operator, running an ultra-high-tech, worldwide intelligence agency out of her remote Scottish castle. Ex–CIA agent Robert Wagner (who exec-produced) helps her steal a Polaris submarine after she kidnaps him and rewires his brain with a ray gun.

The Judge and Jake Wyler, 1972. Retired-judge-turned-private-eye Miss Davis teams up with ex-con Doug McClure as partners in a detective agency—and Bette helps Doug and her clients with their personal problems.

One of Hollywood's greatest stars (no, not Robert Wagner) finds herself stuck in one of television's worst moments (*Madame Sin*) (Photofest)

The Curse of Phil Donahue

When Phil Donahue began his national broadcasts in 1970, he was acclaimed for bringing important topics to the misogynistic wasteland of daytime TV. At that time, engulfed by soaps, game shows, women's talk shows (that focused on makeup, cooking tips, and revolutionary breakthroughs in panty hose), and endless, endless ads for food and cleaning products, women viewers—ninety percent of the daytime audience—felt like female eunuchs just on the cusp of beginning their own diary of a mad housewife. Donahue, though, brought the serious discussion of ideas and issues to women viewers, and he so utterly engaged his studio and home audience in conversations with atheists, lesbian nuns, and KKK members that Erma Bombeck announced, "He's every wife's replacement for the husband who doesn't talk to her. They've always got Phil who will listen and take them seriously," and *Esquire* said, "More women are educated— about sex, morals, trends, and personalities—by Donahue than by any other person—man or woman—in the land."

Now, though, the mood of the country has changed so dramatically that when Phil had a panel looking into whether Iran delayed the release of American hostages during the 1980 Presidential election as part of a deal with Reagan, the Nielsens were a paltry 3.9, but when he showcased avant-garde fashions for men and appeared in a dress, he got a whopping 9. With Oprah!, Geraldo!, Sally! and all the rest, the heat is on, and even though *Donahue!* does plenty of serious shows, it's the ones on teenage strippers and their mothers, a man who married twenty-one times, Catholic priests involved in sex scandals, and bisexuals debating whether men or women are better bedmates that we all watch. Obviously a man who really wants to discuss the important issues of our lives (and one who takes home $8 million a year for his troubles), Phil today is so cursed by his tabloid competition that he recently commented, "We are dangerously close to being referred to as an *intelligent* talk show. If that happens, we're doomed. Please do not call me *intelligent*. I'd rather be called *sleazy* than *intelligent*. That's what it takes to survive on television today."

The Patty Duke Demi-curse

The history of Patty Duked television is a long and torturous one; her first big role was in a 1957 *Kraft Television Theatre* presentation, and, in dramas, she's a three-time Emmy winner for *Captains and the Kings* (1976), a Taylor Caldwell generational saga about a politically influential Irish Catholic family; *My Sweet Charlie* (1970, extraordinary circumstances force the white, unwed, and preggers Patty to meet and fall for the black Al Freeman, Jr., and, together, achieve racial understanding); and the 1979 remake of *The Miracle Worker*, with Patty now in the Anne Bancroft role. Ms. Duke has done memorable work in many other TV dramas— not counting *Call Me Anna*, her autobiography-turned-miniseries, which was easily as distinguished as Shirley MacLaine's *Out on a Limb* (see page 195).

It seems, though, that Patty has never been happy being an award-winning dramatic actress who's achieved great acclaim on Broadway, film, and television—no; she has to be *funny*. Television execs unanimously agree, giving her starring roles in one horrific sitcom after another. Thus: the Duke Demi-curse. Patty's compelled to be a comedienne, and we're equally compelled to cancel her many sitcoms.

This Curse, interestingly, is two sided; it forces Patty to publicly humiliate herself by constantly failing as a comedienne—but, every time out, it gives her a remarkable TV Best Friend.

The Patty Duke Show, 1963. A classic we loved because it was so BAD; you were obsessed with it as a kid, you identified completely with Patty, you still know the theme song by heart—and I *dare* you to watch it now! Cathy Lane is an unbearable Scottish priss who (when substituting for the chemistry teach) gives her own cousin three demerits for talking in class, gets the hiccups when she tries to lie, and will obviously never have sex. Identical cousin (!) Patty is an aggressively insipid, hyperactive American frugathoner, and both share three different facial expressions. Early on when the show's writers ran out of ideas, they brought in a *third* identical cousin, Atlanta bombshell Betsy Lane. If you think *That Girl* is too perky for her own good, these multiple Pattys will give you hives! Knowing that Patty Duke was completely prescription-drugged out during the entire run of *The Patty Duke Show* makes it watchable—but barely.

Patty's best friend: herself.

It Takes Two, 1982. Assistant District Attorney Patty is married to renowned surgeon Richard Crenna; the boffo laughs come from exploring the question of whether a woman can have a career and still be a good wife and mother. Just for sitcom insurance, Patty's grandma (Billie Bird) is hilariously senile.

Patty's best friend: Judge Della Reese.

Hail to the Chief, 1985. Not surprisingly, the Reagan years inspired two sitcoms based on the Oval Office; like real life both were deeply unfunny. George C. Scott and Madeleine Kahn starred in *Mr. President,* while *Hail to the Chief* was the show that asked the burning question: Wouldn't it be a laugh riot to have a woman (Patty) as the President of the United States? And surround her with the kind of wacky-but-adorable characters that are only found on BAD sitcoms?

Just for starters there's a husband who can't keep his zipper shut (*That*

Girl's ex, Ted Bessell); his Soviet spy mistress (obviously inspired by Natasha Badenov); and Patty's sex-crazed senior-citizen mom (a cross between *Soap*'s Katherine Helmond and *Golden Girls'* Estelle Getty). All of this added up to a show so astonishingly laugh free, it has to be seen to be believed. Producer Susan Harris (who surprisingly also produced *Soap* and *The Golden Girls*) blamed ABC's creative meddling— but, Susan, it takes far more than a mere network to make a show this BAD.

Patty's best friend: a zany gay Secret Service agent.

Karen's Song, 1987. Patty divorces hubby Granville Van Dusen, moves to a condo, gives up her successful literary agency to work for a publishing company, and falls in love with a twenty-eight-year-old caterer—a show written and produced by people who obviously know nothing about divorce, condos, the publishing business, twenty-eight-year-olds, or catering.

Patty's best friend: Lainie Kazan.

The Curse of Dying

When Michael Conrad died of cancer while portraying Phil Esterhaus on *Hill Street Blues* (the desk sergeant who warned "Be careful out there"), it was explained at the station that Esterhaus had died while making love to his mistress.

Jon-Erik Hexum starred (with Jennifer O'Neill) in *Cover-Up,* a remake of *I Spy,* as a secret agent disguised as a model (or vice versa; who could tell?). In 1984 Hexum was joking around on the set and shot himself in the head with a prop gun filled with blanks; the force of the gunpowder proved to be fatal. A memorial announcement for Hexum was made during the credits of the next episode. His name was misspelled.

After playing the role of court bailiff on *Night Court* for only a year, the sixty-four-year-old Selma Diamond died of cancer. She was replaced by the sixty-three-year-old Florence Halop, who, after playing the role of court bailiff on *Night Court* for only a year, also died of cancer. She was replaced by the thirty-three-year-old Marsha Warfield, who, as of this writing, is still alive.

The Curse of Jodie Foster

It's hard to imagine Jodie Foster as anything but the acclaimed multi-Oscar owner she is today. Hard to imagine, until you consider her remarkable television appearances:

Bob & Carol & Ted & Alice, 1973. Robert Urich and Jodie Foster try to discover how deeply the subject of wife-swapping can be explored on prime-time television—as you could guess, about two inches.

Paper Moon, 1974. Jodie essays the Tatum O'Neal role as a teen con artist/Bible salesperson.

O'Hara's Wife, 1982. Polaroid-taking tea-drinker Mariette Hartley returns from the dead to aid hubby Ed Asner—and Jodie Foster—in this charm-free imitation of *Topper.*

Svengali, 1984. Obese, tone-deaf Jodie Foster tries playing a would-be lady rock-star and musical prodigy who falls under the tutelage of mentor/lover/hambone Peter O'Toole in this horrifying *My Fair Lady* remake.

Just imagine the impossible—that any of these had turned out to be a hit. Would today's Jodie be a *Hollywood Squares* regular?

The Curse of Gender (Animated)

On the cartoon remake of *The Addams Family* (1973), Jodie Foster provided the voice for favorite son Pugsley Addams. On *This Is America, Charlie Brown* (1988), Charlie's voice is actually a girl's: Erin Chase. On *The Simpsons* (1990), ditto for Bart Simpson, who's voiced by Nancy Cartwright.

The Curse of Inflation

  1973: *The $10,000 Pyramid*
  1976: *The $20,000 Pyramid*
  1979: *The $25,000 Pyramid*
  1981: *The $50,000 Pyramid*
  1985: *The $100,000 Pyramid*

The Curse of Inventory Control

When HBO, Cinemax, Showtime, and The Movie Channel first began cablecasting, twenty-four-hours-a-day commercial-free feature films and sporting events seemed just what cable was made for. Movie lovers and sports fans were in heaven, and the promised brave new world of total-TV pleasure seemed to have come true at last.

Almost immediately, however, disaster struck. With all the competition from the networks, regular cable channels, and each other, the premium channels stumbled on a big problem: it didn't take long before the supply of good features and sports spectaculars that people actually wanted to watch ran out.

The premiums responded by showcasing a staggering number of Z-grade movies that barely made it to the theaters or on videotape; broadcasting would-be pilots rejected by the networks; and allowing us to watch made-fors that should never have been made. Over Christmas week 1992, for example, you could have seen the following features on HBO, Cinemax, Showtime, and The Movie Channel, uncut and without commercial interruption; how many have you ever heard of?

Fast Getaway, The Palermo Connection, Eversmile New Jersey, No Safe Haven, Blood and Concrete, Son of Darkness, Dead Calm, Too Much Sun, Bloodfist 2, Pleasure in Paradise, Mom, Virgin High, Robot Jox, Patterns, Destroyer, Dark Obsession, Rich Girl, Seed People, Dracula's Widow, All-American Widow, Waiting for the Light, The Rage of Paris, A Summer Story, Payoff, The Last of His Tribe, Defense Play, Dreamer, The Other Side of Hell, Talent for the Game, Eye of the Storm, Delta Force 3, Liar's Edge, Ambition, Moon 44, Waterhole #3, Run, Go West Young Girl, Yor the Hunter from the Future, Maniac Cop 3, Common Bonds, Three Warriors, Iron Maze, No Safe Haven, Ski School, Dusty, Hardcase & Fist, Blind Vision, Last Summer, The Oklahoma City Dolls, Big Man on Campus, Black Magic Woman, Demonic Toys, The Man in the Moon, House 4, Eye of the Eagle 2, Young Lady Chatterley, Konga the Wild Stallion, Gibbsville, Dollman, The Long Walk Home, Dead On, Hollywood Boulevard 2, Tripwire, Fair Game, Dolly Dearest, Ring of Fire, and *The Man from Tumbleweeds.*

Finally, the premium channel execs became so desperate that they even began creating original programming too wild and daring for the networks (such as the shock of sitcoms featuring gay men, topless women, and Gary Shandling).

Now TV viewers can test themselves on such important issues as: How many kickboxing, psychic-horror, revenge-rampage, beautiful-girl-in-big-trouble, and zipless porn movies can you watch in one month? Twenty? Fifty? Seventy? A hundred? With the premiums running their semidecent features over and over again, how many times a week can you see *Die Hard, Hook,* or *It's a Wonderful Life*? And how do you feel about paying for all of it?

The Curse of TV Names

The closer you look at television, the more obsessed you'll become with names—fictional, real, and stage. If your parents lost their minds when you were born and came up with a name only a mom could love, a regular guy or gal can always seek relief from the courts. But this issue doesn't even apply to actors in Hollywood, all of whom create *noms de théâtres* to aid in their struggle for stardom; names which should be appealing, distinctive and memorable. So why did these people pick what they did? What kind of brain comes up with *Soleil Moon Frye*? Does *Dack Rambo* want everyone's first thought to be: "Oh, isn't he a cartoon, maybe a relative of Clutch Cargo?" Doesn't anyone try to talk them out of it? Why won't they come to their senses?

Falcon Crest, 1988. One of the cast regulars was the real-life daughter of Jayne Mansfield and her weightlifting husband Mickey, who viciously came up with the mouthful Mariska Hargitay.

A Man Called Sloane, 1979. Mustachioed Robert Conrad stars in this *Man from U.N.C.L.E.* remake, with accursed costar Ji-Tu Cumbuka as "Torque."

Mistral's Daughter, 1984. In this Judith Krantzer, Philippine Leroy Beaulieu stars as Fauve Mistral.

Punky Brewster, 1984. NBC exec Brandon Tartikoff had a New Jersey classmate named Punky Brewster; he gave her name to this show's producers, who tracked down the real Punky, paid her a royalty, and returned the favor by naming the fictional Punky's dog Brandon.

Punky was played by a little girl with the unfortunate name of Soleil Moon Frye; her brother (also a child TV fixture) is actually named Meeno

Peluce. Whether their parents came up with these ideas themselves or let the kids pick, they should be put behind bars.

The San Pedro Beach Bums, 1977. One of the few hour-long sitcoms ever attempted; Buddy, Dancer, Stuf, Moose, and Boychick (five men) live together on a boat and have wacky misadventures. With names like those, misadventures should be guaranteed.

Sugar and Spice, 1976. Two black sisters live together in Oklahoma (but mysteriously fail to encounter redneck racists with guns). Starring Loretta Devine as "Loretta," Vickilyn Reynolds as "Vickilyn," and LaVerne Anderson as "Toby."

The Tex and Jinx Show, 1957. Husband-and-wife interview show, with Tex McCrary (the Oprah of his day) and the remarkably named Jinx Falkenburg. "I still believe in tabloid journalism," says Tex. "For us, the three *r*'s were rape, rot, and ruin."

Uncle Croc's Block, 1975. Charles Nelson Reilly as the Uncle and Jonathan (*Lost in Space*'s Dr. Smith) Harris as Mr. Bitterbottom crock up a parody of a children's Saturday-morning TV show which wasn't all that different from regular children's Saturday morning TV shows.

Just think if a bad speller had to write the credits on *The Cosby Show:*
> Phylicia Rashad
> Malcolm-Jamal Warner
> Tempestt Bledsoe
> Keshia Knight Pulliam
> Sabrina LeBeauf
> Raven-Symone
> Mushand Lee

The other outstanding names and their memorable performances:
Mädchen Amick, *Twin Peaks,* 1990
Sig Arno, *My Friend Irma,* 1952
Buzz Belmondo, *Baywatch,* 1989
Zina Bethune, *Love of Life,* 1965
Mayim Bialik, *Blossom,* 1991
Whit Bissell, *The Time Tunnel,* 1966
Taurean Blacque, *Hill Street Blues,* 1981
Wolf Blitzer, CNN, 1990

Linwood Boomer, *Little House on the Prairie,* 1978

Veda Ann Borg, *The Abbott and Costello Show,* 1952

X Brands, *Yancy Derringer,* 1958

Valri Bromfield, *The Bobbie Gentry Show,* 1974

Ilka Chase, *Glamour-Go-Round,* 1950

Scatman Crothers, *Chico and the Man,* 1974

Khigh Dhiegh, *Hawaii Five-O,* 1968

Fyvush Finkel, *Picket Fences,* 1992

Grant Goodeve, *Eight Is Enough,* 1977

Edan Gross, *Free Spirit,* 1989

Jester Hairston, *Amen,* 1986

Melora Hardin, *Secrets of Midland Heights,* 1980

Rainbow Harvest, *FM,* 1989

Peanuts Hucko, *The Lawrence Welk Show,* 1970

Engelbert Humperdinck, *The Engelbert Humperdinck Show,* 1970

Gunilla Hutton, *Petticoat Junction,* 1965

Mandy Ingber, *Dirty Dancing,* 1988

Taliesin Jaffe, *She's the Sheriff,* 1987

Raé-Ven Kelly, *I'll Fly Away,* 1992

Kaleena Kiff, *Love, Sidney,* 1981

Durward Kirby, *The Garry Moore Show,* 1950

Alf Kjellin, *Combat!,* 1963

Fuzzy Knight, *Foreign Legionnaire,* 1955

Guich Koock, *Carter Country,* 1977

Zohra Lampert, *Kojak,* 1975

Snooky Lanson, *Your Hit Parade,* 1950

Lash LaRue, *Lash of the West,* 1953

Meadowlark Lemon, *Hello, Larry,* 1979

Wink Martindale, *Tic Tac Dough,* 1978

LaWanda Page, *Sanford and Son,* 1973

Aladdin Abdullah Achmed Anthony Pallante, *The Lawrence Welk Show,* 1955

Parkyakarkus, *Playhouse 90,* 1958

Nia Peeples, *Fame,* 1984

Jo Ann Pflug, *Operation Petticoat,* 1978

ZaSu Pitts, *The Gale Storm Show,* 1956

Poncie Ponce, *Hawaiian Eye,* 1959

Dirk and Dack Rambo (twins), *The New Loretta Young Show,* 1962

Rex and Rhodes Reason (twins), *Man Without a Gun,* 1958; *Bus Stop,* 1961

Blossom Rock, *The Addams Family,* 1964
Roxie Roker, *The Jeffersons,* 1975
Menasha Skulnik, *Menasha the Magnificent,* 1950
Olan Soule, *Captain Midnight,* 1954
Tiffani-Amber Thiessen, *Saved by the Bell,* 1989
Lurene Tuttle, *Julia,* 1968
Minerva Urecal, *Tugboat Annie,* 1958
Lark Voorhies, *Saved by the Bell,* 1990
Sheb Wooley, *Hee Haw,* 1969
Ahmet Zappa, Dweezil Zappa, Moon Unit Zappa, *2 Hip 4 TV,* 1988
Zulu, *Hawaii Five-O,* 1968

The Curse of Overtime

All of us want to be considered multifaceted—but who wants to hold down two or more jobs to prove it? As will be seen below, however, television writers and producers are fascinated with the idea of their central characters having multiple careers, especially if these callings are completely unrelated. If you thought the life of a model/waiter/actor was tough, wait'll you see these curses:

Baywatch, 1989. Parker Stevenson is a lawyer, and a lifeguard.

Cowboy G-Men, 1952. In this kids' show Russell Hayden and Jackie (Uncle Fester) Coogan are government agents, and cowboys.

Diagnosis of a Murder, 1992; *The House on Sycamore Street,* 1992. Dick Van Dyke is an eccentric doctor, and an amateur detective.

Ebony, Ivory and Jade, 1979. Debbie Allen and Martha Smith are detectives, and Vegas showgirls. Bert Convy is a detective, a tennis instructor, and a Vegas entertainer.

The Fall Guy, 1981. Lee Majors is a Hollywood stunt man, and a Los Angeles Criminal Courts bounty hunter.

Free Spirit, 1989. Corinne Bohrer is a beautiful ditz, a housekeeper, and a witch.

Hawk, 1966. Burt Reynolds is a police officer working for the New York City DA, and an Iroquois Indian.

Momma the Detective, 1981. Esther Rolle is a New York City detective, and a maid.

Murder in Music City, 1979. Sonny Bono is a Nashville private eye, and a songwriter.

The New Adventures of Beans Baxter, 1987. Jonathan Ward is a teenager, a high-school student, and a spy battling against the evil Mr. Sue.

Nick Knight, 1989. Rocker Rick Springfield is a San Francisco policeman, and a vampire.

Ohara, 1987. Pat Morita is a Los Angeles policeman, and a zen master.

Partners in Crime, 1984. Lynda Carter is a photographer, and a private eye. Loni Anderson is a private eye, and a bass violinist.

The People's Choice, 1955. Jackie Cooper (accompanied by a talking basset hound) is a naturalist, a city councilman, and a real estate agent.

Policewoman Centerfold, 1983. Melody Anderson is a cop, and a *Playboy* playmate.

Quarterback Princess, 1983. Helen Hunt is a winning junior varsity quarterback, and a high school homecoming princess.

Samurai, 1979. Half-Asian Joe Penny is a San Francisco district attorney, and a samurai warrior.

The Sandy Duncan Show, 1972. Sandy Duncan is a UCLA student teacher, a part-time secretary at an ad agency, a struggling actress, "The Yummy Peanut Butter Girl," and the spokesperson for "John E. Appleseed Used Cars in the Heart of the San Fernando Valley."

Sarge, 1971. George Kennedy is a police officer, and a Catholic priest.

Stone, 1980. Dennis Weaver is a Los Angeles detective, and a best-selling novelist.

T and T, 1988. Mr. T is a private eye, a framed ex-con, and a boxer.

Tag Team, 1991. Jesse "the Body" Ventura and "Rowdy" Roddy Piper are police officers, and tag team wrestlers.

Tucker's Witch, 1982. Catherine Hicks is an insurance investigator, a private eye, and a witch.

The Curse of the PBS How-To Superstars

Let's say you're one of the many, many Americans who are dying to move to Hollywood and be a star—but you can't act, you can't sing, you can't dance, you can't read a teleprompter like George Page, you can't turn letters like Vanna White, and you can't chortle like Ed McMahon. There's still one more chance, but only if you're completely obsessive-compulsive about a hobby, and willing to work harder than a dog. You could have a weekly show broadcast to millions, regaling them with your eccentric opinions, and become a megaselling book author—by joining the PBS how-to marathon. Every day, thousands of otherwise obscure American citizens star in their own TV series, telling us everything they know about American cooking, Cajun cooking, Provençal cooking, frugal cooking, Medici cooking, Amish cooking from quilt country, oil painting, watercolor painting, acrylic painting, country painting, quilting, strip quilting, gardening, victory gardening, woodcarving, Yankee woodwork, home repair, home refurbishment, sewing, fishing, golfing, modeling, driving, and yoga.

The curse here is that, on the whole, these stars are easily the hardest-working men and women in the entire entertainment industry. After writing and producing the shows themselves, the hosts must painstakingly demonstrate, moment by moment, their expertise so that any idiot can do it at home, while at the same time talking continuously, and always having in the back of their mind that, at any moment, something will screw up—and they do this every day of the week! For example, Marcia Adams, on one episode of *Amish Cooking from Quilt Country,* makes an immense German apple pancake accompanied by stuffed cabbage rolls, potato pancakes, a cinnamon dessert with edible flowers, and discusses quilt history and Amish hospitality customs, all in a mere twenty-seven minutes!

We now offer merely the highlights of this glowing how-to cornucopia and, as you'll see, most of these shows (and their hosts) are utterly wonderful and don't deserve to be thought of as BAD TV—but who else will preserve them for history?

Adventures in Scale Modelling. Host Mike Lech wants, more than anything, to achieve "realness" in his homemade model airplanes, cars, trains, and oddities—so when you build your Mercedes crash test auto, he'll make sure you don't forget to smash the windshield.

Cooking in America. Who would have ever thought from reading his well-thought-out *New York Times* recipe columns that Pierre Franey is so peculiar? What other TV cook shakes a raw piece of meat right in your face while screaming in a barely intelligible accent, "LOOK! HOW BEAUTI-FUL!" His voice is so slurred, in fact, that you're convinced he's flat-out drunk (although he's not)—so when Pierre brings out the knives, it's absolutely spine tingling.

The Frugal Gourmet. The most popular TV cook since Julia Child is a fifty-four-year-old hyperactive cross of Average Joe, Mr. Science, and Merv Griffin, showing cooking techniques while talking nonstop on history, culture, science, and anything that pops into his head—always punctuated by "Isn't that fascinating?" Onetime preacher Jeff Smith is the James Michener of cooking shows; he makes you feel like you're getting a smidge of education and self-improvement along with all that entertainment. Who else would have as a guest violinist Itzhak Perlman, cooking traditional Jewish recipes? And who else would have dishes like spaghetti with peanut butter or spaghetti with sand?

If you're in the mood, Jeff's mania is gripping—but if not, it's like being smothered with hysteria.

Gourmet Cooking. You'd think that anyone would take one look at the waddling, adipose-encrusted Dom DeLuise, Paul Prudhomme, and *Gourmet Cooking*'s Earl Peyroux and know to avoid their food ideas at all costs—but if you need to murder someone in slow motion, this is the show for you. A typical Peyroux meal: mozzarella salad (drenched in half a cup of olive oil); chicken hash (with three cups mayonnaise, half cup cream, and five eggs); dough ball dessert (fried in olive oil and rolled in a cup of honey).

Gentlemen, start your pacemakers!

The Joy of Painting. Afro-wearer Bob Ross is the king of the many PBS painter shows, and his hypnotic, whispered commentary will lull you into

**The multiafflicted Jack Scalia discovers he's finally reached
the very dregs of his television career on *Tequila & Bonetti***
(Photofest)

fervently believing that all your cares and woes would instantly vanish if
only you'd just start painting, godammit!

Motor Week '93. A show that brings the *Consumer Reports' Special
Automotive Issue* to life, with endless clips of driving, driving, and even
more driving. For those who enjoy spending a quiet afternoon watching
traffic.

The Sewing Connection. Retired Queens high-school teacher Shirley
Adams is a woman who's thought through *every tiny detail* about clothes,
their making, and their embellishment. Like Jeff Smith, Shirley (with her
Lily Tomlin voice) talks continuously while demonstrating her techniques—a nonstop, total-id monologue straight from the subconscious
that rivals anything from Molly Bloom.

Quilt in a Day. Adorably hyperperky Eleanor Burns just can't say enough about the beauty of quilts and the deep pleasure of quilting ("Lemon flavored! The *only* pins to use!"). She's so wonderful and her enthusiasm is so extravagant, in fact, that *Quilt in a Day* is better than any therapist for curing the blues, even if you're don't care a whit about quilts.

The Jack Scalia Curse

Black haired, blue eyed, handsome, masculine, with the affable presence television loves, Jack Scalia seems made for stardom. His career peak, though, came in 1987 with two small roles: as Sue Ellen's banker lover for a year on *Dallas* and as Valerie Bertinelli's magazine art director husband in *I'll Take Manhattan.*

When Jack stars in a series, you'd better watch fast—it'll be gone before you know it. For ten years he was the featured player in five flops. Jack did make it through a full season with Rock Hudson in *The Devlin Connection* (1982) as a private investigator/racketball pro, but only got through three episodes before being axed as an ultramodern security agent in *High Performance* (1983), and four airings as an undercover cop and master of disguises in *Hollywood Beat* (1985). As a San Francisco fisherman/private eye living on a boat, *Wolf* (1989) made it through six episodes in prime time; only insomniacs caught the rest of the series. The worst of Jack's problems, however, wouldn't air until 1991, when he won the Tammi as most cursed TV cop in history on the classic *Tequila & Bonetti.*

The Curse of Being Short, Cute, Black, and Adopted

How many white people do you know who've adopted black children (and don't count Mia Farrow)? In the late seventies to early eighties you'd think it was common as grass, since two of the biggest hits of the time were *Diff'rent Strokes* and *Webster.* While his own flesh and blood works at a Hula Hut, multimillionaire Conrad Bain in *Diff'rent* adopts his dying black housekeeper's children, Gary Coleman and the forgettable Todd Bridges. *Webster* thrusts Emmanuel Lewis into the arms of sportswriter Alex Karras when Karras's black teammate from his football playing days is killed in a car wreck. Both Emmanuel and Gary are adorable beyond belief, never seem to grow up and, since this is pre-*Cosby,* inspired many to think the only way black kids could live well is by having saintly, rich white people adopt them.

In later years Emmanuel would turn into a Michael Jackson mascot (be-

**Sassy scamp Gary Coleman hits the jackpot when he
gets adopted by really rich, really wacky white people on
*Diff'rent Strokes*** (Stephen Cox)

fore being eclipsed by the more successful Macauley Culkin) and Gary
would become a nasty smart aleck and have guest star Nancy Reagan just
saying no on his show; when last heard from he was selling Saturns out
by the L.A. airport.

The Curse of Soap Sex

After a mere glance at the history of daytime soaps you'd swear that all the writers think about all day long is where to have sex—*as long as it's not in a bed.* There's a long history in Hollywood of writers hating actors, and nowhere can this be seen more clearly than in these tawdry moments of daytime TV. Think of the acting greatness your favorite soap stars have achieved in trying to look inflamed under these circumstances! Here are some wild thing location highlights:

> **All My Children:** In a cave and at a beauty parlor.
> **Another World:** In a sealed-up cave (with one partner suffering from hypothermia).
> **As the World Turns:** In a pond and on a hayloft.
> **The Bold and the Beautiful:** In a chemistry lab.
> **General Hospital:** In the hospital's supply closets.
> **The Guiding Light:** Under a waterfall.
> **One Life to Live:** On a desk, in an abandoned theater, and in a deep freeze.
> **Santa Barbara:** On a piano, in a boardroom, and next to a dead body.
> **The Young and the Restless:** In a sauna and in an office.

The Curse of McLean Stevenson

Careerwise, the worst thing that ever happened to Mr. Stevenson was quitting *M*A*S*H;* he never seemed to recover from the loss, appearing in one dreaded horror after another. It all starts, of course, with *The McLean Stevenson Show* (1976), where hardware-store owner McLean's homelife of wife, mother-in-law, and two grown children makes the control tower at Kennedy airport seem tame. Taking a break by cohosting the fondly remembered and quickly canceled *Celebrity Challenge of the Sexes* (1978), our hero that very same year turned to *In the Beginning* (1978), where the new McLean, now family free, follows his calling to become a cranky old priest fighting off the radical ideas of wildly progressive nuns.

In *Hello, Larry* (1979), McLean's a supersuccessful radio talk-show host who can't get anything right at home, even with the help of the cast from *Diff'rent Strokes.* Cut to *Condo* (1983), where snooty McLean and his rich family fall on hard times and have to move from their beautiful suburban home to (gasp!) a condo surrounded by Mexicans. *America*

(1985) finds McLean, Sarah Purcell, and Stuart Damon trying to do a cross between the Barbara Walters specials and *Entertainment Tonight,* but lighter, easier, and fluffier than either. For the "Bastard" version of the teen wet dream *Dirty Dancing* (1988), McLean frets and fumes as a resort owner whose daughter Baby can't keep her hands off of Hollywood construct Johnny (a blue-collar, heterosexual dance instructor). This last outing was the most perfect for McLean's fans, since he seemed so completely at home in the borscht belt.

Film festival, anyone?

The Curse of the Summer-Camp Sitcoms

For some reason network execs feel they have to air a show set in a summer camp every couple of years, and we feel it has to get canceled as quickly as possible. Begin your study of this alarming trend with Maureen *Brady* McCormick and Hermione Baddeley (as Eulalia Divine) in *Camp Runamuck* (1965), the story of bratty kids, goofy adults, and a pair of wisecracking bears. If *Runamuck*'s counselors aren't idiotic enough for you, continue on to *Camp Grizzly* (1980), where the kids have to train the adults, and to *Little Darlings* (1982), the heartwarming "Bastard" camping saga of urban tough Angel and Beverly Hills brat Ferris, who become best friends. But be sure not to miss the bittersweet dramedy *Camp Wilderness* (1980), starring Franci Hogle as "Franci," Stefan Hayes as "Stefan," Ruth Ingersol as "Ruth," Nora Lester as "Nora," and Matt Bronson as "Matt."

The Curse of the Talk-Show Imposters

Some people will do anything to get on television, and one way is to pretend you have a lurid, chat-show life-style. Successful talk-show imposters are not only driven to be broadcast, but they get paid for it via appearance fees, and have to act up a storm. Their compulsion usually catches up with them, however, as they commonly appear, with different problems, on multiple shows. For some reason they seem to prefer *Sally Jessy Raphael* above all others; a sex surrogate on *Sally* appeared as a "wife who hated sex" on *Oprah,* and an impotent husband on *Sally* rematerialized as a wife-free virgin on *Geraldo.*

The Curse of Teen Soaps

Doing a show for teenagers is really, really hard; like, first you have to stay on top of all the excellent happening clothes and slang and everything, and then there's the fact that while they may have a lock on mimicry, teen actors aren't exactly known for their dramatic skills. With all these obstacles it's no wonder that only a lite soap like *90210* can work, while all the heavier-going have failed.

One notable attempt was *Never Too Young* (1965), featuring Tony *Leave It to Beaver* Dow as Chet and Tommy *Lassie* Rettig as JoJo, both living in waterfront property on Malibu Beach and having trouble being understood by their parents. More recently there was *Swann's Crossing* (1992) for the preteen set, starring a group of juvenile hambones the likes of which the world has seldom seen. Both left our sets very quickly, and deservedly so.

The Curse of Tex Antoine's Tongue

Tex Antoine and beloved puppet Uncle Weathby hosted three channels and forty years' worth of New York City weather. On Tex's twenty-fifth anniversary, his co-workers presented him with a cake, and when one of the anchors asked if they could get a shot of it, Tex replied, live and on the air, "They could if you'd move out of the fucking way." He was suspended.

A few years later the newscasters were discussing a young girl's rape and segued to Tex, who announced, "Well, as Confucius say, 'If rape is inevitable, lie back and enjoy it.' " He was fired.

The Curse of Sam Donaldson's Tongue

Donaldson may be one of the most highly regarded, eyebrow-cursed journalists of our time, but his tongue has a life of its own:

> *"Stay tuned for* Nightline, *which tonight focuses on World War II, which began last Friday."*

> *"F. W. deKlerk wants to be the Gorbachev of his time."*

> *"If man had wanted man to fly, he would have given him wings."*

The Curse of Nancy Walker

Tiny Ms. Walker (née name-cursed Anna Myrtle Swoyer) was a triumph costarring with Rhoda, Rock Hudson, and paper towels; her curse, like Tim Conway's, was in not stopping when she was ahead. She first tried to "branch out" by combining her much-loved roles on *McMillan and Wife, Rhoda,* and Bounty ads in *The Nancy Walker Show* (1976), where she was a Hollywood talent agent with a merchant-marine husband, problem-causing daughter and son-in-law, and gay assistant/tenant. Nancy then became the warmhearted Las Vegas producer for a bevy of indistinguishable show girls in *Blansky's Beauties* (1977), where the beauties say things like "They call me Sunshine because I smile a lot!" Lastly, Nancy was mom to Bruce Weitz's post–*Hill Street* tragedy (a sitcom), *Mama's Boy* (1987).

Not stopping when she was ahead brought Nancy her greatest notoriety as a show-business terrorist—not on TV but with her film-directing debut. She had achieved greatness as a television director with the *Mary Tyler Moore Show, Alice,* and *Rhoda* episodes; her film-directing achievement, though, is the must-be-seen-to-be-believed *Can't Stop the Music* (see page 219).

The Curse of Wealth

Rich people are everywhere on TV. Just think of *Dallas* and *Dynasty* with their millions of dollars in real estate; Danielle Steel specials with their millions of dollars in furs and jewelry; *The Cosby Show* with its millions of dollars in sweaters.

When push comes to shove, though, TV skips showing the rich as they really are, almost as if network execs believe regular Americans might find the true-life wealthy too strange and alienating. So they tone down TV rich people into lower-middle-class regular guys and gals—with *big* lines of credit.

If a member of the Ewing family, for example, goes out to eat in a fancy restaurant, it never looks like a genuine chichi restaurant—it looks like the most deluxe Red Lobster ever built. When a character on *Dynasty* goes to a big formal party, it doesn't look anything like, say, a gala that Lynn Wyatt in Houston, Candy Spelling in L.A., or Carolyn Roehm in New York might throw; it always looks like a big bar mitzvah. The women's clothes on all of these programs are especially odd; they never look anything like the dresses real wealthy people wear, but instead like something a novice hooker might throw together for prom night.

Pity poor John Forsythe. A wealthy man in real life, he almost always plays characters on TV who are even richer than he is. But John can't draw on his personal knowledge of himself and his friends and other wealthy people he knows in preparing for his roles.

Instead, he has to think, *If Dan Conner suddenly won Lotto, what would he do?*

> If the television craze continues with the present level of programs, we are destined to have a nation of morons.
>
> —Daniel Marsh

PART 2
·············

The Tammi Awards

⚚ ⚚ ⚚ ⚚ ⚚ ⚚

The warm glow of the carmine-red carpet sweeping from the street to the portals of Hollywood's glamorous Pantages Theater is barely visible through the mob of screaming fans. Two by two, the participants of this much-anticipated evening make their way from sumptuous limousines to the theater's lobby, stopping now and again to give autographs, have their pictures taken, and be interviewed by that greatly admired critic, Michael Medved. A great roar of delight is heard when the biggest stars appear: Jerry Van Dyke, Stubby Kaye, Alex Karras, Suzanne Somers, and Ted Bessell each cause a riotous commotion as they make their way to their front-and-center seats.

Backstage, producers Chuck Barris and Aaron Spelling nervously check on the final, last-minute changes, and try to soothe the delicate egos of hosts Wink Martindale and Bob Eubanks. While the King Family and Pink Lady rehearse their big production numbers, all involved covetously eye the glowing statuettes, finished in real diamanté and dotted with fiery cubic zirconia. There is a hubbub of anticipation in the air as the nominees consider their chances, and nervously await the verdict of their peers.

Earlier that evening talk-show titan Jane Pratt, in a highly anticipated special telecast in conjunction with the proceedings, had interviewed one of the world's greatest entertainers, Robert Urich:

Jane: Bob, people think of you, and they think of *Vega$* and *Spenser: For Hire,* but there's been a lot more to your career, hasn't there?

Bob: Yes, indeed; I've done a number of important dramas, such as *The Hallmark—*

Jane: Well, I actually wanted to ask what our viewers are interested in: your first starring role in a series, *Bob & Carol & Ted & Alice.* Now, how did you decide to take that role?

Bob: Well, you know it was my first big job and—

Jane: I'm sure that's true . . . but you certainly can't use the same excuse for *Tabitha* or *Love Me, Love My Dog* or—

Bob: Now, Jane, you know as well as I do that you read a script and hope for the best and, as an actor, you only have so much control over what the final—

Jane: But, Bob, when you agree to star in a TV movie, and you know it's going to be called *Invitation to Hell,* don't you think its chances of being something you'll be proud of are rather slim?

As Bob's eyes mist over with tears, Jane allows herself a brief, satisfied smile.

The Variety Show Nominees

When I hear whistles, I get bumps all over my goose.

—Maria Rosario Pilar Martinez
Molina Bazza (aka Charo)

V AUDEVILLE ... REVUES ... VARIETY SHOWS ... ONCE THE CORNER-stone of American popular culture; now, almost entirely extinct. Where *The Ed Sullivan Show, The Hollywood Palace,* and *Hullabaloo* (to name just a few) once reigned, now there is practically nothing of the genre still in production; even beloved entertainment figure Dolly Parton couldn't bring it back from the dead.

By trying to merge a little singing, a little dancing, a little comedy, and a little sideshow action into one program, variety shows ended up being about nothing in particular, and they seem undefined and aimless in the face of today's splintering audiences. Now, with cable, there's so much specific entertainment appealing to so many different, specific tastes, that a general show trying to please everyone ends up attracting no one.

Where variety lives on besides *The Tonight Show* is, of course, on the foreign-language channels, especially the Latin Galavision, which is an orgy of the BAD. We felt it was beyond the call of duty to specific-ally analyze the many, many BAD Galavision candidates in this volume, but if you want to see soap operas, game shows, and especially variety programs that have gone completely over the edge of sanity, just touch that dial.

What is the secret to providing sheer entertainment value for millions of Americans? According to variety shows:

97

- There is nothing in the whole world as entertaining as a singing and dancing Mormon family.
- If it can't be Mormons, we like performers who can dance with larger-than-life-sized puppets.
- If it can't be larger-than-life-sized puppets, we like singers who know English.
- If it can't be in English, we like mimes.
- If it can't be Mormons dancing with larger-than-life-sized puppets and singing in English accompanied by mimes, we'll take a Canadian.

The Chevy Chase Show, 1993. When megatalented Goldie Hawn met with Chevy "Under the Rainbow" Chase on the premiere of his notoriously unpopular Fox chat show, their outrageous Mutual Admiration Society of mawkish fawning and autobrownnosing was so over the top that home viewers thought it must be a comedy skit. When Goldie then broke into song praising Chevy's immortal inner soul and remarkable humanity, we realized it was no joke, and had this horror (as well as its giant fishtank) canceled immediately.

Cos, 1976. Before hitting the big time as Dr. Huxtable, Bill Cosby tried his hand hosting this kids' variety show—a cross between Art Linkletter's kiddie shows and those so-cute-you-could-puke Pudding Pop ads. Cos grossly overplayed his signature amiability, and *Cos* OD'd on its own suffocating charm, gone in a mere seven weeks.

Donny and Marie; Marie; The Osmonds; The Osmond Family Show, 1972–1981. Not since the 1960s, with Lawrence Welk and the King Family, had America witnessed so much wholesomeness packed into a mere hour. With "a little bit country, a little bit rock 'n' roll," and lots and lots of ice skating, Donny and Marie Osmond (and their many sequels) aired their Mormon family values with so much sweetness, it kept

You know you've really made it in show biz when your life gets colorful and animated, à la *The Osmonds* (Photofest)

dentists busy for almost a decade. The hyperadorable duo was frequently aided by siblings Alan, Wayne, Jay, Merrill, and Jimmy, with Marie gowned by Cherwear designer Bob Mackie, and the show produced in Utah by puppeteers Sid and Marty Krofft (previously famous for *H. R. Pufnstuf*). The family achieved the ultimate American accolade at the height of their fame in 1972, when they were turned into cartoons on *The Osmonds* for ABC's Saturday morning lineup.

♟ ♟ ♟ ♟

The Edge, 1992. *Fridays* live! Many network execs must remember their teen years as one long drug-induced coma, since they're always airing rock-styled variety shows for the teen set that could only appeal to the pot, tranq, or acid impaired. If you think watching bits like a faux Joan Collins putting on makeup with paintbrushes or the American Gladiators being massacred while leading the forces of a Desert Storm–like invasion are as hilarious as this show's braying laugh track obviously does, then you're in for a real treat.

♟ ♟ ♟

Fridays, 1980. Laugh-free *SNL* rip-off, filled, like *The Edge,* with bits that were funny only to the writers, stoned, dropped by six ABC affils after a mere one episode and sent to cancellation heaven by the one-two punch of *SCTV* and *Nightline.*

♟ ♟ ♟ ♟

The Hanna-Barbera Happiness Hour, 1978. The *Jetsons, Flintstones,* and *Huckleberry Hound* creators try to out-Krofft Sid and Marty with live-action giant puppets (something like Disneyland escapees) in a musical variety hour with skin-crawling music and not enough variety.

♟ ♟ ♟

Hullabaloo, 1965. Many sixties-lovers of today can't remember the difference between NBC's *Hullabaloo* and ABC's *Shindig.* Here's how: *Shindig* was one of the few great network TV shows for teenagers (the *90210* of its day), featuring great performances from great musicians of the time. *Hullabaloo* was put together by Gary Smith, producer of *The Judy Garland Show,* and he thought the way to boost ratings was to combine rock and pop and croon and anything else he could think of.

The result is a show that wanders aimlessly across the wide world of entertainment, showcasing Marianne Faithfull, Jerry Lewis, the Zombies, Jack Jones, the Moody Blues, Mickey Rooney, Woody Allen (in his stand-up days), Joey Heatherton, the New Christy Minstrels, high school bands, and *Hullabaloo*'s greatest contribution to culture: miniskirted cage-dancer Lada Edmund.

▲▲ ▲▲ ▲▲ ▲▲

The King Family Show, 1965. A frightening Osmond-like family with thirty-six energetically dancing, enthusiastically singing, unbearably whole-some members. None of them was named King, and all of them gave the word *upbeat* a bad rep. Every year more and more relatives would be un-covered, and every single one of them wanted to entertain you to death.

▲▲ ▲▲ ▲▲

Late Night with Conan O'Brien, 1993. If you thought 1993 was a tough year for you and your loved ones, just think of what it was like for NBC. First they picked Jay Leno over David Letterman to host *The Tonight Show*—only to see Letterman move to CBS and whomp Leno's pathetic ass in the Nielsens. They then replaced Letterman with this pro-gram—easily one of the most amazing examples of BADness to come down the pike in years.

Cultural anthropologists have conclusively proven that all corporations have at least one employee who makes everyone else working there won-der *How does that person keep his job?* For NBC that person is Conan O'Brien. Plucked from obscurity as a scribe for *The Simpsons,* Conan had never before performed on television (something immediately obvious to viewers), much less tried to replace someone like Dave the Great in our hearts. For those interested in educational programming, in fact, Mr. O'Brien is the perfect lesson in what qualities all good TV performers should have—comic timing, self-assurance, poise, and tone and tempo ex-pertise—since he isn't blessed with any of them.

Conan's opening cartoon credits show him nervous and sweating (his trademark style) which, combined with his unique collection of disturbing tics and itchy quirks—that hair-pulling, that eye-twitching, that squeaking voice—make viewers everywhere tense and disturbed. For a smidgen of variety the producers finally added portly frat-boy sidekick Andy (a would-be Ed McMahon, but without Ed's show-biz subtlety and Hollywood savoir faire), and a series of skits your kid brother would find juvenile.

It all adds up to one thing: a masterpiece.

Mel & Susan Together, 1978. If you wanted to create a smash hit variety show, wouldn't you pair Mel Tillis (the stuttering Nashville singer) with Susan Anton (Muriel cigar spokesperson and Amazon model) as the hosts? The idea here was "Hey, isn't everyone in America dying to see these two together?" and the mystery of the human spirit explored is "How does anyone come up with an idea like this?"

Our Place, 1967. Comedy team Burns and Schreiber and the notorious Doodletown Pipers joined host (and only humanlike element) Rowlf the Muppet in this summer replacement for *The Smothers Brothers*—a show that ended the late sixties trend of prime-time puppet hosts.

Our Time, 1985. Perky-beyond-belief Karen Valentine hosted this yuppie nostalgia show—nostalgia for the childhoods of thirty-year-olds—which, of course, featured lots and lots and lots of TV clips. Guests on the premiere alone included Paul Revere and the Raiders *(Where the Action Is)*, Adam West *(Batman)*, Jay North *(Dennis the Menace)*, Edd Byrnes *(77 Sunset Strip)*, and the dreaded Morgan Brittany (no reason given).

Pink Lady & Jeff, 1980. The Legend. Pink Lady—two very young and very beautiful women, Mitsuyo (Mie) Nemoto and Keko (Kei) Ma-

In the history of BAD TV, many are called, but only a very few reach the staggering, awesome heights of *Pink Lady & Jeff*
(Photofest)

suda—was Japan's #1 music act. Pink Lady wore beautiful gowns, lots of makeup, and giggled simperingly all the time. Pink Lady could dance a little, and could pose in gracious tableaux with wonderful sets. Pink Lady could only speak about five words in English: *hello, good-bye, pink, lady,* and *Jeff*. Pink Lady sang frothy American pop music in tiny, annoying, little-girl voices, with heavy accents that made the songs totally incomprehensible to those who could speak English.

Immediately, America did not like the squeaking Pink Lady (even though the show was developed by Brandon "Golden Gut" Tartikoff and produced by puppeteers Sid and Marty Krofft, who also did *The Brady Bunch Variety Hour)*, and we got rid of it after a mere six episodes. Jeff was American comedian Jeff Altman, whose comedy was as good as Pink Lady's English, with such gut-busting lines as "You just get turned on by my sexy round eyes." He went on to become a regular on *The Starland Vocal Band Show* and *Solid Gold . . .* and he's still trying to have a career in television.

Ii Ii Ii Ii Ii

Saturday Night Live with Howard Cosell, 1975. Not to be confused with the *Saturday Night Live* you know (which premiered a month later and was originally called *NBC's Saturday Night*), this was an ABC variety hour using the miracle of satellite broadcasting to send the acerbic sportscaster on a hosting jaunt across the wide, wide world of entertainment.

Just take a brief moment and think about the gruff, brilliantly cynical (but antiperky) Howard Cosell hosting a variety show, and you'll immediately understand just how BAD this was. A regular was Bill Murray; the remarkable guests included Siegfried and Roy, the Bay City Rollers, Charo, John Wayne (making political comments), Jimmy Connors (singing), Barbara Walters (singing), and Shamu the killer whale.

Ii Ii Ii Ii

Shields and Yarnell, 1977. Husband-and-wife mimes (best known for their husband-and-wife mime robot act) graduate from the streets of San

**When mimedom—and pixie cuts—were in bloom; the
thankfully silent poetry of *Shields and Yarnell*** (Stephen Cox)

Francisco to their own network show during the thankfully brief mime
craze of the late seventies.

———

The Starland Vocal Band Show, 1977. Famous for fifteen minutes due to their lurid novelty chartbuster about lunch and orgasms, "Afternoon Delight," the Starland Vocal Band found its real talent with this show—a talent for BAD TV. It's the show that asks the question: "How did you get this job?" and the horrifying regular guests included tedious political satirist Mark Russell and *Pink Lady & Jeff*'s Jeff.

ⵊⵊ ⵊⵊ

Street People, 1971. Viewers would tune in expecting a program about bums, and instead find host Mal Sharpe wandering around various parts of the United States, bumping into ordinary Joes and Janes on the street, and asking them to sing a capella, tell a joke they heard at the watercooler, or be interviewed about their fascinating lives.

ⵊⵊ

Thicke of the Night, 1983. Some network exec obviously decided that the secret of *The Tonight Show*'s immense success was its wonderfully bland tone, and since Alan Thicke was tremendously popular in his native *tepid rules!* Canada, he got incredible backing and promotional support to try making it on this side of the forty-ninth. So while most disaster shows get canceled right away, this "talk and more!" outing was the bomb that wouldn't die.

As a talk show host Alan Thicke is so excessively amiable and so passively easygoing, he seems barely alive—almost an eighties version of Perry Como. Thicke was so laid back on this show, in fact, that he could never get engaged into any kind of human interaction with his guests. This affectlessness, combined with ridiculously lame opening monologues and a studio audience's artificially forced gaiety, makes this show seem like an alien planet's version of American television.

Thicke and Co. kept tinkering and tinkering, trying to make it work, even though in many cities *Thicke*'s ratings were a 2, and in the others it achieved a landmark 0 Nielsen. A legendary disaster, this show was thought the worst of late night's endless parade of Carson contenders. Since this cavalcade included such compelling luminaries as Pat Sajak,

Tom Snyder, Rick Dees, Ross Schafer, and *The Wilton North Report, Thicke of the Night* is a remarkable achievement. Thicke went on to star in the surprise megahit *Growing Pains*—and later would admit that, when he watched his *Thicke* debut, he fainted.

Toni Twin Time, 1950. A talent show hosted by Jack Lemmon that should be known as *Hair Quiz*. Each show included twin girls, one of whom had a Toni home permanent—but which one could it be?

What's It All About, World?, 1969. A remake of the legendary Smothers Brothers blend of music and political satire with your new host, perky guy-next-door Disney regular, Dean Jones.

And the Tammi for worst variety show ever goes to:

The Brady Bunch Variety Hour, 1977. Even those who loved *The Brady Bunch* (a pretty BAD show, after all) thought this was beyond belief; if you can imagine the stars of *Roseanne* singing, dancing, and starring in their own variety hour, you'll have a bare idea of what's in store for you here. Produced by Sid and Marty Krofft (a pair who deserve their own special BAD TV award; see also *Donny and Marie, Pink Lady & Jeff, The Bugaloos,* and *Lidsville)* with Krofft signature larger-than-life-sized puppets, Lawrence Welk–styled medleys, the worst writing in the history of network television, and the kind of dancing you and your kid sister did late at night in your bedroom when no one was watching, *The Brady Bunch Variety Hour*'s centerpiece was a swimming pool, and the pilot promised "sixty minutes of songs and swimming with America's wettest family!"

The Bradys were all dressed in the worst excesses of the seventies: necklaces and giant collars for the boys; peach Qiana vests and apricot polyester elephant bells for the kids; white disco suit studded with mirrors

All-singing! All-dancing! All-polyester! Call Nickelodeon and demand they broadcast a weekly rerun of *The Brady Bunch Variety Hour* (Photofest)

for Robert Reed; very tight gold lamé and wedgies for Florence Henderson; a maid's uniform for long-suffering Ann B. Davis (whose humiliating musical number involved blond pigtails, rouge dots for freckles, a gingham frock, and a plague of enormous cowboy and farmgirl Krofft puppets). Who but those wacky Kroffts would have thought up these guest stars: Donny and Marie (on roller skates), Tony Randall, Rip Taylor, Rick Dees (singing his novelty hit "Disco Duck" and the unsuccessful follow-up, "Discorilla"), the child stars of *What's Happening!!* and a midget—all in the first two episodes!

The canned, hyperenthusiastic audience applause and gales of laughter at every possible moment is so grossly inappropriate, it only makes everything seem even worse—as if that were possible.

⚊⚊ ⚊⚊ ⚊⚊ ⚊⚊ ⚊⚊ ⚊⚊

I hate television. I hate it as much as peanuts.
But I can't stop eating peanuts.

—Orson Welles

The Music Video Nominees

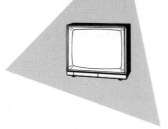

When I was young, we didn't have MTV;
we had to take drugs and go to concerts.

—Steven Pearl

WHEN WE WATCH ROCK VIDEOS, WHAT DO WE WANT? TAWDRY, provocative, eye-catching pictures; enough bare skin to titillate (but not enough so our little brother gets ideas); a world where all singers are heroic and all backups are best friends or sex machines; and tunes you can't get out of your head—in short, one BAD thing after another. Like the soaps and Chuck Barris game shows, the BADder they are, the better they get, so how do you rate this category? Just in the nick of time MTV came through—by polling its readers to create a special, "The Weekend of Triumph and Tragedy" (November 13–15, 1992). The terrible onus is off; we don't have to make the agonizing decisions; we can instead let the most fanatical of MTV's viewers (the ones who care enough to vote) decide for themselves.

Here, then, are the music videos viewers remembered as the worst in the channel's history, with opinions heavily biased to fashion. As will be seen in many cases, yesterday's very popular video is today's object of derision, and a "bad" video is mostly something that's gone out of style. In fact, the fans' pick for #1 "triumph" and best video ever, Guns 'n' Roses' *November Rain,* is an ode to cheap sentiment (at weddings and funerals), smoking cigarettes, playing a mean guitar in the middle of nowhere, and being such a rich rock star that you can afford to hire an orchestra for your videos—how BAD can you get? In fact, after going through four hours of

"Triumphs and Tragedies," one can't help but think about the question Doug Ferrari once raised:

Is MTV the lava lamp of the Eighties?

Quotations found in the following passages are solely the comments of MTV viewers and do not reflect the opinions of MTV, its VJs, or this book's author. And, since MTV doesn't bother with dates, neither can we.

Rick Astley, *Never Gonna Give You Up.* A surprise hit from the Jim Nabors–voiced, J. C. Penney fashion victim, who's accompanied here by cartwheel-spinning jazz dancers.

🕴 🕴 🕴

Toni Basil, *Mickey*. Not-a-teenager-for-a-very-long-time Toni and some of her ditto-aged male peers dress up as frolicsome preteen girl cheerleaders to parody this song's themes of romantic angst. Unfortunately, the enormous amount of makeup and body prostheses needed for their teen transformations makes all involved look undead.

🕴 🕴 🕴 🕴

Culture Club, *Karma Chameleon*. Transvestite-next-door Boy George, his band, and their friends dress up like plantation owners in pre–Civil War Mississippi, and have many amusing adventures (such as catching a riverboat card cheat and making him walk the plank).

None of this has anything whatsoever to do with the song's lyrics, which are about a fishlike person who's always mentally swimming around.

🕴 🕴

Falco, *Der Kommissar*. In a style all his own, Falco (a Eurotrashed Michael Paré wannabe) slicks back his hair, polishes his aviator shades, mutters incomprehensibly in both German and English, practices his sneering, shakes a real Moroccan-leather jacket, and dances like a piece of bacteria—all while supered over flashing police sirens. But how could the MTV voters miss Falco's other masterpiece: *Rock Me Amadeus*?

🕴 🕴 🕴 🕴

———

Gerardo, *Rico Suave*. Another novelty hit's instavideo, this time starring the skirt-chasing gym enthusiast who merged low-rider Latin style with a perky pop chorus. Name-cursed viewer Tigger from New Jersey noted, "¡*Rico Suave* es mucho stinko!"

♟ ♟ ♟

Debbie Gibson, *Electric Youth*. Backdropped by a castle illuminated by laser beams, pop chanteuse Debbie (whom we believe to be a King Family graduate) here tries to bring back a certain style of music, a certain style of fashion, and a certain style of choreography—the "Up with People!" style, that is.

♟ ♟ ♟

Hammer, *Too Legit to Quit*. The man who brought Vegas to rap and rap to Vegas now tries to pound his new record into your head with a musical version of Chinese water torture. Accessorized by small fires, children in double-breasted suits, weightlifting dancers, seven costume changes, and dancing-on-air special effects, Hammer, along with a deadly chorus, yells, "TOO LEGIT! TOO LEGIT TO QUIT!" over and over and over again until you're ready to scream.

♟ ♟ ♟ ♟

Michael Jackson, the censored finale to *Black or White*. Even though this caused instant controversy (and front-page headlines), fans apparently don't much care for the androgynous King of Pop when he's a crotch-grabbing, window-smashing panther morph.

♟ ♟

Journey, *Love Will Find You*. Goofy white teens strain to look both deeply anguished and completely hip while cavorting through deserted alleys in the latest mall outfits.

♟ ♟ ♟

———

Milli Vanilli, *Girl You Know It's True*. Everyone accepts that, when superstars go to make their music videos, they lip-synch. But the record-buying public thought Milli Vanilli went too far when it was revealed that the voices they were lip-synching to weren't even their own. Now that we know the truth, this video is a must-see; having the artifice of the genre thrown in your face makes it all the more enjoyable.

ⅠⅠ ⅠⅠ ⅠⅠ

Nelson, *After the Rain*. Frightening giant-haired blond boy twins hop down from their poster and yank a misunderstood teen out of his bedroom window, through an Indian sweat lodge, and into VIP seating at one of their legendary concerts. "They aren't the sons of Ricky Nelson," a viewer demurred, "but of Larry 'Bud' Melman, and their band should be called *Melman*."

ⅠⅠ ⅠⅠ ⅠⅠ

New Kids on the Block *(You've Got the) Right Stuff*. If MTV hates you but lots of people are buying your albums, do they then try to ruin your career by playing your video so often, everyone wants to see you killed slowly and painfully? *Right Stuff* was aired endlessly when New Kids were in their prime; now it looks like every bit of forced cuteness in the book performed by the worst lip-synchers in history (and choreographed by Popeye).

ⅠⅠ ⅠⅠ ⅠⅠ ⅠⅠ

Sinéad O'Connor, *The Emperor's New Clothes*. As part of the backlash against Sinéad for performing badly and then tearing up a picture of the pope on *Saturday Night Live,* MTV connoisseurs now claim she's "spastic and froglike."

ⅠⅠ ⅠⅠ

—

Right Said Fred, *I'm Too Sexy*. Bald English bodybuilders in fishnet perform a satiric ode to the joys of runway modeling that became one summer's throwaway novelty hit with its own throwaway novelty video, both of which aged very quickly.

Michael Sembello, *Maniac*. Wouldn't it be great if they made a movie about the travails of an ironworker who practices for her entrance exam to a snooty dance academy by working nights in the world's greatest topless bar? Thankfully, they did; the first motion picture inspired by MTV itself, *Flashdance* is the ultimate eighties megahit, and to get it, you had to be there. This video is one of many hit singles from the film, which also introduced us to glamorous sweatpants, setting fashion sense for the decade.

Bart Simpson, *Do the Bartman*. White boy rap from the popular cartoon character done (by a woman) in his signature pubescent screech with an equally screechy pubescent chorus.

Styx, *Mr. Roboto*. Movie soundtrack paean to Oriental robots called Mr. Roboto in order to rhyme with *oregato* (Japanese for hello). "You know, Styx is a river in hell, and that's where this video belongs."

Vanilla Ice, *Ice Ice Baby*. The sensation when it appeared is now the definitive reason why white boys shouldn't be allowed to rap.

And the Tammi for worst rock video ever goes to:

Warrant, *Cherry Pie*. An ode to cunnilingus ("She's my cherry pie . . . tastes so good makes grown men cry") illustrated with servile, pie-bearing waitresses, uncontrollable firehoses, and dripping pie slices plopping down on female crotches.

"I respect women," said the lead singer in defense; "we did this just for fun."

ᴌ ᴌ ᴌ ᴌ ᴌ ᴌ

I invite you to sit down in front of your television set . . . and stay there without a magazine, newspaper, or book to distract you—and keep your eyes glued to that set until the station signs off. I can assure you that you will observe a vast wasteland. You will see a procession of game shows, violence, audience participation shows, formula comedies about totally unbelievable families, blood and thunder, mayhem, violence, sadism, murder, western bad men, western good men, private eyes, gangsters . . . and, endlessly, commercials. . . .

—Newton Minow, FCC Chairman,
1961

The Game Show Nominees

We're in the same position as a plumber laying a pipe. We're not responsible for what goes through the pipe.

—David Sarnoff, founder, NBC

THOSE WHO CLAIM TO HATE TELEVISION (AND WE USE *CLAIM*, SINCE those who say they hate it frequently never watch it) have lots of bad things to say about game shows, and for the most part they're right! Successful game shows usually pander to the worst in both their audience and their contestants. If you're a squealer, a jumper, can easily flush with excitement and howl, "Big bucks! big bucks! big bucks!" in a convincing, mantralike way, you'll probably get on the air; if you're mildly educated (but not too educated), you could even win some money— and that's on the *good* game shows. The bad ones have incomprehensibly bad concepts, contests impossible for viewers to enjoy, and a habit of humiliating the contestants so often and with such intensity that watching them is like watching Lions versus Christians in the good old days.

Alarmingly, game shows have become one of Hollywood's biggest exports. *Wheel of Fortune* now appears in fifteen countries and is a sensation in Poland; Spain's gaga over *The Price Is Right;* and the Turks can't get enough of *The Dating Game* (which in Turkish comes out as *Saklambac*).

Though we in the U.S. haven't reached the point of German television with its amazing *Tutti Frutti* (a cross between *Jeopardy!* and strip poker), from the looks of the BAD game shows below (and the current desperation of cable programmers), we're well on the way.

115

What do game shows reveal?

- There's nothing more fun than watching people being utterly humiliated on nationwide television while practically the entire U.S. population looks on.
- Greed is is not just good—it's great!
- There's nothing more fun than watching a truly pathetic creature win big prizes.
- Americans really are willing to do *anything* to get on television.
- Explicit sex and explicit sex talk are *verboten* on TV—but try to come as close to it as you can.

Born Lucky, 1991. The only game show with contestants yanked from a screaming mob at "your local mall" who might win "mall money" and therefore have to spend it there. The blow-dryer-impaired host will give you tiny prizes for easy trivia answers, but to get the grand prize he'll put you through an unwinnable endurance contest from hell.

Crime Time, 1960. Mobsters' favorite recipes, "I was framed!" accounts playing to audience sympathy and applause, and safecrackers trying to beat the clock for valuable prizes, are just a few of the highlights here.

ESP, 1958. Vincent Price himself hosted this testing of guests (called "sensitives") to see if they had extrasensory perception, but no one could figure out how to make ESP look interesting or dramatic on the air.

How's Your Mother-in-Law?, 1967. Produced by genius Chuck Barris and hosted by *Ur*–game show host Wink Martindale, this legendary outing had three women contestants compete before a panel of comedians to see who is America's best mother-in-law, who could tell the most mother-in-law jokes, and how long a show based on such a thin premise could last.

Ⅱ Ⅱ Ⅱ

It Pays to Be Ignorant, 1949; It Pays to Be Stupid, 1973. Game-show parodies (as if there could be such a thing) where the celebrity contestants try to think up funny ways of not being able to answer obvious questions. "Who's buried in Grant's tomb?" "Uh . . . uh . . ."

Ⅱ Ⅱ Ⅱ Ⅱ

Laugh Line, 1959. Host Dick Van Dyke showed fabulous celebrities (such as Orson Bean and Mike Nichols) cartoons. The famous had to—live!, on the air!—provide the captions. When these megastars fished around to think up a line, it was boring; when they had a snappy comeback, it looked fake.

Ⅱ Ⅱ

Lie Detector, 1983. Notorious criminal lawyer F. Lee Bailey explored such questions as: Will Ronald Reagan's barber admit to dyeing the then-President's hair? Is Melvin Dummar telling the truth about his important role in Howard Hughes's will? Is it even a tiny bit interesting to watch someone take a polygraph test?

The answer to all three? No.

Ⅱ Ⅱ Ⅱ

Lip Service, 1992. If you feel that there's not enough going on in today's game shows, then MTV has the answer with this combination of *Name That Tune,* improvisational dancing, Spinderella, close-ups of mysterious music video lips, homemade choreography, karaoke lip-synching, typewriter prizes, and last but not least, Dr. Joyce Brothers.

Ⅱ Ⅱ Ⅱ

The Pop 'N' Rocker Game, 1983. Music quiz show with surly, ignorant teen contestants and guest rock stars.

Puttin' on the Hits, 1985. Big prizes awarded for that crucial life talent, lip-synching—one of the many things MTV filched from drag queens, and not something an awful lot of fun to watch at home when it's performed by the people next door.

Shop Till You Drop, 1989. Another *Price Is Right* imitation for an all-new generation of hysteric yuppie consumers in a set that mimics a California Plaza strip mall. Winners know all there is to know about jingle lyrics, brand names, ad slogans, important new makeup developments, and how to decipher a J. Crew catalog (where the clothes colors are things like soviet, anodyne, fingersnap, missionary, libra, electricity, and matisse). Winners fly to shopping sprees around the world; nonwinners receive electric sandwich-toasters.

Showdown, 1966. Losing contestants of this quiz show would have their chairs fall apart, sending them sprawling across the floor.

Sit or Miss, 1950. The riveting drama of five contestants playing musical chairs.

So You Think You Got Troubles?!, 1982. Contestants with odd problems consult with a panel of experts, ventriloquist Jay Johnston and his nasty dummy, Bob. Winners correctly guess which expert's comments the studio audience liked best.

Starcade, 1983. The thrill of spending a half hour watching preteens play video games.

Stop Me If You've Heard This One, 1948. Host Ted Brown told fabulous celebrities (such as Morey Amsterdam) jokes sent in by the viewers at home. The famous had to—live!, on the air!—provide the punch line.

Strike It Rich, 1951. A gender-free version of *Queen for a Day,* with needy people telling their pathetic, maudlin stories to make the audience sob and win big bucks. Even losers had a chance at something, since the show included a "Heart Line," where the home audience could call in and offer money to the prizeless. New York City wasn't thrilled that the show was produced in Manhattan; in 1953, fifty-five families came to New York trying to get on the show, didn't make it, and ended up on welfare.

Stump the Stars, aka Pantomime Quiz, 1949. Screaming internationally famous superstars like Stubby Kaye, Ruta Lee, Deanna Lund, and Tom Poston dress up in formal wear at an ersatz Hollywood penthouse, play an incredibly difficult game of charades, and almost always lose—on a show that lasted for twenty-one years.

Supermarket Sweep, 1965. How good are you at guessing what the most expensive thing in a grocery store might be? How quickly can you run through the store's aisles, throwing things into your cart? The answers to these questions have fascinated Americans for over twenty-

If you've ever said to yourself, "I'd do *anything* to have a freezerful of meat," you're just what the producers of *Supermarket Sweep* are looking for (Photofest)

eight years on one of the longest-running shows in the history of television.

🙍 🙍 🙍 🙍

Treasure Isle, 1967. Practically every successful game show in history (just think of *Concentration, Jeopardy!, Let's Make a Deal, Password,* or *Wheel of Fortune*) is based on a simple premise that anyone can understand, with low production costs that make them some of the most profitable outings in television. John D. MacArthur, source of the MacArthur "genius" grants, owned the Colonnades Beach Hotel in Florida, and decided that what his hotel needed in its never-ending quest for fame and glory was its own game show—a game show that would ignore the cardinal rules of success.

Wildly complicated in both costs and gaming, *Treasure Isle* was based on an immense man-made lake built at the hotel. Contestants were all married couples, who first had to paddle furiously around the lake, putting together a giant floating crossword puzzle, and then row off to the eponymous island, where the words of the puzzle would be the clues for the exhausting treasure hunt.

Instead of the frothy pleasure that a good game show provides, *Treasure Isle* had an undertone of pity and sadness. You couldn't help but feel sorry for these pathetic couples, who worked harder at playing this game than any prize could possibly be worth.

🙍 🙍 🙍 🙍

You're in the Picture, 1961. Celebrities would stick their head through the cutout holes of a carnival painting and, by asking host Jackie Gleason questions (à la *What's My Line?*), try to guess what the painting was. The show was supposed to focus on Gleason's impromptu jokes and comments (like *You Bet Your Life*), but the first broadcast was so tedious and amateurish that the Great One (on a bare stage with a bottle of whiskey) spent the first fifteen minutes of the next broadcast apologizing. He then launched a chat show guesting his friends, which would last an entire season.

🙍 🙍 🙍

The Chernobyl Lifetime Achievement Award:

To producer CHUCK BARRIS

The Dating Game, 1965; The Newlywed Game, 1966. American classics on the air for over twenty-five years, with a host of imitators and no sign of ending, *Dating* and *Newlywed* are really the same show. Created by BAD TV mogul Chuck Barris, the point of both is to see how much explicit sex can be discussed without falling beyond the Standards and Practices bounds of network television (on HBO both shows would be like *Dream On*—topless). If you don't think Americans have mixed feelings about sex, just turn on your TV; every *Dating* and *Newly* question is loaded, and every answer walks the line between being revealing . . . and being coy.

In 1968 Howard Hughes wanted to buy ABC. That is, until he saw *The Dating Game*. Said Hughes: it is "the largest single collection of poor taste I have ever seen . . . it abused any conceivable moral standard by arranging a sexual rendezvous between a beautiful white girl and a Negro man in Rome, which may even be in violation of the law." Hughes was, of course, mistaken; the beautiful white girl was in fact black. And he never bought ABC.

In 1987 *TV Guide* called *The New Newlywed Game* "the worst piece of sleaze on television today." The most amazing *Newlywed* moment has been described by many on the Nominating Committee, who insist it's true. Bob Eubanks has denied it and I don't believe it for a minute; even so, it would be criminal not to include it in the pages of this important volume, at least as an example of TV legend:

Bob Eubanks: "Where will your husband say is the *strangest* place the two of you have ever made whoopee?"
Female Contestant: "In the butt, Bob!"

Mr. Eubanks himself told the *Village Voice* "I always figured I could sell about a million IN THE BUTT, BOB T-shirts if I wanted to." And, as Mr. Barris himself noted: "If a newlywed couple loved and respected each other, they probably would never have thought about doing the show in the first place. And even if they had, we would most likely not have

The Genius (Chuck Barris) prepares for another quiet, sophisticated evening on *The Gong Show* (Stephen Cox)

selected them for the program. They would have made lousy contestants."

The Gong Show, 1976; The Chuck Barris Rah-Rah Show, 1978; The $1.98 Beauty Contest, 1978. Chuck strikes again; he even served as host for *The Gong Show,* which took Ted Mack's original idea to an all-time low. Featuring a bevy of grade-Z celebrity panelists (like Jayne Mansfield remake Jaye P. Morgan, Don Drysdale remake Steve Garvey, Charles Laughton remake Rex Reed, and Dr. Joyce Brothers remake Dr. Joyce Brothers), a gong that would instantly terminate the competing acts, low-rent prizes, and the kind of talent never before seen on television (such as an immensely fat woman who sings with burps and an ancient man pirouetting in a tutu), the insistently BAD *Gong Show* was a unique vision that both made its mark in television and found a real following.

Barris then tried to recreate his legendary success—twice. What *The Gong Show* did for *Ted Mack's Original Amateur Hour, The $1.98 Beauty Contest* tried to do for *The Miss America Pageant.* Sadly, Chuck's vision was gone; it's one thing to make fun of someone's singing and dancing, but quite another to make fun of their intense ugliness. For mysterious reasons *Gong* shortly thereafter lost its magical booking abilities, and ran out of bizarre but lovable contestants. The *Rah-Rah Show* was an attempt to recycle the bad performers and bad panelists (Jaye P. Morgan again) from *Gong* into an hour-long prime-time variety format—like, for sure.

Many TV shows—most notably, *Late Night with David Letterman*—deliberately try to have BAD elements, with the cast offering their home and studio audiences vicious, knowing winks that say, *Don't confuse these poor suckers with us. Gong* and *$1.98,* however, are unique in television history since both, from start to finish, lovingly wallowed in BADness whole-hog—and gave our rating system a fit. Does *Gong* get more points for being good BAD, or should *Rah-Rah* and *$1.98* get more for being bad BAD? As of press time we were still baffled by this question . . .

The Dating Game ♟♟ ♟♟ ♟♟ ♟♟; *The Newlywed Game* ♟♟ ♟♟ ♟♟ ♟♟ ♟♟; *The Gong Show* ♟♟ ♟♟ ♟♟; *The $1.98 Beauty Contest* ♟♟ ♟♟; *The Chuck Barris Rah-Rah Show* ♟♟.

The *Newly Dating* Clones: *Love Connection,* 1983; *The Gay Dating Game,* 1989; *Studs,* 1989; *Personals,* 1989; *Night Games,* 1991; *Perfect

Score, 1992; *Infatuation,* 1992; *That's Amore,* 1992, *How's Your Love Life?,* 1992. If you've ever considered a career as a professional voyeur, these shows can test if you're right for the job. The ultimate in audience safe sex, they all offer three possible thrills; the half-coy, half-explicit descriptions of sex that made *The Newlywed Game* such a classic (normally); the successful date where love is in bloom (rarely), and the date from hell, with the postmortem contestants bitterly attacking each other (always).

Like the rest *Love Connection* (with a full ten years on the air) seldom features a love connection; the show's main attraction is watching two vicious singles publicly humiliate each other in front of a live TV audience. We get to discover, in explicit details, how bad your breath is, what crummy ideas you have for a date, how rudely you treat people of the opposite sex, what bad taste you have in clothes, how repulsive you are sexually, and more: "He's a fasting psychic—so he didn't want to eat, and he spent a lot of time telling me bad things he knew about me already—it was an endurance test." "He kept telling me about his cat's gross urinary infection." "She was such a bad kisser, Chuck, I mean, when you kiss you don't want to bump noses and things like that, and, you know, blood is a bad scene."

The good news, though, is that Bob Eubanks is back, and *Infatuation*'s got him! Compared to the others of its ilk *Infatuation* takes the high road, putting together duos who already know each other. One's a secret smitten kitten, while the other finds out about the crush on the air, and the two then discuss their relationship. It's a very sweet and touching show, strangely hosted and produced by our very own Oil King Eubanks.

Such nice things can't be said for *That's Amore,* where longtime married couples air their dirty laundry and the audience votes on who's got the most valid set of gripes, all overseen by a Chef Boyardee sound-alike.

Personals is such a clone, it even has a *separated-at-birth?* Bob Eubanks wannabe for a host. The crux of the show is having a passel of gorgeous gals fill out an application, answering multiple-choice questions like "Are you concerned about nuclear proliferation?" and "Did you ever make love in an amusement park?" to get a date (how lifelike). While the studio audience sits around a mock singles bar, you the home viewer can leave answering-machine messages for any of the contestants for a mere $2.95 a minute. The finale comes when two would-be couples compete against each other on a compatibility test rated via the *Love Thermometer* to discover whether their date will be at Club Med Haiti or the Solana Beach Ramada Inn—advertised on the air as "the best place to do it."

Since it's on Fox, *Studs* goes as explicit as television can; a recent night featured lines like "I gripped his gun until it exploded all over me," "One look at his big banana and my cherry was tied in knots," and "He grabbed the back of my head and slipped it right in." One contestant, obviously inspired by Tom Arnold, dropped trou to show everyone the artistic tattoos on his butt. Host Mark DeCarlo (*Sale of the Century*'s biggest winner ever) gets to encourage his guests nightly into lines like "One munch of my maraschino and he went limp"—but also "I've fallen in love and I can't get up!" *Spy* magazine shockingly revealed that, as far as can be determined, all these lines (including "Any guy who can eat more meat than me is my kind of guy"—about a date at a steakhouse) arise from completely innocuous dating moments and were written by the show's producers.

At the end of every *Studs* two guys pick future dates from three women (who prefer their clothes very small and their hair very big)—so there's always one woman left, rejected, who becomes the camera and audience's complete focus of attention. Will she be a good sport about being judged a loser with 20 million people watching—including everyone she knows?

The only one of these shows that plays it for laughs is New York City's *The Gay Dating Game,* whose top prize is a ten-dollar tourist boat ride around Manhattan ("the world's most complicated island!"), and whose hosts are a leather queen and a loopy transvestite.

The great and true mystery of the universe explored by all these programs is: If you've ever watched one and seen what kind of total humiliation most of the "guests" have to endure, why on earth would you ever agree to be a contestant? Are Americans so desperate to get on television they're willing to be made fools of in front of millions of viewers around the world?

Watch, and judge for yourself.

Love Connection 🕹🕹 🕹🕹 🕹🕹 🕹🕹; *Infatuation* 🕹🕹 🕹🕹 🕹🕹; *That's Amore* 🕹🕹 🕹🕹; *Personals* 🕹🕹 🕹🕹 🕹🕹 🕹🕹; *Studs* 🕹🕹 🕹🕹 🕹🕹 🕹🕹 🕹🕹; *The Gay Dating Game* 🕹🕹 🕹🕹 🕹🕹.

Treasure Hunt, 1974. A Chuck Barris Productions recreation of a popular 1956 show, where contestants tried to figure out which of many boxes held the big prize (not unlike the "what's behind the curtain?" fun of *Let's Make a Deal*). In its new, turgidly moving version, however, *Treasure* host Geoff Edwards sadistically tortured and humiliated his contestants by constantly tricking them into thinking they'd made the wrong choice and lost out on everything. With few "thrill of victory" moments

Treasure Hunt was the only game show ever focusing on "the agony of defeat."

♟♟ ♟♟ ♟♟

♟♟

And the Tammi for the worst game show ever goes to:

Queen for a Day, 1956. On the air (via radio and then television) for over nineteen years and, during much of the fifties, the top-rated program on daytime TV, *Queen for a Day* had a simple premise: Have women describe something they want and why they should get it. After the all-important applause meter recorded the judgment, the winner would be robed in sable and crowned in a tiara, would lug a dozen long-stemmed roses over to a tatty throne, and be presented with exactly what she asked for, and more!

Strategic thinkers soon realized that if they could induce the audience and judges into hysterical crying fits, they'd win, and the show turned into a sobfest of who could most dramatically tell the most pathetic, heartbreaking story anyone had ever heard (though not every would-be queen followed this strategy; one contestant's wish was to have host Jack Bailey do her nails). To win, not only did you have to be a terminally ill paraplegic who'd spent all your money on medical bills and all you wanted before your imminent death was to visit your only child who you hadn't seen in twenty years (and who happened to live in Hawaii), but you had to be able to tell this story convincingly, and with maximum dramatic impact, in less than eight minutes.

Were tens of thousands of American women up to this challenge? You bet—here are some real-life *Queen for a Day* contestants, many of whom wring their hands in woe, are constantly suppressing sobs, and look like those classic *Let Us Now Praise Famous Men* photographs from the Depression era:

"I want *saw*curity: My father-in-law had a heart attack and he'll stay in bed for about three or four more months and he's awfully depressed because he won't be able to go back to a steady job, and he's worried he'll be a burden to us. So I want some power tools for him to work with since he's awfully handy with that stuff when he has good equipment."

"I want a washer-dryer. I do all my wash for my husband and five children by hand."

**Less-than-gracious runners-up pose with a gushing fountain
of pathos (the winner) on *Queen for a Day*** (Photofest)

"I'd like a secret meeting with my real mother. When I was three weeks old, she adopted me out, and I had very wonderful foster parents who are dead now, and I would like to meet my own mother, and I have located her but I've found out that the man she married doesn't know she gave me away. She didn't want to; she tried to get me back, but my foster parents moved away."

"I'd like a bicycle for my boy. He had one, it was an old one, and he got a paper route in November. Now the bike is broke and it needs welding, so I have to get up at four in the morning to take him on his paper route before I go to work at St. Francis hospital cafeteria and put in my eight hours. He let me have the money to come here and he didn't know what I was going to ask for. And today is his birthday."

"I want a house and some food. We live in a trailer camp and we haven't paid our rent and the man came over last night and said we had to be out by tomorrow. I have four children and my husband's been in one accident and had pneumonia twice. We don't have any money. My mother and father live with us and they're not able to work. We sleep on the floor. I'd give anything to get out of it."

Of course the trailer camper won, getting four dozen long-stemmed roses, a Max Factor makeup case, a compact vacuum cleaner, forty pieces of sterling silver, sixty-seven pieces of china, a dinette set, a refrigerator, a sewing machine, a Spiegel catalog gift certificate, a vacation in New Mexico, six months of rent on a house, a shopping spree at a grocery store, and beds for everybody!

The Twelve Titans
If they're involved, it's a must-watch

Susan Anton
Ted Bessell
Bob Cummings
Bob Eubanks
Alex Karras
Sid and Marty Krofft
Wink Martindale
Geraldo Rivera
Sherwood Schwartz
Suzanne Somers
Aaron Spelling
Shelley Winters

Television is the literature of the illiterate, the culture of the lowbrow, the wealth of the poor, the privilege of the underprivileged, and the exclusive club of the excluded masses.

—Lee Loevinger

The Drama Nominees

Is there that much, kind of, uh, sex on the show? I don't think so. Aren't there more sexy shows on, or is ours the sexiest? We really don't have sexy things happening, do we? I don't know, maybe people watch the show because they think it's good. Of course, everybody appreciates watching women. I know I have a big following among young little boys. Now, that can't be all sexual, can it?

—Farrah Fawcett Majors, on
Charlie's Angels

IT'S HARD ENOUGH DOING SUCCESSFUL DRAMA IN ANY MEDIUM, and even harder when you have to produce it week after week, day in and day out, to fit with our cherished and long-standing TV series format. The following, however, aren't just the also-rans and tries that didn't measure up; they're out-and-out catastrophes that many remember with great fondness. How BAD they really were can only barely be described, as the terribleness of many of these shows is truly humbling. They do, however, offer many lessons worth learning:

- If you find a corpse, don't take it home and try to bring it back to life.
- If you're on a quest for inner peace and spiritual harmony, don't go looking for it in the Wild West.
- If you're a cop, it may be more trouble than it's worth to have a partner who's from another planet.

- If you have to fall madly in love, don't do it with the Devil's girlfriend.
- Every day many saintlike people are falsely accused of a crime and get chased across the country by savage FBI agents and obsessed sheriffs.
- Sometimes when a group of lawyers wins a big case, they sing songs and tap-dance down the street together.
- Every day many saintlike people are falsely accused of a crime and get sent to the worst prison in the country where they're menaced by savage inmates and obsessed wardens.
- If you're attacked by a supernatural creature and all else fails, microwave it.

Action in the Afternoon, 1953. A Western broadcast live (and shot on location in the suburbs of Philadelphia), remembered by crew member Hugh Best as "violence—that's what it was all about—drowning, stoning, trampling, hanging, burning, impaling, and so on."

Alexander the Great, 1968. The pageantry! The drama! The history! The stars: William Shatner (Alexander), John Cassavetes (Kronos), Joseph Cotten (Antigonus), and Adam West (Cleander). How could it miss? Says Shatner: "The nine months I spent working on *Alexander the Great* came in handy for *Star Trek*. Captain Kirk is in many ways the quintessential hero, and the Greek heroes in literature have many of the same qualities I wanted to explore. . . . It was like *Combat*, in drag." Says West: "It just didn't work. The audience and Madison Avenue just weren't ready for orgies with Shatner and West lying there on their backs, eating grapes, with belly dancers beside them."

Automan, 1983. Renegade police officer Desi Arnaz, Jr., plays around with the force's computer and accidentally creates a magical humanoid being, Automan, and his equally magical sidekick, Cursor (a holograph who can create any object needed in the fight against crime). Magical, but utterly charm free.

——

Baywatch, 1989. The wild lives and searing drama of Speedoed L.A. lifeguards who frequently save bikinied girls in trouble, shot on location at one of those beaches with a strict door policy (no unattractive swimmers, please). It's as if *Charlie's Angels* changed sex and rid themselves of personality, becoming Chippendale dancers armed with flotation devices. If you're incapable of imagining an exciting, dramatic story that takes place on the beach, and if you can't think of humanlike dialogue, you can probably get a job writing for this show. Single-dad star David Hasselhoff has a *Wonder Years* clone child, but the writers, after running out of lifeguard ideas, couldn't even do family drama. The original series was dropped after two seasons by NBC, but it now seems to be doing exceptionally well in syndication and in foreign climes.

In Germany *Baywatch* is a huge hit and Hasselhoff is immensely popular. Who can explain this mystery? Says the leader of his biggest German fan club (but only one of many such clubs): "It can't be explained with the intellect. He is relaxed, he is looking very, very good, his contact with the fans is relaxed and easy . . . and very, very important, he loves children."

                                                                    ▲▲ ▲▲

Diamonds, 1987. When their married-couple-who-are-also-detectives TV show is canceled, a pair of actors start a married-couple-who-are-also-detectives agency. For an amazing coincidence, see the made-for-TV movie *Shooting Stars* (page 203).

                                                                    ▲▲ ▲▲

Doctor Franken, 1980. Robert Vaughn (Victor Frankenstein's great-great-great-grandson) drives by a car wreck and can't stop himself from doing what must be done. He takes the unknown dead driver back to the hospital, performs many grueling transplant procedures, and revives him. Sadly, John Doe doesn't want to hang around with his new dad; he has his own ideas—as well as the memories and souls of the people who donated his new organs and limbs. Every week Doe goes off in search of a different donor/ancestor/relative, finding self-awareness, a sense of family, and learning how to help everyone with their personal problems.

ıı ıı ıı ıı

Dream Street, 1989. Have you ever watched a beer commercial and thought, *Gee, if only all those people had their own show!* Well that's exactly what the creators of *thirtysomething* must have been thinking when they came up with this titanically superficial refrigerator biz drama.

ıı ıı ıı

The Dumplings, 1976. In the wake of his massive success with *All in the Family, Maude,* and *The Jeffersons,* Norman Lear could get anything on the air—even this sitcom starring the three-hundred-pound James Coco and the padded-so-she'd-look-fat Geraldine Brooks about the incredibly funny and charming lives of immensely fat people who LOVE LOVE LOVE each other so much it makes you want to SCREAM.

ıı ıı ıı

Fitz and Bones, 1981. Magnavox spokespeople and noted singing co-medians Tom and Dick Smothers try to prove the immense range of their acting talents by starring as unrelated television journalists in an hour-long drama that was the year's lowest-rated program.

ıı ıı

Ghost Story/Circle of Fear, 1972. A supernatural anthology; the most memorably BAD episode concerns a zombie doll coming to life and trying to bite off Karen Black's ankles . . . until she successfully microwaves it.

ıı ıı ıı ıı

Good Against Evil, 1977. Dack Rambo falls madly in love with the Devil's girlfriend (who's kidnapped by satanic worshipers), and travels the world searching for her, aided by noted exorcist Dan O'Her-lihy.

ᴧᴧ ᴧᴧ ᴧᴧ

The Immortal, 1970. Christopher George leaves *The Rat Patrol* to discover he can't age because of something in his blood. Chris's secret gets out, so he spends the rest of the series burdened by eternal life and pursued endlessly by rich old men (who dream of transfusions) and their willing sycophants.

ᴧᴧ ᴧᴧ ᴧᴧ

Kung Fu, 1972. After being kicked out of Beijing on a murder rap, demi-Chinese priest David Carradine searches the Wild West for a spiri-tually pure existence. Sadly, the American frontier isn't ready for zen mysticism—and Mr. Fu is constantly forced to use his expert martial arts to kill and maim.

ᴧᴧ ᴧᴧ ᴧᴧ

Lady Blue, 1985. Frightening redheaded *Falcon Crester* Jamie Rose does a "Dirty Harriet" turn as a Chicago policewoman with a big gun. The National Coalition on Television called this the most violent show on the air and, thankfully for the BAD connoisseur, it is.

ᴧᴧ ᴧᴧ ᴧᴧ

Lucan, 1977. A simultaneous remake of *L'Enfant Sauvage* and *The Fugitive, Lucan* is a boy raised by wolves who's falsely accused of a crime and chased across the country by greedy bounty hunters and flint-eyed sheriffs.

ᴧᴧ ᴧᴧ

Man and the Challenge, 1959. Hollywood scapegoat George Nader plays your typical athlete/host/scientist/doctor testing the abilities of hu-man beings to withstand the rigors of the elements and giving the home viewer unendurable high-school science lectures.

ᴧᴧ ᴧᴧ ᴧᴧ

———

A Man Called Shenandoah, **1965.** Cowpoke Robert Horton gets shot in the head, has total amnesia, and wanders the Old West searching for clues to his identity. *Shenandoah* fans have bitter arguments over what was worse about this show: that every episode ended with someone who knows the answer saying "You're . . . you're . . ." and suddenly dying, leaving the mystery intact—or that Horton himself sang the show's theme song.

♟ ♟ ♟

Manimal, **1983.** Simon MacCorkindale is a scientist studying animal behavior who learns "the secrets that divide man from animal" from his animal behavior-studying scientist father. With this fantastic ability he can turn himself into any creature at will, and so of course volunteers to help the New York City Police, where he meets the one person who knows his secret: quasi–love interest (and BAD Queen) Detective Melody Anderson.

Narrated by *Jake and the Fat Man*'s William Conrad, *Manimal*'s only real suspense was in waiting to see what Mr. Manimal would turn into— since it could be anything, he was invincible (even Superman had kryptonite troubles, for chrissake). With TV audiences used to shows like *Flipper*, it never occurred to the producers that trained animals might add a little something; *Manimal* fans were treated to such exciting animal cameos as a raven flying off, or a wolf walking away into the forest, or a leopard looking at the camera.

Even PBS knows better. *Manimal* does live on in TV history, though; it's what's on Jay Leno's *Tonight Show* coffee mug (Carson's was a decal portrait of himself).

♟ ♟ ♟

Mariah, **1987.** Staggeringly depressing Sartrean series about hopelessness and constant suicide in the dank hole of Mariah State Penitentiary.

♟ ♟ ♟ ♟

Look! Up in the sky! It's a bird, it's a snake, it's a gorilla, it's a lizard, it's a wolf, it's a gnat—no, it's *Manimal* (Photofest)

—

McClone, 1988. Both a remake of *The Six Million Dollar Man* and a parody of *McCloud,* with Howie Long as an android pursued by vicious clones.

Men into Space, 1959. Department of Defense post-Sputnik propaganda hyping the space race by featuring the imagined and deadly-dull perils of tomorrow's astronauts.

Middle Ages, 1992. Three guys in a remake of *thirtysomething.* The theme, reiterated over and over again, was that it's not the sixties anymore. Everyone's moping and moping about how it's not the sixties anymore. Said *Entertainment Weekly:* "a show that gives the word *downer* a good name."

Misfits of Science, 1985. Mad scientist hunk Dean Paul Martin works for a defense contractor making giant bunnies (but not the ones that attack Arizona in *Night of the Lepus*). Through various means he creates the Misfits—a shrinking black man, a blue-skinned, icicle-haired guy whose touch can freeze, a rock star who can run like the Flash and throw lightning bolts, and a pretty juvenile delinquent who uses her *Carrie*-like powers to throw things and people around—and leads them to deeds of glory. The whole thing's a cross between *90210* (if those teens had magic powers and were racially integrated) and *The A-Team,* but without either show's witty scripts, engaging pacing, philosophical depths, or fine acting.

Movin' On, 1974. Socially conscious Teamsters Claude Akins and Frank Converse truck the open road, aiding the needy, defending the innocent, and helping people with their personal problems.

—

The New People, 1969. Desert island plane-crash survivors—all-American, with-it youths, many in turtlenecks—start a new, hip society on an ex-nuclear test site; the kind of test site that's filled with mannequins and supplies. What do *New People* talk like?

> **Mod white teen:** "There's a piano in there!"
> **Mod black teen:** "Groovy! I'll play some blues!"
> **Sole adult** (who soon dies): "Wait a minute! So you're the ones who are going to inherit the earth? Give ya one lousy piece of it, and your first order of business is a crying jag in a ghost-town saloon!"

Think of *The Mod Squad* cloning themselves into a species and taking over *Gilligan's Island,* and you'll get some idea of the searing drama and incisive commentary on crucial social issues in store for you here.

♟♟ ♟♟ ♟♟ ♟♟

Nightingales, 1989. Aaron Spelling and Douglas Cramer tried to recreate their *Charlie's Angels* jiggly success with this student nurse show. Though the premise is ripe with drama—one student being a recovering alcoholic, and another a member of the feds' Witness Protection Program—the nurses spend more time getting dressed and aerobicizing their young, hard, big-breasted bodies than they do nursing.

The show was sold to NBC when Spelling ran into topper Brandon Tartikoff in a parking lot and beautifully pitched: "Student nurses . . . in Dallas . . . and the air conditioner's broken!"

♟♟ ♟♟ ♟♟

Paper Dolls, 1984. Another *Charlie's Angels*–inspired jiggle show, based on the surprise hit made-for of the same name and set in the ultradramatic world of modeling. The series was written and produced by people who don't know a damn thing about the ultradramatic world of modeling, and it starred Lloyd Bridges, Morgan Fairchild, Nicollete Sheridan, and Mimi Rogers.

♟♟

The best hopes of our nation confront the decay of Western civilization—mannequins—on *The New People* (Photofest)

A Peaceable Kingdom, **1989.** Lindsay Wagner gives up bionics to run the Los Angeles Zoo in a heartwarming tour de force that was the *Daktari* of the eighties.

—

The Phoenix, 1982. Alien being (and peroxide user) Bennu of the Golden Light is freed from his Egyptian tomb by E. G. Marshall and goes off to search for his companion Mira and to help earthlings with their personal problems.

AI AI AI AI

The Powers of Matthew Star, 1982. When this series began, it was about a mind-reading alien with ESP (who pretended to be a high school student) and his African-American guardian (who pretended to be a science teacher). When the ratings didn't gel, the same two stars abruptly became government agents, and the alien could also astral-project.

The Powers of Matthew Star had a brief life, but it was a remarkably cursed one. Producer Allan Balter had a heart attack and died in the middle of a meeting; costar Lou Gossett, Jr., was arrested for drug possession; and lead Peter Barton spent several months in the hospital undergoing skin grafts after catching on fire.

AI AI AI

Prisoner: Cell Block H, 1980. Relentlessly downbeat and harrowingly violent women-in-prison drama featuring international terrorists, vicious murderers, drug kingpins, and of course, lesbians. Housewife Karen is a devout Roman Catholic sentenced to life imprisonment for murdering her abusive husband; she did nothing to defend herself at the trial, and has burn marks all over her back. Nanny Lynnette is in the can for kidnapping and attempting to murder her charge. Hairdresser Bea murdered her husband and a co-worker. Kleptomaniac Lizzie Lee is in for multiple murders. "Qualified fashion model" Mandy is in for hooking. Thief "Franky" is in for murder (and has naked women tattooed on her breasts).

An immense hit in its native Australia, the show was so intense and so depressing that most American stations wouldn't air it until very late at night, sealing its Nielsen doom.

AI AI AI

——

Sam, 1978. UCLA quarterback Mark Harmon began his Hollywood career playing second banana to the LAPD's most misunderstood, most belittled, and most ignored new police officer—a dog.

Sara, 1976. Feisty Brenda Vaccaro combats evil and bad manners amid the savagery of the Wild West in her new job as town school-marm.

Seaway, 1965. Another riveting Canadian drama, this time concerning the torrid adventures of a security man working on the St. Lawrence Seaway.

Second Chance/Boys Will Be Boys, 1987. Kiel Martin left *Hill Street Blues* to star as a dead man given a second chance to reform his bad ways by trying to convince his fifteen-year-old self to be a good person. Both the teen and adult Kiel are about as charming as *Mr. Sunshine;* when we avoided this show like the plague, the producers dropped the death angle and retitled—to no avail.

Shangri-La Plaza, 1990. One of 1990's deeply troubled drusicals (the other being *Cop Rock)*, *S-L P* explored the all-singing, all-dancing adventures of a widowed mom who inherits a donut franchise (and a sassy black waitress) in a pastel California strip mall. Three minutes of mediocre singing and dancing followed by thirty seconds of plot followed by three minutes of mediocre singing and dancing did not grip viewers to their screens.

———

She-Wolf of London, 1991. Why don't we get to see more television from other lands? A quick look at this *East Enders*-with-bad-special-effects snoozefest will tell you exactly why. The horror geniuses of London's Hammer Studios must be spinning in their bloody graves.

ʌ̣ ʌ̣

Skag, 1980. Karl Malden, Piper Laurie, and Peter Gallagher live the high life at a Pittsburgh steel mill in this brilliantly titled drama.

ʌ̣ ʌ̣

Something Is Out There, 1988. Alien Maryam d'Abo teams up with an L.A. cop to track down a criminal from outer space. The cop soon learns that on Maryam's planet, hands are considered wildly erotic; she likes his fine pair, and romance blooms.

ʌ̣ ʌ̣ ʌ̣

Space: 1999, 1975. *Mission: Impossible* launched the careers of husband-and-wife actors Martin Landau and Barbara Bain, who at the height of their fame left the show to make *Space: 1999*—one of the most notorious flops of the seventies. While we loved Barbara and Martin on *Mission* for being cool beyond cool, when they played husband and wife moon colonists on *Space* and did the same icy thing, it seemed like they hated each other's guts. Though the show looked great, since the FX director was a *2001* designer, the entire astronaut team (launched into adventure when an atomic explosion throws the moon off orbit) seemed like they'd rather be doing anything than be together. Think of what *Star Trek* would be like if Kirk, Spock, Scotty, and Uhura were only there to do their jobs, and couldn't stand each other; it's antichemistry, and it makes *Space: 1999* unwatchable.

ʌ̣ ʌ̣ ʌ̣

Stop Susan Williams, 1979. Beautiful yet enormous Susan Anton proves once again that she's a model, not an actress in this show's leading role: a journalist who wants to keep a bad man from destroying the world.

♟ ♟

The Storefront Lawyers, 1970. A trio of do-gooder lawyers (including Robert Foxworth) who are wealthy, pro-bono renegades like *The Mod Squad* and just as believable, link elbows and skip down the streets of Los Angeles together, letting the wind tousle their hair, and looking for cases that prove indisputably that all poor people are good and all rich people are bad.

♟ ♟ ♟ ♟

Strange Paradise, 1969. An overt *Dark Shadows* imitation set in the Caribbean featuring séances, black magic, voodoo, and popular characters coming back from the dead—not like Bobby Ewing or Fallon Carrington, but as zombies.

♟ ♟ ♟

The Survivors, 1969. Instantly forgettable generic Harold Robbins yarn, notable for the massive amounts of money it lost in lensing on location around the world and starring the very well paid Ralph Bellamy, George Hamilton, Lana Turner, and Rossano Brazzi.

♟ ♟

The Sword of Freedom, 1957. Painter and revolutionary Marco del Monte battles Prince Machiavelli and the entire Medici family in Renaissance Florence.

♟ ♟

Tate, 1960. A one-armed man with a bad temper wanders aimlessly around the Wild West, killing people.

♟ ♟

———

Tattinger's, 1988. A dramedy like *Cop Rock* and *Supertrain,* this confused program featured Stephen Collins, Blythe Danner, Mary Beth Hurt, and an old-fashioned, elegant Manhattan restaurant. After nine showings the show was demicanceled and completely made over as a frothy half-hour sitcom about New York's most "in" nightspot. Now called *Nick and Hilary* with the original cast more or less intact, this new version was appreciated even less than *Tattinger's* and fully canceled after a mere three episodes.

⚜ ⚜

Trauma Center, 1983. Week in, week out, one damn accident victim after another goes to the hospital, and their life is or is not saved.

⚜ ⚜

TV Reader's Digest, 1955. Dramatic re-creations of heartwarming true-life stories from *Reader's Digest* magazine, which followed such a rigid format they were practically indistinguishable from each other.

⚜ ⚜

2000 Malibu Road, 1992. The most quickly discarded and the most fun of all the *Beverly Hills, 90210* clones came from *90210* producers Spelling and Cramer themselves in a program that bit off far more than any mere TV series should ever try to chew. The drama of a wealthy, beach-living prostitute, Jade (essayed by former infotainment hostess Lisa Hartman Black), whose financial troubles force her to rent rooms to lawyer Jennifer Beals, devious hippie chick Tuesday Knight, and would-be actress Drew Barrymore, *Malibu* was a catalog of the darkest impulses of women on the make—all done in a languid, "just another day at the beach" manner—which made the characters' schemes and plottings appear even more loathsome than the law of character likability can allow.

On top of this the show tried to resuscitate simultaneously the careers of not one but two of yesteryear's superstars. They failed miserably with Jennifer Beals (who, post-*Flashdance,* seems to be deliberately withholding her humanity from the audience), but Madonna-blond Drew Barrymore's hyp-notically eerie presence (she always looks deeply content, like she either just finished having the greatest sex of all time, or killing someone) was the show's shining moment, and it would be fine-tuned in her star turn as the eponymous heroine of *Out of Control: The Amy Fisher Story* (see page 176).

▟▙ ▟▙ ▟▙ ▟▙ ▟▙

The Young Rebels, 1970. A cross between *The Mod Squad* and *Young Guns* (from *Mod* producer Aaron Spelling) but set during the American Revolution, with cool, hip, glamorous kids (including Lou Gossett, Jr.) surreptitiously fighting the Brits. Up against the wall, redcoat mothers!

▟▙ ▟▙

▟▙

And the Tammi for the worst drama of all time goes to:

Cop Rock, 1990. The bigger they are, the harder they fall: Norman Mailer had his *Ancient Evenings;* Woody Allen had his *Shadows and Fog;* Steven Bochco (acclaimed producer of *Hill Street Blues* and *L.A. Law*) had *Cop Rock.* How does it happen?

At the end of the 1980s many TV producers and executives got very ex-cited thinking about radical new shows that mixed standard television genres. This technique, however, frequently ended up creating mongrels, something like a cross between a dachshund and a St. Bernard. The pro-ducers especially liked mixing drama with comedy to make dramedies—*The Days and Nights of Molly Dodd,* for instance—but none of these mongrel programs did well enough to stay on the air.

This trend of failure and humiliation might have stopped lesser men, but not the mighty Bochco, who flew in the face of reason to imagine the winning combination for a new show as being a drusical (dramatic musi-cal): the notorious *Cop Rock.* The show attempted to merge gritty New York realism (Bochco's signature more-ironic-than-thou aesthetic) with the best artifice Hollywood has to offer—music from popsters like Randy Newman (whose biggest hits were the novelties "I Love L.A." and "Short People").

Just like the other 1990 television drusical, *Shangri-La Plaza, Cop*

The jury erupts into joyous gospel singing after sending a man to prison on Cop Rock (Photofest)

Rock had every problem that almost all musicals face, and more! The drama (which was tough, urban, and edgy, as good as anything on *Hill Street*) would suddenly stop dead in its tracks to have its characters burst into song, usually for no apparent reason. At a time when the biggest thing in urban music was hard-edged rap, *Cop Rock* specialized in New-manized Rodgers-and-Hammerstein lite, all accompanied by cops, criminals, lawyers, and judges boogying down in music-video-style choreography.

In a typical scene the town's mayor (Bochco's wife, Barbara Bosson) and her Vegas-styled aides sing a paean to the joys of graft while worshiping a neon-glowing suitcase of money. During the premiere's big trial scene the verdict is read, the court reporter's desk turns into a synthesizer, the jury becomes a gospel choir, and the judge and accused do a call-and-response. Finally, a pathetic crack addict sings a lullaby to her baby before selling it off to infertile yuppie scum. The whole show is so goofy and inane, you can't even give Bochco credit for trying.

Even though each episode seemed to get more and more ludicrous and pathetic than the last, ABC bravely kept *Cop Rock* on for a full season—

especially brave, since everyone financially involved took a huge loss, with each episode costing just under $2 million to produce.

ᴸᴸ ᴸᴸ ᴸᴸ ᴸᴸ ᴸᴸ ᴸᴸ

Most Common Jobs in the U.S. (in 1993)	**Most Common Jobs on TV** (in 1993)
Salesman	Cop
Teacher	Lawyer
Secretary	Doctor
Accountant	Restaurateur
Truck driver	TV reporter
Cashier	Nurse
Janitor	Newspaper reporter
Nurse	TV producer
Cook	Coach; Disc Jockey; Interior Decorator (a tie)

First I see the wife and she's whining, "What about my needs?" Then they cut to the husband, and he's whining, "What about my needs?" And I'm sitting there saying, "What about my needs? I want to be entertained. Can't you blow up a car or something?"

—Jay Leno discussing
thirtysomething

The Kids' Show Nominees

Never put a child in show business. Kids are just pieces of flesh.

—Lauren Chapin ("Kitten" on *Father Knows Best*)

IT'S EXTREMELY DIFFICULT FOR AN ADULT TO PASS JUDGMENT ON THE merits of kids' shows, since as can be seen with *Gilligan's Island, The Patty Duke Show, The Facts of Life, Barney & Friends,* and their ilk, what children judge to be classic entertainment can drive adults mad. The nominees here, then, either were suggested by children, or come from those who used to be children and have long memories, or are so obviously due a nod that they speak for themselves. What we think of ourselves, and what TV thinks of us, is readily apparent with these shows:

- Real people are a lot more fun when they're turned into animals.
- Recombinant DNA technology is alive and well in the animation studios of Tokyo.
- Video games are a lot more fun when they're turned into cartoons.
- If a singing group's recording career falters, they can always get a job hosting Saturday-morning kiddie shows.
- If animals could talk, they'd be just like you and me.

Baggy Pants and the Nitwits, 1977. NBC took great silents from the early career of Charlie Chaplin and "animated" them with a cartoon alley

Ruth Buzzi and Arte Johnson *are the* **Nitwits** (Photofest)

cat in the "Little Tramp" role, assisted by *Laugh-In*'s Ruth Buzzi and Arte Johnson (as the Nitwits).

🎭 🎭 🎭 🎭

The Barkleys, 1972. A cartoon remake of *All in the Family,* with the Bunkers essayed by a family of dogs.

🎭 🎭 🎭

——

Barney & Friends, 1991. Every preschooler in America seems to adore this waddling, eggplant-tinted dinosaur and his really ugly kiddie friends (perhaps since there's nothing else specifically for them on the air except *Shining Time Station*), but we think this show is a conspiracy to drive adults insane. Made on the cheap with tatty production values, low-grade "fun" that brings new meaning to the word *insipid,* and a lead who sounds like a broken dishwasher, *Barney & Friends* makes *Ding Dong School* look like Shakespeare.

Writer James Gorman notes, "Next to Barney and his friends, Sandy Duncan is a flesh-eating succubus," and the May 3, 1993, issue of *The New Yorker* included this chilling tale:

> . . . a serenely good-natured mother of a four-year-old girl made a confession in midtown Manhattan: "I bought the Barney book. I admit it. I read it to my daughter in the Barney voice. My husband looked at me with mistrust and dismay, but I did it."
>
> Did she hate herself?
>
> "Yes," she said, and then, louder, and with a flicker of viciousness, "I wish I could shoot Barney."

If you've never seen this show, try one of its signature elements by singing the following to the tune of "This Old Man," as slowly as possible:

> I . . . love . . . you . . .
> You . . . love . . . me . . .
> We're . . . a . . . great . . . big . . . family . . .

If you're concerned at all about the effects of television on your children, here's one program you really should be worried about.

🔫 🔫 🔫

Bigfoot and Wildboy, 1979. Krofft Bros. live-action adventures of the crime-fighting Abominable Snowman and his young human teen son, who are frequently confronted by space aliens. One of the great BAD kids' shows of all time, *Bigfoot and Wildboy* must be seen to be fully appreciated, and some episodes are now available on video. A fan notes, "This is so bad, it's practically a religious experience; it makes *Plan 9 From Outer Space* look like *Last Year at Marienbad.*"

Bonkers, 1978. After the cancellation of *The Hudson Brothers Razzle Dazzle Comedy Show,* the much beloved Hudson singing sensations continue to bring their unique blend of comedy and music to television viewers everywhere in a show so madcap and so zany, it completely fulfills the promise of its title.

The Bugaloos, 1970. Witch Benita Bizarre (Martha Raye) tries to enslave a quartet of mod, Carnaby Street bee musicians—the *Herman's Hermits* of the insect world—since they're her competitors in the shark-eat-shark world of kiddie tunes writing.

Clutch Cargo, 1961. Tepid adventure series with creaky animation starring the *Steve Canyon* clone Cargo. The show's only memorable feature was what made it so BAD: Superimposed on top of every character's otherwise immobile cartoon face were *real human lips.* The effect was so creepy that it was used on the dead models for the Joker's Gotham City cosmetics ad in the movie *Batman.*

Cowboy G-Men, 1952. In the fifties little boys wanted to be either a cowboy or a G-Man (a government agent; i.e., FBI). *Cowboy G-Men* cynically and brilliantly exploits these dreams by starring Jackie Coogan (Uncle Fester) as a G-Man who goes undercover as a cowboy.

Dear Alex and Annie, 1978. Kids would write in about their personal problems, and the answers would be the advice of child psychologist Eda

LeShan, magically turned into song lyrics, which were then sung by Alex (the name-cursed Bing Bingham) and Annie.

ĿĿ ĿĿ ĿĿ

Dynomutt, 1978. If all kids love superheroes, dogs, and robots, wouldn't it be great if they made a cartoon about the adventures of a superhero dog robot? Thankfully, they did.

ĿĿ ĿĿ

Fangface, 1978. A boy and his cat see the moon and become werewolves who help kids with their personal problems.

ĿĿ ĿĿ

Gigantor, 1966. Another epic of Japanimation, this time featuring a twelve-year-old boy who controls an immense super-robot, and nominated by many as the worst kids' show of all time.

ĿĿ ĿĿ ĿĿ ĿĿ ĿĿ

The Groovie Goolies, 1971. Frankenstein, Dracula, Mummy, and Werewolf sing songs and play practical jokes on each other.

ĿĿ

Kid Gloves, 1951. Children meet and compete in the wonderful sport that really prepares you for all that life has to offer: boxing.

ĿĿ ĿĿ ĿĿ

Kimba the White Lion, 1966. Japanese cartoon about a benevolent African ruler orphan who lugs around his mother's carcass.

ĿĿ ĿĿ ĿĿ

The Krofft Superstar Hour, 1978. Larger-than-life puppet show hosted by then-ubiquitous Bay City Rollers, the world's only known Scottish rock band.

ĿĿ ĿĿ

Bad hair days can't stop Lancelot Link's and Mata Hairi's crucial undercover work in a show described by ABC's PR Dept. as a "Swiftian satire in which a world like ours is peopled entirely by chimpanzees." (Photofest)

Lancelot Link, Secret Chimp, 1970. Chimpanzees (suffering the curse of overtime by being simultaneously spies and rock stars) star in a simultaneous remake of *The Man from U.N.C.L.E.* and *The Monkees,* with a chimpanzee in the Robert Vaughn role, a chimpanzee in the David Mc-Callum role, a chimpanzee in the Leo G. Carroll role, a chimpanzee in the Peter Tork role, a chimpanzee in the Mickey Dolenz role, et cetera. All the chimps had dubbed human voices and names like Mata Hairi; they took time off from sleuthing by performing in an all-monkey band, the Evolution Revolution.

The basic idea—monkeys playing on the set, while humans offstage provide their voices—is also a remake, from NBC's *The Darwin Family* (1956).

♟ ♟ ♟ ♟

Land of the Lost, **1974.** Another Sid and Marty Krofft masterpiece: Ranger Rick and his two kids time-warp to the dino era and meet the monkeylike Pakunis and the lizardlike Sleestacks.

♟

Lidsville, **1971.** Curious about the mechanics of a magician's hat, shag-wearing *Munster* child Butch Patrick meets and explores the singing, dancing, and dramatic lives of hats—with special guest appearances by Witchiepoo, Weenie the Genie, and Charles Nelson Reilly as the evil green Hoo Doo.

♟ ♟ ♟ ♟

The Littlest Hobo, **1963.** From those wacky Canadians, the story of a traveling German Shepherd who helps people with their personal problems.

♟

Maya, **1985.** Jay "Dennis the Menace" North runs through India with his best friend Raji and the show's only entertainment value, an elephant.

♟

McDuff, the Talking Dog, **1976.** Not just a talking English sheepdog, but a talking English sheepdog *ghost,* who can only be seen and heard by his ex-veterinarian.

♟ ♟ ♟

Real Live Sea Monkeys, **1991.** Wouldn't it be great if the ever-popular brine shrimp pets got their own show? Thankfully, they did. In this jaw-dropping concept the live-action Monkeys (who look like *Star Trek* guest alien rejects) may remind you of the Three Stooges—but with three giant nipples subbing for hair or comic abilities. Their unbelievably funny (if you're a toddler) slapstick arises from not understanding our world.

Tape now; this is one show bound to become a collector's item.

👣 👣 👣 👣 👣

Rubik the Amazing Cube, 1983. The animated adventures of the much-loved puzzle toy, which (when its colors were aligned) became a superhero.

👣 👣 👣 👣

Rude Dog and the Dweebs, 1989. Speeding along in his 1956 pink Cadillac, Rude Dog was a hero to alienated preschoolers, teaching his many fans how cool it was to be an antisocial misfit, and showing them tips on how you yourself can get that way. Parents' outrage kicked the show off the air, but it lives on at your local video store and is still immensely popular with the tot set.

👣 👣 👣

Run, Joe, Run, 1974. A remake of *The Fugitive,* with Heinrich the German Shepherd in the David Janssen role. Accused of attacking his master, Army dog Joe runs away; he's pursued by both the law and his owner, who's got the evidence to restore his good name. Joe travels the country, looking for shelter, and helping people with their personal problems.

👣 👣 👣 👣

Saturday Supercade, 1983. A collection of cartoons originating from the immensely creative world of video games, including *Donkey Kong* and *Q*Bert.*

👣

Science All-Stars, 1964. Child science fair winners from across the country discuss their projects with guest scientists.

👣 👣

——

Scorch, 1992. A CBS series so quickly yanked off the air that I couldn't find anyone who's ever seen it, and starring what *Entertainment Weekly* called a "flame-barfing" puppet.

Sigmund and the Sea Monsters, 1973. Two brothers help a sea monster avoid his vile relatives, featuring witch Margaret Hamilton, midget Billy Barty, and "comedian" Rip Taylor.

Skippy, 1969. The adventures of a pet kangaroo, filmed on location in Australia, where kangaroos are usually eaten.

Sleepy Joe, 1949. On a Los Angeles local station, a storyteller in blackface delights his child audience. On national ABC, the same thing—with puppets.

Smilin' Ed's Gang, 1950; Andy's Gang, 1955. One of the great moments of kiddie surrealism of our era, this show (which lasted through two hosts) began with the seemingly very drunk Ed McConnell or Andy Devine pulling out a book and reading some odd tale that would turn into an even stranger movie; perhaps the adventure of an elephant-riding Indian teen (not *Maya*) and his encounter with a scary rhino, who he runs into a pit. Next would come Midnight the Cat (one of those really mean-looking, flat-faced Persians), a perpetually frightened hamster, Squeaky Mouse (?), and their pre-ASPCA special effects, which could make Squeaky play a guitar while Midnight did a hula dance (and purr her famous "NIIIC-E!").

Bringing up the rear was the show's real star (who some fans consider the Antichrist), Froggy the Gremlin. An innocuous-looking plastic frog, Froggy had the personality of a *Batman* villain, a deep, malevolent chuckle (like Darth Vader's), the ability to perform black magic (he once turned Andy into a black-faced Zulu with a bone through his nose),

**Andy Devine and his Indian chum introduce malicious
Froggy the Gremlin to their not-so-innocent child audience—
Andy's Gang (Photofest)**

and the desire to teach fifties children how to be rotten brats. Occasionally, Uncle Fishface would put in an appearance, and on Fridays Andy would announce, "Don't forget church, synagogue or Sunday school!" After this show, everyone involved would need some religious cleansing.

———

The Storybook Squares, 1969. A remake of *The Hollywood Squares* for kids, the big new idea being that the celebrities in the tic-tac-toe box wear funny costumes.

The Three Robonic Stooges, 1977. Cartoon variety show with three actors in giant bird suits on skateboards.

The Toxic Crusaders, 1992. Campy joke-horror movie *Toxic Avenger* (a vengeful mutant) comes to kiddie time as a deformed but sincere cartoon superhero.

Turbo-Teen, 1984. When a cartoon teen gets hot, he turns into a car.

Wait 'Til Your Father Gets Home, 1972. A cartoon remake, with lots of screaming, of—not again!—*All in the Family.*

And the Tammi for worst kids' show of all time goes to:

Smurfs, 1981. The staggering number of television programs wildly popular with preschoolers but which drive anyone else completely insane is remarkable, but few shows are as legendary as *Smurfs*—a series guaranteed to eliminate any and all adults from the room within minutes. Tedious, grating, sexist, repellent; for nine long years these horrid blue creatures dominated Saturday morning children's programming; at one point their show expanded to an hour and a half! Part dwarf, part elf, and part

**The *Smurfs* try to destroy another holiday—Valentine's Day—
with their relentlessly saccharine life-style and
"My Smurfy Valentine"** (Photofest)

leprechaun, with squeaky, screechy voices and robotlike behavior, the
Smurfs' only drama in life was to avoid being captured and put into slav-
ery by an evil wizard. Tragically, he never succeeded.

Created by a Brussels cartoonist known as "Peyo," the Smurfs' adventures were translated into twenty languages. They are known as Schtroupfs in France, Smurfies in South Africa, Lah-Shin-Lins in China, and Strunfs in Brazil. Peyo said he made the Smurfs blue because it's a child's color; he thought yellow meant illness, and red was violence. In the movie *Slacker* one monologuist believes the Smurfs are a plot by Krishna devotees to get American children used to seeing blue people.

For many years all the Smurfs were uniform, like androids; finally for a point of mild variety, an old Smurf, a bad Smurf, and a girl Smurf ("Smurfette") were introduced. The show was finally canceled in 1990, and we were no longer confronted with the Smurfs' squealing war cry— "It's a Smurfy world!"—and their ubiquitous presence in the toy stores, the Ice Capades, and on the air.

ਪ ਪ ਪ ਪ ਪ ਪ

My husband runs what is called an educational television network. You must have seen some of the wonderful work they put on. Who else gives you a close look at gum surgery? Just as you're sitting down to dinner?

—Chris Chase

The Made-for-TV Movie Nominees

Having your book turned into a movie
is like seeing your oxen turned into bouillon cubes.

—John le Carré

IF "IMITATION IS THE SINCEREST FORM OF FLATTERY" . . . AND HOLLY-wood is a town famous for brownnosing . . . is it any wonder that band-wagon-jumping is so popular out there? Make a suprise hit or two and soon enough, every low-rent movie and TV producer's got a deal to make a knock-off. What was once surprising and original becomes an orgy of photocopying, and you'd think they'd learn after all these years that we're bored with it, want something new, and won't cough up at the box office or in the Nielsens to make it worthwhile.

Made-for-TV movies, which industryites like calling either MOWs (for their original name, Movies-of-the-Week) or made-fors, historically be-gan as part of this Hollywood urge. Practically every MOW was a clone of a successful theatrical release. If you liked *Airport,* this theory goes, you'll love *Cruise Into Terror* and *Fer-de-Lance.* When *Towering Inferno* is a hit, can *Fire!* and *Flood!* be far behind?

While that's still somewhat true (especially in the made-for-cable realm), the current crop of network made-fors is almost completely fo-cused on one subject: true crime, especially with a woman's touch. Just as tabloid shows like *A Current Affair* and *Hard Copy* have replaced news hours, so have tabloid specials knocked out the knock-offs of yesteryear. *Torn from today's headlines*—and then mangled beyond recognition—is the byword for made-for Nielsen heaven today.

If you're one of the seeming flood of pistol-packin' mamas following in the footsteps of Betty Broderick (who killed her ex-husband and his new wife), Carolyn Warmus (who murdered her lover's wife), Amy Fisher (who shot her lover's wife), and Wanda Holloway (who tried to kill a neighbor so that neighbor's daughter Amber would do badly in a cheerleader contest and Wanda's own daughter Shanna could win), you'll now only have to wait a mere four months or so to see your bloody deeds turned into prime-time entertainment. The networks love these tales, since they come with a ready-made audience of viewers who already know the outlines of the story from Oprah, Geraldo, Phil, Sally, and their ilk. You, the killer, might even get to see multiple versions of your true-life story; Carolyn got on both CBS and ABC, Wanda made it on both ABC and HBO, and Amy hit the grand slam: CBS and ABC simultaneously, with her own sale to NBC beating the competition by a week. Development desire has become so hysterical that Wanda's intended victim, Texas housewife Verna Heath, received fifty-six phone calls from TV producers trying to capture her rights the week that the news accounts first appeared.

If so much of these made-fors are completely made up by the writers, why do the producers bother getting anyone's rights in the first place? The secret of the MOW true-life-story business is that, when you get a criminal's rights, the major right that you in fact acquire is the ability to fictionalize conversations and dramatic moments without the fear of getting sued. Without those rights you'd have to make sure that every single thing that happened and every single word that's said by any of the participants in your movie actually happened, or the network lawyers won't approve the script.

⚑⚑

These BAD made-for-TV movies are the ultimate in tease. Their titles (and ads) seem to offer everything we want from a quality tabloid afternoon: steamy sex and revelation, passion and "the story behind the headlines." How little they actually deliver—either through television timidity or, more often, outright Hollywood incompetence—is a real shock. MOWs make up an unusually depressing landscape for tube lovers, since you watch these grave disappointments and can only think: what a great show could have been made from this material if only the right people were involved! All those potentially great TV moments, *ruined forever.* If only someone like John Waters would switch to TV, just think of the wonderful made-fors we could be watching!

One reason for this is that practically everyone working in the television industry didn't have TV as their first career pick—they originally wanted to work in features, but didn't make it (and this in fact is what comprises the third category of made-for-TV movies, which were originally made to *be* features, but didn't make it). TV writers, producers, actors, and execs are furious that they have to work on the small screen instead of in the far more admired 70 millimeter (it's odd that such an obsession with size isn't strong enough to keep alive the glories of Cinerama). With their self-image reduced to twenty-one inches (measured diagonally), it's no wonder television professionals love to take their career frustrations out on the audience—by assaulting us with contemptuous dreck.

The situation has become so out of control that finding a made-for that shouldn't be included here is almost harder than finding the deservedly BAD. Between the tabloids, the imitative mimics, and the theatrical failures, MOWs are ripe with the shimmering promise of trash, and in deciding what should and shouldn't be included here, there's a question: *Where do you even begin?* Frequently, the most popular made-fors are ravenous trashfests; 1979's biggest hit, for example, was investigative reporter Jane Seymour going undercover to expose the secrets of the *Dallas Cowboy Cheerleaders,* while 1981's topper was *Fallen Angel,* about a runaway's involvement in child pornography, and two of 1992's top-rateds simultaneously covered the dramatic story of Long Island temptress Amy Fisher.

As always, our picks below are items so ludicrously off the mark you won't want to miss a single moment. Even the extreme disappointments—MOWs so distorted from reality, so incompetently made, so utterly worthless as to seem instantly forgettable—have moments that must be seen to be believed.

What hidden thoughts and desires, you must be asking yourself right now, do made-fors reveal about us as a culture? What educational reasons are there for watching; what are the American beliefs and philosophies we can discover from researching this amazing topic? Here are just a few:

- 📺 The Devil exists, in many forms.
- 📺 Mentally retarded people should find love and have sex.
- 📺 If you ever see Bette Davis or Shelley Winters, run for your life!
- 📺 There is a spirit world, and it's filled with malevolent beings.

- All methods of transportation—trains, planes, boats, even submarines—are just disasters waiting to happen.
- You are the only woman in America who hasn't murdered someone.
- If you can't get a job, you can always become a prostitute.
- The fences at safari parks are not very strong.
- In the very near future, the world will be full of clones.

Acceptable Risks, 1986. Instamovie starring Brian Dennehy and Cicely Tyson, who struggle over corporate responsibility in the wake of the Bhopal toxic chemical leak.

A.D., 1985. Five-part, twelve-hour, $30-million free-for-all between Jews, Romans, and proto-Christians, with Ava Gardner, Fernando Rey, Richard Roundtree, and Elizabeth Taylor's son (as Jesus).

Alexander: The Other Side of Dawn, 1977. Unbearable sequel to the classic *Dawn: Portrait of a Teenage Runaway,* with Leigh McCloskey as a teen boy who foolishly abandons his loving parents and can't find any kind of job whatsoever and so is forced against his will to become a male streetwalker and develop a relationship with a Dave Kopay–styled footballer.

All the Kind Strangers, 1974. Scary *Children of the Damned*–like orphans and their nasty *Cujo*esque dogs entrap tourists in a musty old farmhouse and demand to be adopted.

**When Sally Struthers didn't come through, bereft orphans
try another strategy in *All the Kind Strangers*** (Photofest)

Amber Waves, 1980. Tense, riveting drama ensues when Manhattan male model Kurt Russell moves to the middle of nowhere but surprisingly doesn't get along well with wheat farmer Dennis Weaver.

🄻🄻

Amerika: It Can't Happen Here, 1987. ABC, which had aired the left-leaning *The Day After* about what life was like in the U.S. in the wake of atomic war, decided to give the Commies-under-every-bush thinkers their day in the sun and so produced this fourteen-hour-plus epic about the Soviet takeover of the United States. According to *Amerika* the Soviets have a secret plan in store; it involves making all the homeless live in low-rent refugee camps, forcing women to wear babushkas, and having everyone in the U.S. talk like Latka on *Taxi*.

In the four years that it took to create this masterpiece, the world had changed so much that *Amerika* was completely outdated by the time it aired; in fact, a mere three years later the Soviet Union would disappear.

🥃 🥃 🥃 🥃

The Babysitter, 1980. Crazed and childless, Stephanie Zimbalist worms her way into the lives of that awesome supercouple, Patty Duke Astin and William Shatner, in a made-for amazingly similar to 1992's *The Hand That Rocks the Cradle.*

🥃

Bad Ronald, 1976. After killing his mother a teen evades the law by Sheetrocking himself into the house, and is still there years later to surprise the home's new owners and their three teenage daughters.

🥃 🥃 🥃 🥃

The Beasts Are on the Streets, 1978. Carol Lynley and Philip Michael Thomas live in a Norman Rockwellian small town under attack by exotic marauding animals when a car accident destroys the fence at the local safari park.

🥃 🥃 🥃

Beg, Borrow . . . or Steal, 1973. Legless Mike Connors, eyeless Kent McCord, and handless Michael Cole join forces to successfully steal priceless museum treasures.

🥃 🥃 🥃

Beulah Land, 1980. Just as African-Americans thought they were making headway into prime time, along comes this four-hour *Gone With the Wind* rip-off, which, when it wasn't sleep inducing, was offensively exploring in great detail just how terrific life on a Southern plantation really was—especially when you had all those devotedly happy stepin fetchit slaves around.

🥃

———

Bionic Showdown, 1989. Bionic Lee Majors and bionic Lindsay Wagner meet and fall in bionic love; Lindsay proposes marriage, and Lee cute-oafishly accepts. Before the vows, however, the two are menaced by an evil bionic blond cyborg aided by his bionic ex-girlfriend. With $24 million dollars' worth of bionic heroes and bionic villains racing everywhere, the big climactic moments are so filled with blurry bionic slo-mo special effects, you'll think there's something wrong with your set.

♟ ♟

Black Market Baby, 1977. When the unwed Linda Purl gets a bun in the oven, she and Desi *"Of course I want to marry you, honey"* Arnaz, Jr., must outwit a gang of vicious baby sellers.

♟ ♟ ♟

Born Innocent, 1974. The men who get turned on by lady chain gangs are obviously a real classy bunch; as will be seen time and again in this volume, they produce and direct a whole genre that's instantly BAD. When *Born Innocent* first aired, it was considered wildly shocking, since TV wasn't ready for the show's soft-core sadomasochism, bondage, and domination—but without that, why watch? As the title suggests, the central drama is the same as every other women-in-prison movie: a young, naive, beautiful girl (aka straight virgin) is tortured by old, nasty, ugly convicts (aka dyke whores). Wouldn't the guys who love this stuff be happier if these movies would just cut to the chase—and feature half-naked females being torn apart by vicious Dobermans?

When the supposedly fourteen-year-old Linda Blair (looking just as sweet and untouched as she did puking guacamole in *The Exorcist*) runs away from home for the sixth time, her folks sign her over to Juvie Hall where, as a ward of the state, she gets thrown into the California Home for Girls, a world of scary teen lezzies, typical black best friend Josie, and a morose suicidal roommate. Linda spends all her time looking pathetic, so we get to spend, say, an hour and a half watching her simper in the shower, doodle longingly in the classroom, and mope pointedly on her bunkbed. The evil teen dykes finally get so fed up, they gang-rape her with Tommy the bottlebrush.

The whole thing is low-rent junk trying to be serious social commentary, as if you had to watch Roseanne Arnold do Lady Macbeth. *Born Innocent* did, however, make tragic TV history: Linda and Tommy's sex scene allegedly became a copycat crime.

♟♟ ♟♟ ♟♟ ♟♟

The Boy in the Plastic Bubble, 1976. Match up acclaimed teen director Randal Kleiser *(The Blue Lagoon)* with teen sensation John Travolta, and what do you get? This unbearably maudlin medical drama about a bizarre immune disorder. As accurately "Based on a True Story!" as *Helter Skelter* (see page 184), watching Travolta forlornly paw away at his plastic cage—desperate for human touch—is great for a few laughs.

♟♟ ♟♟

But I Don't Want to Get Married!, 1970. Unattractive widower accountant Herschel Bernardi is mysteriously chased by a husband-hunting mob of gals, including Shirley Jones, Nanette Fabray, June Lockhart, Tina Louise, and Sue Lyon.

♟♟

Calendar Girl, Cop Killer? The Bambi Bembenek Story, 1992. The story of this Wisconsin woman-with-a-gun who was perhaps framed by a corrupt small town, and who kept escaping from prison and living an outlaw life on the lam, is heaven sent for TV; ABC, however, couldn't make what should have been a classic and mangled the drama with this Instant Oats quickie.

♟♟ ♟♟

Casino Royale, 1954. TV's "Golden Age" produced many memorable moments, and this, the very first screen adaptation of an Ian Fleming novel, is certainly one of them. Who alive today doesn't have a very strong image of James Bond and what his movies are like (even though he's been played by several very different actors)? This *Casino Royale* upends all those religiously held beliefs by being, from start to finish, remarkably BAD. Here, "Jimmy" Bond is an American and, as played by Barry Nelson, he's about as soigné as Bluto: "You know, women can lie as well as men" is a typical snappy riposte. "There is one special effect," noted critic Leonard Maltin, "if you count the elevator." Even the requisitely buxom Miss Manners and Peter Lorre as the nefarious Russian bad guy can't save this disaster.

🩲🩲

The Clone Master, 1978. A government scientist makes thirteen crime-fighting copies of himself.

🩲🩲 🩲🩲

Cocaine: One Man's Seduction, 1983. Noble real estate agent Dennis *Gunsmoke* Weaver is forced to take cocaine by Pamela *Dynasty* Bellwood, becoming addicted after listening to harangues from his sniveling "drug-free and proud of it!" son, James *Sex Lies* Spader. At one point Weaver becomes so out of control that he knocks an ounce and a half of Bolivian Marching Powder into the toilet; at the time this was considered one of the most horrifying scenes in the history of television.

🩲🩲 🩲🩲 🩲🩲

Child Bride of Short Creek, 1981. Just invite someone over who preaches "family values," pop this on, stand back, and watch the fun! "Based on a True Story," *Blue Lagooner* Christopher Atkins throws a temper tantrum when polygamous Mormon dad Conrad Bain gets the hot pants for a fifteen-year-old. Chris gets so mad, in fact, that he does what any decent son would do—calls the police and gets his father thrown in the can!

But does all this ensue because of Chris's strong moral convictions—or because he wants the child for himself? As Chris and his child love stride off into the happy ending's sunset, you'll be sorry there's never been a *Child Bride of Short Creek Returns.*

🩲🩲 🩲🩲 🩲🩲 🩲🩲

A Cold Night's Death, 1973. In this sci-fi shocker, squabbling scientists Robert Culp and Eli Wallach discover they're being experimented upon by giant monkeys.

🩲🩲 🩲🩲 🩲🩲

———

***Companions in Nightmare*, 1968.** You're in group therapy with wealthy, renowned psychiatrist Gig Young—and one of the group is a bloodthirsty killer!

🎬 🎬

***Cruise into Terror*, 1977.** An ancient Egyptian curse terrorizes an ocean liner filled with such TV megastars as John Forsythe, Stella Stevens, Lee Meriwether, Ray Milland, Hugh O'Brien, Dirk Benedict, Lynda Day George, and Frank Converse. Whenever you see a nutty lineup like this, be sure to watch—it's guaranteed to be BAD.

🎬 🎬

***A Cry in the Wilderness*, 1974.** When farmer George Kennedy gets rabies from a skunk, he chains himself up in the barn so that when madness strikes, he won't imperil his family. Too bad it's been raining cats and dogs and the whole damn county's going to be flooded any minute now!

🎬 🎬 🎬

***The Darker Side of Terror*, 1979.** Scientist Robert Forster finds trouble brewing when his clone falls in love with wife Adrienne Barbeau.

🎬 🎬 🎬

***The Dark Secret of Harvest Home*, 1978.** A family foolishly leaves Manhattan for the idyllic American countryside only to find Bette Davis practicing occult fertility ceremonies with lots of sheet-draped, keening pre-teen girls in a two-night, five-hour spectacular.

🎬 🎬 🎬 🎬

***The Daughters of Joshua Cabe*, 1972.** Prime-time whore Karen Valentine, thief Lesley Ann Warren, and pickpocket Sandra Dee pretend to be Buddy Ebsen's daughters to help him guard his land against greedy homesteaders.

♟ ♟

Dawn: Portrait of a Teenage Runaway, 1976. Brady gal Eve Plumb leaves home only to discover she can't make the rent and so becomes a whining, bedraggled whore, whose hideous fate and operatic angst drove teen viewers wild, and made this one of the year's biggest hits—even spawning a sequel.

♟ ♟ ♟ ♟ ♟

The Demon Murder Case, 1983. A much-cherished TV moment: psychic Cloris Leachman, priest Eddie Albert, and demon scholar Andy Griffith perform the rites of exorcism—with Harvey Fierstein as the Devil.

♟ ♟ ♟ ♟

Devil Dog: The Hound of Hell, 1978. Richard Crenna and Yvette Mimieux find trouble at home when their dog is possessed by Satan.

♟ ♟ ♟

Devil's Daughter, 1972. The Devil (Shelley Winters) forces a mortal girl to marry a demon.

♟

Diary of a Teenage Hitchhiker, 1979. *Dallas* butterball Charlene Tilton, *Soap* sister Katherine Helmond, and *Poltergeist Coach* Craig T. Nelson show the nation why beautiful young girls with big luscious breasts and very tight, very skimpy clothes shouldn't get into strange cars driven by big, drooling *Deliverance* costars while listening to a thundering grade-Z horror flick soundtrack.

♟ ♟ ♟ ♟

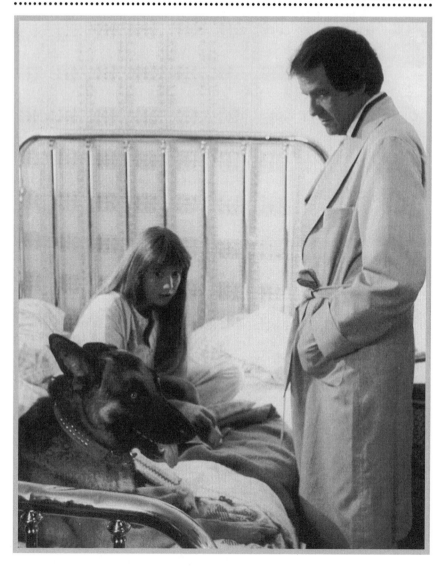

**Satan—disguised as a German shepherd—tries to ruin the
lives of a wonderful all-American couple in *Devil Dog:The
Hound of Hell* (Photofest)**

***Elvis*, 1979.** Three whole hours of Shelley Winters as Ma Presley, the
ubiquitous Pat Hingle as Colonel Parker, and Disney kid Kurt Russell as
the King—all exec produced by Dick Clark.

———

Elvis and Me, 1988. If you're a nobody who becomes a somebody because of your marriage, but it doesn't work out and you're forced to leave hearth, home, and millions, then what's a girl to do? If you're the very savvy Priscilla Presley or Roxanne Pulitzer (see page 199), you write a best seller, sell the rights to TV, and simultaneously get vicious revenge in public and a nice piece of change.

According to the gospel of *Elvis and Me* Priscilla Beaulieu was a sweet, innocent girl who didn't love Elvis for his money and fame; she loved him for being the Tennessee hick that he was deep down inside. But was her pure love and devotion rewarded? No! Being married to Elvis was torture incarnate; he manipulated her, cheated on her, lied to her, kept her all isolated from everyone in that big mansion, and he was, like, real weird to boot. Ultimately, Priscilla achieves freedom and maturity through divorce . . . and guest-starring on *Dallas.*

Was it all Elvis's fault? Is there such a thing as a marriage where the husband is the devil and the wife is a blameless angel? Is being married to Priscilla and having Lisa Marie as your daughter such a dream come true? You'll never know from this made-for . . . but you can get a hint from the sequel, *Elvis, Priscilla and Me,* written by Priscilla's kung fu fighting boyfriend, which sadly never made it to television.

Ⅱ Ⅱ Ⅱ

The Eye Creatures, 1965. One of the cheapest sci-fis ever created. When exposed to car headlights aliens (in costumes made out of things found in the Dumpster and covered in waving, waggling eyes) explode.

Ⅱ Ⅱ

The Feminist and the Fuzz, 1971. Radical libber Barbara Eden and macho chauvinist cop David Hartman are forced to be zany roommates in a made-for costarring the much-missed JoAnne Worley and Julie Newmar.

Ⅱ Ⅱ Ⅱ

Fer-de-Lance, 1974. How'd you like to be stuck at the bottom of the sea in a broken-down submarine filled with David Janssen, Hope Lange, and vicious, poisonous snakes slithering everywhere you turn? It's almost as good as *Night of the Lepus.*

ʌ ʌ

Fire, Flood, 1977. From disaster-prone producer Irwin Allen, a TV double bill aired back to back. Watch a huge forest blaze threaten a small American town filled with Patty Duke Astin, Erik Estrada, Vera Miles, Donna Mills, and Ernest Borgnine, then see Richard Basehart, Barbara Hershey, Martin Milner, Carol Lynley, and Roddy McDowall flee a cracked dam.

ʌ

The Amy Fisher Extravaganza: If MOWs in the nineties became all about women with guns and who they kill, no one aroused the networks like Amy Fisher, the "Long Island Lolita" whose story was a "real-life *Fatal Attraction.*" The basics of the tale are simple: suburban teen princess Amy falls so hard for car repairman Joey Buttafuoco that she shoots his wife, Mary Jo, in the head, partially paralyzing her, and is sent off to the can for five to fifteen. The drama, however, was in the telling: Amy, Joey, the DA, and the lawyers fought the case in the media with daily revelations; Amy says Joey seduced her, got her involved in a prostitution ring, and encouraged her to shoot Mary Jo; Joey says Amy's obviously insane and a pathological liar and he never even touched her—but one time they did go out for pizza.

All three networks rushed out made-fors within days of the sentencing (two of which, for the first time on TV, aired simultaneously), and all got fantastic ratings—over a third of the American population watched at least one. We were obsessed with Amy, Joey, and Mary Jo because they were such regular-guy, suburban-people-next-door types . . . with a nightmare story so disputed that the mystery of what exactly happened remains to this day.

NBC's *Amy Fisher: Her Story* (1992) was first, and especially considering how quickly it was made, is actually pretty good as these things go. The Buttafuocos had won the case in the media, with Amy coming off as a crazed, bratty tramp, and her story a cautionary tale for married men thinking about cruising high schools for dates. In this MOW, Amy gets to tell her side, and it's both believable and completely compelling.

By her own account Ms. Fisher is a naive, giggly teen so desperate for love, she's bereft of free will or common sense—and she's dumb as a post. Amy's completely over the moon about Joey, while he's obviously just happy to be getting his peppers popped. At one point her best friend asks, "What do you see in this guy?" and Amy answers, "He loves me, we have great sex, and he fixes my car!" After the shooting Amy washes up and sees blood everywhere in the bathroom; her reaction? "My dad's gonna *kill* me."

To show how lifelike all this actually is, on a TV interview aired just before the movie, Amy said, "I got upset if I got a traffic ticket and now I'm in prison—I can't believe it!" Amy was shown pieces of the made-for on that same interview, and she started sobbing because it was so close to real life, which is even further proof that she really was madly in love. Who besides Amy Fisher could look at Ed *Hill Street* Marinaro (her made-for star) and see Joey Buttafuoco?

While the producers couldn't stop themselves from upscaling the characters' socioeconomics, they did retain the Fishers' flocked wallpaper, and the Lon Guyland accents are perfect. There are three oddities, however:

- Of all three movies Amy actually comes off the worst here—she's patently stupid—and it's her own movie.
- While the actors portraying Amy and Joey are much better looking than their real-life counterparts, the TV Mary Jo isn't as attractive as the real wife.
- The makeup artist forgot the common Hollywood courtesy of rouging Marinaro's tiny nipples.

📺 📺 📺 📺

The Buttafuocos got to respond with CBS's *Casualties of Love,* featuring Joey as a would-be rock star who can heroically drive a car and snort multiple lines of coke at the same time. He goes in for six months of rehab and comes out as Jack Scalia, world's greatest husband and father, and a man so pure, he doesn't even drink coffee. Even Amy's own father tells her that Joey's "the kind of man I hope you end up with," and after the shooting, Joey's really, really nice to his wife in the hospital, even though she looks like the Elephant Man.

Speaking of Elephant Man—though she was involved with this production, Mary Jo Buttafuoco doesn't get glamorized like Joey and Amy do. Once again, the actress playing her isn't much better looking than the real Mary Jo, and she has incredibly dopey dialogue—after being shot she says, "This is, like, the worst thing that could ever happen!" Lifelike Mary Jo got the raw end of the stick all over again, and while watching the TV shooting of her own shooting, she collapsed.

Casualties is so strongly Joey's movie that it's the least exciting and the least plausible of the three. Since there's no sex here (at one point Joey tells his lawyer, "Between you and me, I did flirt with her"), the only juicy stuff comes via innuendo:

    Amy: I wanna be wearing your shirt on my body.
    Joey: It may be a little big for you.
    Amy: I can handle your size.
    Joey: You can handle extra large?
    Amy: I can handle anything you give me.

♟ ♟

The third and best of all was based on a *New York Post* reporter's stories and access to the Fishers. *Beyond Control: The Amy Fisher Story* features who must be the actress made for the role, Drew Barrymore. Only Drew gets down the mechanical, birdlike way Amy always looked at her lawyer for prompting, only Drew gets to portray her two suicide attempts, and only Drew conveys both a sex-hungry Lolita and a teen brat living within one young, mysterious girl.

Beyond Control is the only one to show both sides of the story and convey the mystery of what really happened; it includes such interesting tidbits as that while Amy's bail was set at $2 mil, Robert Chambers (the "preppy killer" who actually did murder someone) only had to cough up $200 thou. And it has great dialogue such as this, from Ma Fisher: "She always hated being trapped. When I was carrying her, she'd kick so hard, I'd get bruises. Now, the only one to bruise is herself." It's also by far the sexiest of the three, making Massapequa, Long Island, New York, look like the center of some kind of hormone experiment.

♟ ♟ ♟ ♟ ♟

As can be seen from the chart below, watching all three made-fors is like attending a minimalist opera and seeing repeated, with slight variations, the "Aimee" on the side of the 1989 Dodge Daytona, the herpes revelations, the escort service beeper, the disputed T-shirt, the candy sale, the shooting, the sex in her parents' house, the sex with the tile man, the sex with the escort-service customers, the sex with the gym instructor, the sex in the motel with the deli sandwich, et al. The story's details pile up—but the truth never surfaces.

	AMY FISHER: HER STORY	CASUALTIES OF LOVE: THE LONG ISLAND LOLITA STORY	BEYOND CONTROL: THE AMY FISHER STORY
Source:	Amy Fisher	Joey & Mary Jo Buttafuoco	*NY Post* reporter Amy Pagnozzi
Who received:	$80,000	$300,000	a consultant's fee
TV Amy Fisher vs. real Amy Fisher	3 times better looking	about as good looking	10 times better looking
And she's a	naively stupid girl	pathetic psycho	both enigmatic nymphet and bratty teen
TV Joey Buttafuoco vs. real Joey	8 times better looking	10 times better looking	3 times better looking
And he's a	working-class cad getting his rocks off	bighearted, studly family man	both innocent and a married guy on the make
TV Mary Jo Buttafuoco vs. real Mary Jo	not as good looking	about as good	not as good looking

	AMY FISHER: HER STORY	CASUALTIES OF LOVE: THE LONG ISLAND LOLITA STORY	BEYOND CONTROL: THE AMY FISHER STORY
TV Ma and Pa Fisher	living on Pluto and sexually abusive	parents trying to do what they can with a psychoteen daughter	living on Pluto
How Amy says the word Joey	CHO-ee	CHO-ee	CHO-ee
When Amy tells Joey she lost her virginity to the tile man at age 12, he gets	completely aroused	naively shocked at her wanton ways	ideas for what she might do with him
Sex scenes	suburban trysts; ****	none; only eat pizza	uncontrollable lust; *****
When Amy shoots Mary Jo,	she says, "Don't you think a 40-year-old man on top of a 16-year-old girl is disgusting?" and the gun goes off in a confused scuffle	she says, "Don't you think a 40-year-old man on top of a 16-year-old girl is disgusting?" and shoots her right in the face	she says, "Don't you think a 40-year-old man on top of a 16-year-old girl is disgusting?" and there's both a confused scuffle and an off-screen shooting

Highlight:	Amy comes off the worst here, even though it's based on her own account	Driving, percussion soundtrack depicting Amy and Joey's crazed obsessions	Drew Barrymore's sensuous nail biting
Extraordinary revelations:	Amy intimates her father molested her and sees herself as being incredibly stupid	The bullet in Mary Jo's head sets off metal detectors	Amy nearly gives her father a heart attack and does her guns-for-sex deal with an Oriental short order cook
Great lines:	"What do you see in this guy?" asks Amy's friend. "He loves me, we have great sex, and he fixes my car!" Amy: "When you said go out, I didn't know you meant a deli sandwich and a motel."	A Buttafuoco co-worker says, "It's the wires. The wires aren't buried underground like in other parts of the country, so with all this electricity in the air, it fries some people's brains. Midisland syndrome—that's what Amy's got."	Joey to Amy: "I got scars older than you." Reporter to Mrs. Fisher: "Can't you at least see that she's a monumental brat?" Mrs. Fisher: "You mean, she's spirited?"

———

The Five-Hundred-Pound Jerk, 1973. Adman James Franciscus tries to turn hillbilly Alex Karras into a weightlifting superstar and breakfast-cereal spokesperson.

♟♟

Forbidden Love, 1982. A title that seems to promise bestiality, or at least some juicy incest, for chrissake, turns out to be about sex between the young Andrew Stevens and the older Yvette Mimieux. *How will they face their friends and family?* Obviously created and produced by the bimbo-obsessed—as if sex with Yvette would be such a torture.

♟♟ ♟♟

Frankenstein: The True Story, 1974. Will the greats of British thespianism do anything for a buck? This nutty made-for (written by none other than Christopher Isherwood) includes cameos from Ralph Richardson and John Gielgud, with Agnes Moorehead, David McCallum, Michael Sarrazin as the monster, and Jane Seymour as his bride. The big BAD moment is when Michael gets so excited meeting Jane, he pulls her head off. And just what is this "true story" bit?

♟♟ ♟♟

Fresno, 1986. Carol Burnett, Dabney Coleman, Charles Grodin, Teri Garr (as "Talon"), and Gregory Harrison (as "Torch") gamely try to parody the hit eighties prime-time soaps *(Dallas, Dynasty, Knots Landing, The Colbys,* and especially *Falcon Crest)* in this family drama of the raisin industry. The writers couldn't pull it off, though, since these shows are already so nutty (with such moments as Fallon's abduction by a UFO), how much farther can you go?

♟♟ ♟♟

Genesis 2, 1973. NASA scientist wakes up in 2133 from suspended animation to discover a world where heroes dress like Viet Cong, villains are outfitted in caftans and medallions, everyone else is reduced to hospital-gown couture, and Mariette Hartley looks great. The director loves nothing more than endless shots of people running, running, running, from and to everywhere, which makes the future look like an awfully exhausting place. Another Gene Roddenberry spectacular.

♟ ♟

The Ghost of Flight 401, 1978. In 1972, 163 passengers and 13 crew members on a jetliner crashed into the Everglades. Mysteriously, six years later, as Captain Ernest Borgnine is landing in Miami, the landing signal light on his jet won't work and he, too, crashes into the Everglades.

♟

The Girl Most Likely to . . . , 1973. An intensely ugly woman undergoes plastic surgery to become Stockard Channing and extract revenge on everyone who was mean to her when she looked like an ape. Oddly, the script was written by the ever-gorgeous Joan Rivers.

♟ ♟ ♟ ♟

Gold of the Amazon Women, 1979. Explorers Donald Pleasance and Bo Svenson bring Amazon queen Na-Eela (Anita Ekberg) and some of her tribe (including Jasmine, Sarita, and Lee-Leeo) to New York City.

♟ ♟

The Great Houdinis, 1976. Paul Michael Glaser (*Starsky and Hutch*), Sally Struthers *(All in the Family),* Vivian Vance *(I Love Lucy),* and Bill Bixby *(The Incredible Hulk)* confuse us completely by appearing together in this biopic.

♟

The Great Niagara, 1974. Another *Based on a True Story*—nasty old gimp Richard Boone forces son Randy Quaid to go over Niagara Falls in a barrel.

♟ ♟ ♟

———

***Gridlock,* 1980.** Desi Arnaz, Jr., Shelley Fabares, Lisa Hartman, Rue McClanahan, and Abe Vigoda are stuck in traffic.

ⅈⅈ

***The Gun,* 1974.** The remarkable life story of a pistol and its various owners.

ⅈⅈ

***Happiness Is a Warm Clue,* 1970.** *Laugh-In's* Ross Martin *is* Charlie Chan in a telepic so awful, it wasn't aired until nine years after being made.

ⅈⅈ ⅈⅈ ⅈⅈ

***The Haunting Passion,* 1983.** When Jane Seymour hits the marital rocks with hubby Gerald McRaney, salvation appears when she catches the roving eye of a handsome, sexy, stud ghost.

ⅈⅈ ⅈⅈ ⅈⅈ

***Helen Keller: The Miracle Continues,* 1984.** Instead of the searing, raw drama of the original, this sequel is so sugar coated you'd think Helen was an angel, just an angel, so adorable in her deaf/dumb/and blindness. Mare Winningham in the Patty Duke role looks like a collectible Victorian bisque doll, and Blythe Danner in the Anne Bancroft part looks like she's got a thyroid disease (or perhaps is Rodney Dangerfield's sister). With Perry King as Anne Sullivan's ardent but superfluous suitor, and Jack Warden as Mark Twain.

ⅈⅈ ⅈⅈ ⅈⅈ

***Helter Skelter,* 1976.** By itself this is a great movie, with excellent acting (especially Nancy Wolfe as Susan Atkins and Sondra Blake as her horrified prison roommate), a brilliant ability to make Beatles music seem ominous, and a serious talent for turning the Los Angeles Police Department's professional incompetence into riveting drama. The movie shows the revolution in how we prefer our psychos (with Manson as the old-fashioned bug-eyed, hysterically giggling ranter and Atkins as the very modern cold, flat, emotion-free robot), and it does a great job with courtroom transcripts, like Manson's trial soliloquy:

> *I look at what you do and I don't understand it. You eat meat, and you kill things that are better than you are, and then you say how bad, what killers your children are. These children that come at you with knives; they're your children. You taught them; I didn't teach them. I just tried to help them stand up. The people you call my "family" were people you didn't want. People alongside the road their parents had kicked out so I took them to my garbage dump and I fed them. . . . I'm only what lives in each and every one of you. My father's a jailhouse; my father's your system; I'm a reflection of you. I'm what you made me.*

However, *Helter Skelter* is one of the first docudramas, and as such, its playing fast and loose with the facts set the style of almost every docudrama to come. L.A. DA Vincent Bugliosi cowrote the original book; apparently, he felt the story of the Manson gang and their brutal killings wasn't exciting enough, so he stretched a few things. The TV producers felt the book didn't go far enough dramatically, so they stretched a few more things. In real life Charles Manson was an ex-con and cult leader who encouraged others to murder. In *Helter Skelter* he has supernatural powers! In real life Leslie Van Houten, Susan Atkins, and Patricia Krenwinkel were hippie chicks who dropped so far out of mainstream society that they found comfort in Charlie's "Family." In *Helter Skelter* they're satanic harpies!

Apparently, in 1976, America was desperate to have hippie monsters, and Bugliosi & Co. gave it to us in spades. Manson and his family weren't mere killers; they were the Devil and his hellish minions (guess it's hard to complain when you're a murderer on death row). Who says we no longer believe in myths? When this book and movie came out, we bought it all.

The lesson? When Hollywood uses the words *Based on a True Story,* it usually means "We got this idea from the newspaper, but made it all up anyway."

———

***Hit Lady*, 1974.** Yvette Mimieux wrote and starred (with the one and only Dack Rambo) as a bikini-clad killer-for-hire.

♟ ♟

***Hollywood Wives*, 1985.** Even Candice Bergen, Angie Dickinson, Anthony Hopkins, Roddy McDowall, and producers Spelling and Cramer spending six hours of creative willpower couldn't make Jackie Collins's homage to Joyce Haber's *The Users* take off and fly.

♟ ♟

***Human Feelings*, 1978.** Las Vegas is threatened with total destruction if Billy Crystal and Pamela Sue Martin can't find six decent people in a week's time. With Nancy Walker as God.

♟ ♟ ♟ ♟

***Invitation to Hell*, 1984.** After scientist Robert Urich joins his new neighborhood's superlavish country club, he discovers it's the portal to Hades. With Susan Lucci as the Devil.

♟ ♟

***It Happened at Lakewood Manor*, 1977.** Suzanne Somers, Robert Foxworth, and Lynda Day George are attacked by man-eating ants.

♟ ♟ ♟

***The Jayne Mansfield Story*, 1980.** Jayne Mansfield was a colossal goddess of American popular culture. Even with an IQ of 163 the only thing she ever wanted in life was to be a big movie star, so she analyzed exactly what Hollywood wanted and gave it back to them in buckets. With skintight clothing, eye-popping colors, Betty Boop voice, muscleman husband, and foundation garments that made her look like a Buick, Jayne gave the world a how-to in stardom, as well as providing an explicit analysis of the Hollywood psychosis toward women.

Instead of the great show that could have been made from all this, *The Jayne Mansfield Story* is a fascinating, epic portrayal of prime-time timidity. Even with the mighty Loni Anderson (so popular at the time, her *Jayne* drew a 39 share) and the then-brunette Arnold Schwarzenegger, it looks like a Disney product; we don't even get to see Miss Mansfield's notorious decapitation. The whole thing is a parade of big clothes, big cars, and big hair—just think of how disappointed the "photo-ops at any cost!" Jayne would have been.

▲▲

Katie: Portrait of a Centerfold, 1978. Since Lesley Ann Warren wasn't available, Kim Basinger was forced to star in this, the first of the magnificent *Portrait* series, as a young, naive girl who leaves her friendly desert home to seek stardom in nasty Hollywood. Kim loves L.A., even though she has to live with the unemployed Melanie Mayron and a bunch of common street mimes. Strangely, Ms. Basinger has lots of trouble getting work as an actress (even though she acted just as superbly then as she does today), and poverty forces her into her moment of shame. Posing topless—why, she might as well be a common streetwalker! In the very happy ending, however, Kim overcomes the terrible stigma of centerfolding, and has all her dreams come true by meeting Tab Hunter and Fabian.

▲▲ ▲▲ ▲▲

Keeping Secrets, 1983. Suzanne Somers struggles to play herself as both adult and teen in this adaptation of her very own true-life abused-child story.

▲▲ ▲▲

Killdozer, 1974. *Cheyenne*'s Clint Walker and *Donna Reed*'s Carl Betz are attacked by a *Duel* imitation—an outer-space-alien-controlled bulldozer—whose murderous rampages are never explained.

▲▲

Killer Bees, 1974. In her TV debut Gloria Swanson is the German-accented matriarch of a California vintner family, à la Jane Wyman on *Fal-*

con Crest. Unlike Jane, however, when someone gets in Gloria's way, she has them attacked by swarms of man-eating bees.

Ii Ii Ii

KISS Meets the Phantom of the Park, 1978. The dramatic debut of much-beloved rock group KISS, who must fight a mad scientist and his greatest invention, KISS robots.

Ii Ii Ii Ii

Lace, 1991. Ravishingly memorable for introducing us to the idea that a woman can be named "Pagan" and for Phoebe Cates's shining career moment: "All right, which of you bitches is my mother?"

Ii Ii

The Last Days of Pompeii, 1984. Obviously someone decided that Pompeii must have been just like Sodom, Gomorrah, and *Dallas,* so we got this great BAD classic. The seven-hour *Last Days of Pompeii* was written exactly like the other prime-time soaps of its day, but everyone's running around in togas—everyone being Ned Beatty (Diomed), Ernest Borgnine (Marcus), and Lesley-Anne Down (Chloe).

A special thrill is knowing in advance the surprise ending—that we'll get to see all these people smothered to death by torrents of boiling lava.

Ii Ii Ii

The Legend of Lizzie Borden, 1975. An emaciated Elizabeth "Samantha Stevens" Montgomery strips naked (to avoid getting evidence on her clothes) and axes her mom and dad into bloody bits. Believe it or not, *Lizzie* was a big Emmy-winner in its day.

Ii Ii Ii

Leona Helmsley: The Queen of Mean, 1990. Why should the life of this snakebit hoteltress deserve the two-hour attentions of a made-for? Because it stars that madly scenery-chewing, unstoppable force of nature, Suzanne Pleshette. With lavender contact lenses borrowed from Liz Taylor, Suzanne teaches us a valuable parental lesson: Ignore one needy daughter while giving all your attention to her sisters and you, too, may create a Queen of Mean. One of many highlights here is Suzanne's second (of three) weddings: "Leona Rosenthal needs it all," sayeth mama, "and no one has that much to give!" "You're jealous of me, aren't you?" La Pleshette screeches, and we're off and running in this life story of a woman who doesn't have much time for any of her family since she's too busy clawing, scratching, and screwing her way to the top, all the while spouting dialogue so pungent, it could set off car alarms: "I said no calls; are you deaf or are you stupid? Do that again and you're fired!"

Assisted by *Murphy Brown*'s Joe Regalbuto as the underling/friend and *Sea Hunt*'s Lloyd Bridges as the very rich Harry Helmsley (whom Leona zombifies), Pleshette deserves universal industry praise for turning this drecky idea into utterly compelling television. Even as an on-the-prowl single gal, trying to put the hooks into the very married Harry and birthday-gifting him with desktop sex and a co-op conversion, Pleshette throws off power and charisma like there's no tomorrow—a philosophy of life that rings completely true as a depiction of the real Leona.

⚏ ⚏ ⚏ ⚏

Liberace, 1988. In the wake of Wladziu Valentino Liberace's death and employee Scott Thorson's lawsuit against the estate claiming Lee'd given him AIDS, this life story must've been seen as an exciting, provocative idea. Just think of all those fans Liberace had, and how much they'd want to know about the hidden secrets of his life! What TV did, though, was decide that those senior citizen fans didn't actually want to know *too* much (not to mention Liberace's successful lawsuit against *Confidential* magazine), and so created one of the oddest tormented heroes in TV history.

The drama here is that Lee (eerily recreated by Andrew Robinson) can't make his beloved mama (a role hamboned into the ground by Rue McClanahan) happy by getting married and having kids. He keeps trying, and even announces during dinner with Mom, Lee's traveling companion, and a miniature poodle, that he's engaged to a poor girl named Joanne—but Joanne's dad won't allow it because of Lee's "reputation."

Liberace can't understand why he has this reputation, even though he keeps hiring cute young guys to essentially do nothing, and flatters them to death over milkshakes in his spiffy vintage convertible.

Even with this major entertainment defect, however, *Liberace* is a must for both his serious fans and for BAD connoisseurs. See! the moment when a candelabra was first applied to a piano . . . the lavish re-creations of Liberace's lavish Las Vegas performances . . . and the dramatic highlight when Lee throws out that conniving employee Scott Thorson after Scott has all his druggy friends come over to Lee's mansion and they turn up the easy-listening music *real* loud.

ʟ ʟ ʟ

Little Ladies of the Night, 1977. If you survive being a teenage hitchhiker, maybe you can become a teen runaway, and be forced into a tragic life of prostitution. This is just what happens to bedraggled Linda Purl, who, thank her lucky stars, meets up with concerned, dedicated, sexy social worker David Soul. Together they make the long struggle back home, reuniting Linda with her family—a family that doesn't want her back.

ʟ ʟ ʟ ʟ

Live Again, Die Again, 1974. Dreamy Everygirl Donna Mills shows why we should all be happy that we won't be alive for the nightmarish horror of tomorrow's technology, cryonics. It turns out that, after being frozen alive for twenty years, when you're brought back out of the deep freeze, your husband's an old cudge and your kids are your peers.

ʟ ʟ

The Loneliest Runner, 1976. The stirring drama of a teen athlete troubled by uncontrollable bedwetting, written by and starring Michael Landon, and based on his own true-life story.

ʟ ʟ ʟ

———

Look What's Happened to Rosemary's Baby, 1976. An unbearably trashy sequel with the cursed Patty Duke and George Maharis in the Mia Farrow/John Cassavetes roles, Ruth Gordon and Ray Milland as the covenheads, and featuring the ever-talented Tina Louise and Donna Mills.

Patty's best friend: the son of Satan.

🐾 🐾 🐾 🐾

Mad Bull, 1977. Susan Anspach finds the tender, sensitive heart buried deep, deep inside crazed wrestler Alex Karras.

🐾

Maid in America, 1982. Alex Karras so badly wants to be a maid that he takes his lady-lawyer would-be employer to court when she wants to hire a woman instead.

🐾

Mafia Princess, 1986. If you wonder why Susan Lucci has never won an Emmy . . . if you're curious why Tony Curtis doesn't get more work . . . if you think it might be exciting and dramatic to be a part of a *Cosa Nostra* family . . . learn the bitter truth with *Mafia Princess.* What should have been great, great television is instead the story of a whining brat who's upset she'll never get into "High Society" (like maybe partying with Donald and Ivana Trump) because of her ratty, criminal heritage.

🐾 🐾

Maneater, 1973. Written and directed by none other than Vince Edwards—two couples out camping become the victims of an insane animal trainer and his starving tigers.

🐾

Mars Needs Women, 1966. The citizens of Mars, who wear scuba wetsuits, headphones, and walkie-talkies, fall completely in lust with nightclub dancer/scientist/Batgirl Yvonne Craig, and create a soundtrack that inspired a 1989 dance hit.

ᴧᴧ

***Mayflower Madam,* 1987.** Before her big break in telejournalism, Candy *Murphy Brown* Bergen tramped her way through this glorious piece of tabloid TV. According to *Mayflower Madam,* Sydney Biddle Barrows was a perfectly nice, lovely William Brewster descendant who hit a bad spell moneywise and—because of her snooty heritage and never learning how to type—what could she possibly do but run a glamorous prostitution ring? Employing the stiff, wooden, robotic acting style of her older brother, Charlie McCarthy, Candy is a woman whose lot is so low that the only job she can get is as phone girl for Exclusive Escorts, where her scuzzy pimp boss Eddie teaches her the searing realities of the world's oldest profession. Candy is so offended by the whole thing she decides to start Cachet—a feminist operation filled with earnest medical students and adorably naive thespians. She's the Eileen Ford of escort operators, taking her girls shopping, getting them *noms de coucher* from a book of baby names, and teaching them how to be "real ladies"—they even go on balloon rides and picnics together! It was all a perfect, caring, and sharing business, until Candy's surly, loutish landlord sics the vice on her.

Even though some may think it's a big step up portraying an imitation Diane Sawyer instead of a whoremonger, Murphy Brown gets to spend lots of time with dreary Republican politicians—while the Mayflower Madam got to meet fun people like boyfriend Chris Sarandon and lawyer Chita Rivera. One thing: If what Sydney did was illegal, what are all those escort ads doing on cable?

ᴧᴧ ᴧᴧ ᴧᴧ ᴧᴧ

***Mirror, Mirror,* 1979.** To keep their men, Janet Leigh, Lee Meriwether, and Loretta Swit are forced to undergo cosmetic surgery.

ᴧᴧ

***Miss America: Behind the Crown,* 1992.** Two nights after bequeathing her tiara to next year's model, our 1992 Miss America, Hawaii's pineapple-sweet Carolyn Sapp, followed up her *People* magazine feature story by starring as herself in this nightmarish re-creation of her nightmarish life story. Not that being Miss America is so terrible; the terror was in dating the fiancée-beating, name-cursed Samoan football star Nuu Faaola (portrayed, of course, by Ray Bumatai), and then having to go through the whole thing all over again in *Miss America: Behind the Crown.* The dramatic highlight of the show is Faaola/Bumatai pummeling Sapp's head against the wall and screaming, "WHY DO YOU DO THIS TO ME? WHY DO YOU MAKE ME SO ANGRY?"

Perhaps Miss Sapp still hasn't recovered from her ordeal, since her performance here seems Xanax-controlled—and you'd think she could at least play *herself.* Said *People:* "There were infomercials with more energy and imagination than this."

▲▲

Money on the Side, 1982. Housewives Jamie Lee Curtis, Karen Valentine, and Linda Purl need pin money, so they become whores.

▲▲ ▲▲ ▲▲

Moses the Lawgiver, 1975. A trash classic remake of *The Ten Commandments* with Irene Pappas as Zipporah, BAD Queen Mariangela Melato *(Swept Away . . . , Flash Gordon)* as a leering Egyptian princess, and Burt Lancaster as Moses.

▲▲ ▲▲

Murder on Flight 502, 1975. A terrorist lunatic attacks, and the passenger list includes Sonny Bono, Farrah Fawcett, and Danny Bonaduce.

▲▲

A Murderous Affair: The Carolyn Warmus Story, 1992; The Danger of Love, 1992. Crimes of passion are probably the easiest murders to understand (and therefore the least interesting to spend time thinking about). If you finally met your one true love, and your passion was so deep it was like nothing anyone's ever felt before, and he said time and again that he loved you so much he could die but there was someone in the way of you two becoming happily ever after (i.e., his wife), wouldn't you get ideas? It's as common as the day is long, but murderous women (even in our enlightened age) are still thought so exotic that these "Fatal Attraction" stories get lots of press and, frequently, multiple made-fors.

Such is the case with the love-obsessed (but otherwise dreary) high-school student Amy Fisher, and the equally love-obsessed (but otherwise dreary) schoolteacher Carolyn Warmus, who was convicted of offing boyfriend Paul Solomon's wife and then having sex with him in a car. At one point in the two-year, two-trial case, suspicions were raised that the boyfriend planted some evidence and that Carolyn wasn't criminally sophisticated enough to doctor her phone bills (the main alibi). The twists and turns got so confusing that the real story was more like *Jagged Edge* than *Fatal Attraction*—filled with "did she or didn't she?" questions (Warmus maintains her innocence to this day)—but all this great stuff is skipped completely by our two "based on a true story" outings.

At least Carolyn got lucky on TV. For the ABC *Affair* she's never explicitly ID'd as the killer; she and the boyfriend are sexpot clotheshorse Virginia Madsen and shirt-free sunlover Chris Sarandon, and the show was moved from the tedious New York suburb of Westchester to sunny, glamorous L.A. (or at least it looks that way). In bed, that romantic Virginia wonders, "Who's the best you ever had?" and Chris moans, "You . . . you . . . you . . . you you you!"

Ia Ia Ia

On the CBS *Danger* Carolyn and Paul are done by gorgeous Jenny Robertson and hardbody Joe Penny (all in all, not a bad way to be remembered by millions of viewers). *Danger* explicitly, coldly details the murder; Joe's name is changed to "Michael Carlin," and he hires comedian Richard Lewis as his lawyer.

Ia Ia

Like all made-fors based on a true crime both of these MOWs orient the viewer to identify with the poor "victim" while simultaneously having the "villain" be the only interesting, fun person in the whole show—letting us both feel morally superior and vicariously enjoy a good murderous rage, all at the same time.

—

Mysterious Island of Beautiful Women, 1979. An oil-rig crew arrives on an uncharted isle to discover a tribe of man-murdering Amazons named Chocolate, Snow, Flower, Jo Jo, and Bambi.

♟♟

Night of the Ghouls, 1959. The only TV movie done by notorious director (*Plan 9 from Outer Space, Glen or Glenda,* etc.) Edward Wood, Jr. A conman bilks mourners by claiming to contact their beloveds from beyond the grave, but the con's on him when he actually ends up reviving a whole bunch of low-rent cadavers—who murder him for interfering with the natural order of things.

♟♟ ♟♟ ♟♟ ♟♟

Nightmare in Badham County, 1976. Two beautiful, buxom coeds are on vacation in the American heartland when they're framed by sheriff Chuck Connors. Luckily, in prison they meet guard Tina Louise, warden Robert Reed, and fellow jailbirds Della Reese and Lana Wood.

♟♟ ♟♟ ♟♟

No Other Love, 1979; Like Normal People, 1979. In *No Other Love* mentally retarded Richard Thomas and mentally retarded Julie Kavner fall in love and arrange to be wed despite their parents' and society's harsh disapproval. In *Like Normal People* mentally retarded Shaun Cassidy and mentally retarded Linda Purl fall in love and arrange to be wed despite their parents' and society's harsh disapproval.

Seems that in 1979 our thoughts turned to love and mental retardation.

♟♟

Out on a Limb, 1987. In 1984 Shirley MacLaine published the story of her adventures in the spirit world, and three years later played herself in a four-hour dramatization of her adventures in the spirit world, and two years after that published *It's All in the Playing,* the story of her adventures in the spirit world while playing herself in a four-hour dramatization of her adventures in the spirit world. Hopefully *Playing* will also become a made-for, so we can watch Shirley playing herself making the TV movie where she plays herself in a four-hour dramatization of her adventures in the spirit world.

"Did you ever feel that you're not seeing what you're looking at because you're not real sure about what you see in yourself?" asks Shirley of her longtime confidante, Bella Abzug. This is only the beginning of Shirley's exploration of many mysteries (later she'd tell Bella, "I can't go to your fund-raising garden party next week . . . because I'm going to Peru to look for UFOs!"). In *Out on a Limb* she's a learner, an explorer, someone who's just trying to understand such things as: Why would Shirley MacLaine be attracted to a young, gorgeous, brilliant, aristocratic British politician about to become that country's PM? Is it because they were once husband and wife on Atlantis? Does she write her books (and make this movie) because Mayan the extraterrestrial wanted her to teach people about reincarnation, trance channeling, and the spirit world? And is her spiritual adviser John Heard (your typical painter/spiritualist hunk type) doing the right thing when he tells her "everything is happening as it should . . . everything you want to know is right inside of you; you are the Pacific Ocean; you are the universe!" and then makes her stare deeply into his eyes and scream, "I AM GOD!"

Soon enough, however, *Out* makes you, the viewer, ponder many mysteries, such as: How can a great actress like MacLaine (still knocking us dead in *Terms of Endearment* and *Postcards from the Edge*) do such a bad job playing herself? Is she in real life such a coy, winsome stiff? Does she really eat out of saucepans in bed with her lovers? Does she actually buy her friends ugly New Age paintings for their birthdays? And why is it that she only comes alive as an actress when she's throwing a temper tantrum?

Like Madonna in *Truth or Dare,* Shirley MacLaine, in *Out,* is creating her own tabloid. Watch as she jets from New York to Malibu to Hawaii to Hong Kong to London to Paris to Stockholm to Lima, and see her perfectly dressed to the teeth for every occasion, and wonder: Could the *National Enquirer* come up with anything more embarrassing than this stuff?

Out does, however, have one saving grace: like Shirley, the trance channelers play themselves.

———

Overboard, 1978. Angie Dickinson falls off a boat and, while waiting the entire two-hour length of this movie to be rescued, floats around in the water thinking about husband Cliff Robertson and lover Andrew Duggan.

♟♟

Paper Dolls, 1982. Teen model Daryl Hannah, mom Joan Hackett, and ruthless agent Joan Collins face the horrors of fashion together. In the quickly canceled series made from this shockingly successful special, Morgan Fairchild took the Collins role.

♟♟ ♟♟ ♟♟

The People, 1972. *True Grit*'s Kim Darby goes to a small town filled with William Shatner and other levitating, telepathic aliens-in-disguise.

♟♟ ♟♟ ♟♟

Planet Earth, 1974. *Star Trek* creator Gene Roddenberry exec-prodded this adventure set fifty years into the future, when the world is ruled by Amazon women and the men are all servants (known as Dinks), starring John Saxon, Ted Cassidy, and Diana Muldaur.

♟♟ ♟♟ ♟♟

Portrait of a Stripper, 1979; Portrait of a Showgirl, 1982. Before her breakthrough in the masterpiece *Choose Me,* Lesley Ann Warren starred in the middle two of the *Portrait* tetralogy—tragically, she never got around to making the finale, *Portrait of a Naked Bimbo Slut on Drugs.* Like *Mayflower Madam* the two *Portraits* depict in an oh-too-realistic fashion how a perfectly normal, nice young single woman can, when trouble hits, become enslaved by the sex industry.

In *Stripper* single mom Lesley is made to become a tawdry stripper in order to support her woeful son—but since she's a stripper and obviously an unfit mother, she may end up losing him to a foster home. A mere three years later *Showgirl* Lesley makes her way to Las Vegas (in an update of the many 1960s wacky stewardess flicks), where she discovers that show-girlhood is not the wildly glamorous job it's cracked up to be. Her Vegas life is a boring rut of going to work and going on dates and going to work and going on dates where the men have the strangest ideas since they've just seen you onstage in front of hundreds of strangers wearing nothing but feathers and sequins.

Two great classics, not to be missed.

Pray for the Wildcats, 1978. Robert Reed, Andy Griffith, and Marjoe Gortner go dirt-biking for the weekend and end up in a TV remake of *Deliverance.*

Rainbow, 1978. Judy Garland's wonderful childhood years, with Piper *Carrie* Laurie as mom and the sickening Andrea *Annie* McArdle as our Judy.

Rape and Marriage: The Rideout Case, 1980. *Wild Orchid* Mickey Rourke screams at, beats, and rapes his wife, *Terminator* Linda Hamilton, until she sues. A fascinating true story is here turned into an annoying soap opera, starring one of the strangest couples in the history of show business.

Revenge, 1971. Shelley Winters thinks Bradford Dillman was responsible for the death of her daughter, and so kidnaps and tortures him in her basement. Thank goodness Brad's wife is blessed with ESP, 'cause that's what it takes to rescue him from Shelley's madness.

Roll, Freddy, Roll!, 1974. Computer-obsessed Tim Conway tries to recapture his name-cursed son Moosie Drier's love by winning "longest time spent on roller skates" in the *Guinness Book of World Records.*

⁙⁙⁙

Roxanne: The Prize Pulitzer, 1989. When rich white trash Peter and Roxanne Pulitzer divorced, their vicious fighting (and his bitter accusations of her sleeping with both women and trumpets) made for lurid headlines around the world. After losing a big, messy divorce trial (and getting gouged in both the custody and money departments), Roxanne brilliantly cashed in with her memoir, *The Prize Pulitzer,* and this made-for, which portrayed her (via fresh-faced newcomer Chynna "Wilson" Phillips) as an innocent regular gal like you and me who got swept up in the decadence of Palm Beach wealth and got done wrong by those rich Florida snoots.

"Based on a true story," the script portrays the Pulitzers as so sexually insatiable, they go at it in the bathroom during a chichi party, and so wealthy that the nanny takes precedence over Rox in taking care of their twins, Mack and Zack. Peter (done well by a handsomely decayed Perry King) has *Happy Birthday, Rox* written in coke on a mirror to pass around at her party, and brings in the big present later that night: a masseuse with a yen for three-ways. Being the sweet thing that she is, Rox whimpers in protest, but Peter incessantly nags her about it, so Rox turns to her best friend for advice—and a ménage is born. Later, the best friend will tell Rox the facts of life: "In Palm Beach, when your marriage is over, *you're* over."

Roxanne: The Prize Pulitzer is a classic, but what's even more fun is to wonder, scene by scene, what the real story might have been—and to share the coldly delicious revenge Ms. Pulitzer achieved with this brief, shining moment.

⁙⁙⁙⁙

The Runaways, 1975. A teen falsely accused of stealing runs away from his foster home only to become best buddies on the road with a runaway leopard who's escaped from one of those dangerous safari parks.

⁙

———

Salvage, 1979. Trashman Andy Griffith flies to the moon in a home-made rocket to start a new business salvaging abandoned NASA junk.

▲▲

Sarah T—Portrait of a Teenage Alcoholic, 1975. A BAD master-piece (written by Richard and Esther Shapiro of *Dynasty*) centering on the whiny, pouty, dour Linda Blair, who helps out at her parents' party and, unseen in the kitchen, throws back a whole lot of leftover Scotch to thun-derous strings. The next day's hangover ruins her Glee Club audition, but does Linda learn? Her parents are separating, what's a poor girl to do, but Linda does admit her love for travelin' artist dad Larry Hagman when he gives her a hundred dollars, all of which goes to buy the latest thing, an appliquéd jean jumpsuit with elephant bells. Linda's first date in her new town is with thuggy next-door neighbor Mark Hamill, who obviously thinks she's the biggest drip this side of Niagara Falls, but encourages (nay, forces) her to drink. Unpopular, unattractive Linda gets all the teens hopping by singing a Carole King medley, dancing wildly to Elton John covers, and getting bombed.

Why the Shapiros and all the execs involved thought two hours of watching Linda drink has entertainment value is one of those unknown mysteries of the human spirit.

▲▲ ▲▲ ▲▲ ▲▲

Satan's School for Girls, 1973. Kate Jackson, Cheryl Ladd, and many other beautiful, lingerie-wearing girls worship the Devil (Roy Thinnes) in a cult disguised as a private school.

▲▲ ▲▲

Scream, Pretty Peggy, 1973. Sculptor Ted Bessell hires comely co-eds to take care of mom Bette Davis and a mysterious sister.

▲▲

The Screaming Woman, 1972. The loony bin sets free dowager (and small-screen debutante) Olivia de Havilland but, because of her psycho past, no one will believe her when she claims to hear a voice yelling from underneath the ground, and no one will help her when she wants to dig the body up.

♟ ♟ ♟ ♟

Scruples, **1980.** Efrem Zimbalist, Jr., Connie Stevens, and Gavin MacLeod hit the boards in this cleaned-up version of Judith Krantz's megaseller, which launched the "sex and shopping" women's novels of the 1980s. The kind of BAD TV that's so scummy, it makes you feel like taking a shower, *Scruples* is a classic period piece that contains everything the decade had to offer: Fat teen moves to Europe, drops a ton of flab, and turns into model Lindsay Wagner, who marries a rich old coot moments before his death, inheriting everything, and uses the dough to launch the most fab Bev Hills boutique ever. Krantz's brilliance was in combining the festive panic of Giorgio's with a whole new attitude about conspicuous consumption—why settle for a mere closetful of gorgeous gowns when you can *own the store*?—and she would parlay the idea into an entire book and MOW career.

♟ ♟ ♟

Second Serve, **1986.** Joined by a brilliant assemblage of boyish wigs, binding undergarments, body doubles, basso voice, and stubble makeup, Vanessa Redgrave stars here as a man, a woman, a transvestite, a she-male, an ophthalmologist, and a tennis star—yet believe it or not, it's all one wild, wacky person, Renee Richards. Redgrave is brilliant beyond belief (even though she's the ugliest transvestite to hit the small screen since Peter Kastner); but watching *Second Serve* makes you feel slimy and creepy and ooky since you spend the whole two hours looking for Vanessa behind the man, Vanessa behind the trannie, and Vanessa behind the preop. It's a movie as eerily voyeuristic as *Chained for Life* (see page 221).

♟ ♟ ♟ ♟

Secrets of a Married Man, **1984.** William Shatner commits adultery with Michelle Phillips, and wife Cybill Shepherd just won't even try to understand.

♟

Vanessa Redgrave as the man/drag queen/woman (you decide) in *Second Serve* (Photofest)

***Seven in Darkness*, 1969.** Milton Berle, Dina Merrill, Alejandro Rey, Lesley Ann Warren, and other megastars survive a plane crash even though they're all blind.

                                                    🍿 🍿

——

Shooting Stars, 1983. After being fired from their starring roles as private eyes in a TV series, Billy Dee Williams and Parker Stevenson try to become private eyes in real life.

🁣

Sins, 1986. Joan Collins and her then-husband Peter Holm capitalized on Joan's newfound American stardom as *Dynasty*'s ultimate bitch-from-hell to make this self-aggrandizing piece of trash, supposedly the story of a Helen Gurley Brown type who scratches, bites, and claws her way up the corporate ladder only to use her money and power to track down the Nazi who destroyed her family. Actually, *Sins* is the story of Joan Collins's magnificent thespian talents—and her ability to wear eighty-seven different outfits in a mere two hours.

🁣 🁣

Sole Survivor, 1970. Ghosts Vince Edwards, William Shatner, and Brad Davis haunt General Richard Basehart for the bad, bad things he did in World War II.

🁣

Someone I Touched, 1975. The searing drama of a man and two women squabbling over who gave whom herpes.

🁣 🁣 🁣

The Specialists, 1975. U.S. Public Health scientists investigate a strange outbreak of itching at an elementary school and mysterious accidents at a soap factory.

🁣

Spectre, 1977. Another failed pilot exec prodded by Gene Roddenberry, featuring Robert Culp and Gig Young scared out of their wits by

Druid-worshiping John Hurt, a humanoid green lizard, and tarty women.

♟ ♟ ♟

SST—Death Flight, 1977. Before the *Concorde,* many were frightened by the idea of supersonic transports, so Regis Philbin, Bert Convy, Tina Louise, Billy Crystal, and Robert Reed appeared in *Death Flight* to prove their paranoid suspicions were completely valid.

♟

Stranger in Our House, 1978. Linda Blair's teen witch uses supernatural powers to control her family in an MOW directed by horrormaster Wes Craven that isn't even a little bit scary.

♟ ♟

The Stranger Within, 1974. In a subtle nod to pro-choice, preggers Barbara *Jeannie* Eden (in a Tammy Wynette hair extension) is menaced by an alien fetus that forces her to drown her food in salt, drink coffee like there's no tomorrow, eat with her bare hands, keep the house at freezing temperatures, and run to the window to stare at the moon.

♟ ♟ ♟ ♟

Strays, 1991. Timmy Busfield leaves Patty Wettig for Kathy Quinlan (not the coma victim), a lovely house in the woods, and a rampaging mob of vicious cats. Since the movie is completely unbelievable and the kitties less than fearsome, the *New York Post* called *Strays* "the worst movie ever shown on the USA channel."

♟ ♟ ♟

Sweet Hostage, 1975. Criminally insane Martin Sheen escapes from the loony bin, kidnaps Linda Blair, and takes her to his remote mountain hideout . . . where love blooms.

♟ ♟ ♟

———

Tarzan in Manhattan, **1989.** A remake of the Johnny Weissmuller classic with mouth-breathing Joe Lara as Tarzan, a Brooklyn cabbie as Jane, and Tony Curtis as the friend, searching throughout New York for the man who killed Tarzan's ape mother—a man who says things like "There are all those bleeding hearts who don't like me taking the top off chimps' heads and grinding up the brains!"

ⅠⅠ

Three Sovereigns for Sarah, **1987.** Even The Legend (Vanessa Redgrave) can't save this highfalutin university press treatise on the origins of the Salem witch trials. Instead of a yummy TV version of Ken Russell's *The Devils* (with plenty of self-flagellation, clothes-rending, screaming attacks of hysteria and eye-rolling, and tongue-shooting demonic possessions), *Three Sovereigns* turns out to be a lot of trial chat in stuffy Puritanese.

ⅠⅠ

Twin Detectives, **1976.** Two PIs use their twindom to foil and confuse criminals in this dramatic TV debut of both *Hee Haw*'s Hager Twins and Lillian Gish.

ⅠⅠ ⅠⅠ

Wake Me Up When the War Is Over, **1969.** German baroness Eva Gabor convinces dashing American pilot Ken Berry that World War II is going on, and on, and on, so he'll stay undercover in her chateau and satisfy her woman's needs.

ⅠⅠ ⅠⅠ ⅠⅠ

Women in Chains, **1972.** Parole Officer Lois Nettleton goes undercover as a femme con returning to the can in order to investigate the notorious brutality of Head Matron Ida Lupino. Lois's cellmates are the standard late-sixties microcosm of our troubled American society: one harmonica-playing black, one dirty-haired spaz, one nerdy virgin who's falsely accused, one tough Rican killer, and one backwoods mama. Ida is in perfect form as a sadist with absolute power who helps her fish pummel a disliked inmate, jabs people with her keys to make a point, and schedules Lois to be killed on a Sunday with the whole prison knowing about it. She even *smokes* mean.

♦♦ ♦♦ ♦♦

♦♦

And the Tammi for the worst made-for-TV movie in history goes to:

Guyana Tragedy: The Story of Jim Jones, **1980.** The ultimate made-for-TV movie. James Earl Jones, Colleen Dewhurst, Ned Beatty, Amy Irving (in her alien/zombie contact lenses), and Randy Quaid costar with BAD TV sensation Powers Boothe, and his riveting portrayal of Jim Jones. A bisexual psychiatrist who hears the word of God and begins his People's Temple by selling capuchin monkeys door to door, Powers's new religious sentiment immediately causes trouble at home:

Mr. Jones: Don't stand in my way as I travel from this miasma of mortal confusion to the path of salvation and righteousness!
Mrs. Jones: But I found you in the arms of another woman!
Mr. Jones: I have to be all things to all men and all women!

A series of successful faith-healings, charismatic public appearances, and compelling religious visions (inspired by late-night TV movies) brings Powers the hysteric cult he craves, even though he can't keep his zipper closed:

Cult follower wife: How could a married preacher lie with a woman, and then with her husband! It's obscene and it's insane!
Cult follower husband: He has special needs.

So successful is Jones (even when wearing white ties and aviator glasses) that the people of the People's Temple follow him everywhere—even to Guyana! Perhaps the wildest aspect of this movie is the fact that, when it aired, it was greeted with immense acclaim. *The New*

York Times, normally not attuned to the BAD, gave *Guyana Tragedy* a rave, *TV Guide* gave it four stars, and that year's Emmy went to . . . Powers Boothe.

There is a standard formula for success in the entertainment medium, and that is: Beat it to death if it succeeds.

—Ernie Kovacs

The Bastards!
(My Parents Were Movies)
Nominees

Imitation is the sincerest form of television.

—Fred Allen

Just think back and remember those magic *TV* moments: *Diner; The Flamingo Kid; Shaft; 9 to 5; Serpico; To Sir, With Love; Dirty Dancing; Catch-22; Lilies of the Field; The Jerk; Guess Who's Coming to Dinner; The Best Years of Our Lives; Mother, Juggs and Speed.* Don't ring a bell, do they?

It's amazing how many television executives must walk around with the successes of *M*A*S*H* and *The Odd Couple* ringing in their ears. Every television season brings with it a hit, semihit, or even not-hit movie turned into a TV series—which is then immediately canceled. Watching these shows gives viewers a serious nostalgia problem; you can't help but remember the original and how much better it was in every way. The stars were bigger; the writing better; the special effects more exciting; the camera and lighting work much more sophisticated; "we had faces then!" Just looking below at who on television replaced whom in the original quickly proves why successful bastards are so rare. A similar problem is bowdlerization; when TVizers tone down the extremes of the film roles, the results are usually so tame, no one wants to watch.

These outings are called "Bastards" not only for their illegitimate heritage, but also because this category is easily television's lowest moment. Watching TV's attempt to clone a feature is almost an exercise in pity, since the outcome is so miserably pathetic. Not only do these shows awkwardly mimic a movie you've already seen (or didn't want to see in the first place), but they frequently are written, directed, and art-directed by Hollywood's least original scripters, directors, and designers.

Additionally, we provide the following as cautionary tales for all you would-be entertainment executives. In fact, considering recent history (*The Addams Family, The Flintstones, Wayne's World, Star Trek I–VI),* your Hollywood careers will go far if you recommend translating from the small to the big screen—and never vice versa.

▲▲

The African Queen, 1962; The African Queen, 1977. Twice tried, with James Coburn and Glynis Johns and, a decade later, Warren Oates and Mariette Hartley, in the Humphrey Bogart/Katharine Hepburn roles.

▲▲ ▲▲

Bates Motel, 1987. *Harold and Maude*r Bud Cort plays a lunatic who inherits Tony Perkins's *Psycho* resting place, which is now haunted, and so provides every guest with a first-class supernatural experience.

▲▲ ▲▲ ▲▲

Butch Cassidy and the Sundance Kids, 1973. Cartoon teenage FBI agents go undercover as the world's greatest rock band.

▲▲ ▲▲ ▲▲

Cat Ballou, 1971; Cat Ballou, 1971. NBC decided to try something utterly bizarre by making two different pilots from the same movie—one starring Lesley Ann Warren, the other Forrest Tucker—giving them both the same title, and airing them a day apart from each

other. Generating total viewer confusion probably wasn't the best programming strategy.

La La La La

Co-Ed Fever, 1979. All three networks tried bandwagon-jumping on
the hit movie *Animal House,* with ABC's *Delta House* (starring Michelle
Pfeiffer as "Bombshell"), NBC's *Brothers and Sisters,* and CBS (the so-
called "Tiffany" network) with this—a thing so dreadful, it thankfully
lasted for one mere episode.

La La La

Down and Out in Beverly Hills, 1987. Fun Fun Fun! as weekly misunderstandings occur between a family of rich snoots and their live-in
bum—who, of course, teaches them about real life and helps them with
their personal problems. A third-generation remake (the original being
Renoir's 1932 *Boudu Saved from Drowning*), savvy Fox aired the pilot in
April, but didn't start the series' run until July.

La

Goodbye Charlie, 1985. This saga of a skirt-chasing mobster who
is reincarnated as—gasp!—a woman, was essayed on Broadway by
Lauren Bacall, on the big screen by Debbie Reynolds and Ellen
(Switch) Barkin, and on the small screen by BAD TV legend Suzanne
Somers.

La La La

Holly Golightly, 1969. Stefanie Powers—aka *The Girl from
U.N.C.L.E.*—skips breakfast at Tiffany's to go to an all-night party
that's a walk on the wild side—but only in the mind of prime-time television standards and practices.

La

Johnny Belinda, 1967. One of four TV remakes of the Jane Wyman
spectacular (the others popping up in 1955, 1958, and 1982), this jejune

attempt featured the much-married Mia Farrow. Watching her over-the-top, sappy performance made viewers around the world lunge for their insulin.

♙♙

The Man Who Fell to Earth, 1987. A series that proves David Bowie's greatness in portraying thirsty, emaciated aliens is uniquely his own.

♙♙

9 to 5, 1982. Rita Moreno, Valerie Curtin, Rachel Dennison (and later on, Sally Struthers) recreate the Jane Fonda, Lily Tomlin, and Dolly Parton roles (Dennison being Parton's sister). For four years, on ABC and in syndication, the show searched in vain for an audience, but without the movie's beautifully handled feminist tone and the chemistry of the film's stars, the TV *9 to 5* never struck ratings gold.

♙♙

The Oddball Couple, 1975. Fleabag the dog and Spiffy the cat in a cartoon version of the Jack Klugman/Tony Randall roles.

♙♙ ♙♙

The Owl and the Pussycat, 1975. Writer George Segal and whore Barbra Streisand are TV-replaced by writer Buck Henry and actress Bernadette Peters.

♙♙ ♙♙

Roman Holidays, 1972. Hanna-Barbera cartoon remake of *A Funny Thing Happened on the Way to the Forum,* featuring the wacky Holiday family.

♙♙ ♙♙

W.E.B., 1978. A reincarnation of the theatrical feature *Network* (with *Dynasty*'s Pamela Bellwood in the Faye Dunaway role), produced by television exec Lin Bolen—reportedly the model for Dunaway's character in the movie.

ʟɪ ʟɪ ʟɪ

ʟɪ

And the Tammi for the worst bastard ever goes to: A three-way tie:

Bring 'Em Back Alive; The Quest; Tales of the Gold Monkey; 1982. Bruce Boxleitner, Perry King, and Stephen Collins simultaneously try to TVize Harrison Ford/Indiana Jones and *Raiders of the Lost Ark*. All three programs were beyond miserable (even considering their utterly BAD competition) and easily won this category. Bruce, Perry, and Stephen couldn't even come close to pulling off believability in either the scientist or the adventurer facets of their roles, and of course no prime-time series could remotely afford to have special effects as lavish as the original. Where Indiana reignited the fun and adventure of Hollywood's Golden Age kiddie serials, these three seemed like pale imitations of the already wan and faded-by-age originals.

Though the *Raiders* heritage of all three of these clones was completely obvious to even their hoped-for preteen audience, *Monkey*'s producer insisted his show was inspired by *Only Angels Have Wings* (1938), and *Bring 'Em*'s producer vehemently argued his show was based on the true-life adventures of 1930s explorer Frank Buck. Even though both got plenty of airtime and publicity explaining this artificial controversy, all three series bombed and were canceled faster than a whip-crack.

ʟɪ ʟɪ ʟɪ ʟɪ

I've got a uvula, you got a uvula, all God's children got a uvula!

—Barney Fife, *The Andy Griffith Show*

Special Bonus Section:
The Remarkably BAD Movie
Nominees

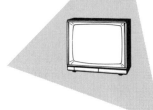

Bad movies . . . become documentaries of people trying to make a good movie. With their preposterous narratives, fractured editing, tatty sets, and monotonous line readings, they play like doomed dress rehearsals. First, you are drawn into the catastrophe of the filmmaking process, like a rubbernecking motorist passing a road kill. Then you notice that these movies are doubly subversive: they not only subvert themselves, they rebel against the timid rules of traditional filmmaking.

—Richard Corliss, *Time*

THOUGH THERE'S A TREASURE TROVE OF GUIDES TO BAD MOVIES already available, and though this is a book whose real love is television, features comprise so much of today's TV that not including at least a few standouts would be ignoring our duties to you, the discriminating viewer. Besides the hundreds of "normal" films shown around the clock, many cable programmers are now deliberately showcasing BAD features—and this has become such a pronounced trend that it's a wonder there's time on TV for anything good. Between USA's *Up All Night!*, Comedy Central's *Mystery Science Theater 3000,* and the frequent TNT and Cinemax festivals (to mention only a few), for us to ignore TV's dreadful motion pictures would be omitting what has become a programming mainstay.

It's also interesting to take a look at features because, for a number of reasons, BAD TV tends to be very different from BAD movies. Where the movies are nutty, quirky, and rich, the television is nutty, evasive, and thin. In a BAD movie such as *Faster, Pussycat! Kill! Kill!* you not only have the bizarre central idea (a gang of psychotic dragster-racing go-go dancers terrorizes the Nevada desert), but the follow-through is equally idiosyncratic (the star is half Apache, half Japanese; the costars are named "Boom-Boom" and "the Vegetable," and you'll want to memorize practically the entire script).

BAD TV has the nutty central idea, and it's frequently far more insane than any movie could be; *The Hathaways,* for example, concerns a couple who think they should treat their family of performing chimpanzees just as they'd treat real human children, while *Pink Lady & Jeff* is a variety show hosted by a Japanese singing duo whose musical interpretations could never in a million years become popular in the U.S. and, by the way, they don't speak English. The TV follow-through, however, isn't as peculiar as it is in film, since TV-hatching is far more of a committee effort than moviemaking. Instead, you get to watch, in explicit detail, a gaggle of TV execs try to figure out: *How do we get out of this mess? The Hathaways'* answer was to make chimp ma Peggy Cass the most obtuse woman in the history of entertainment (she makes Gracie Allen look insightful), while *Pink Lady*'s rescue attempt involved a fortune in costume changes and endless moments of rapturous giggling . . . all of which only made these shows even more enjoyably BAD.

There is such an abundant wealth of remarkable BAD features that what follows is a very personal, very select list of only the very, very worst—only those definitely worth spending a little videotape on late at night.

⚏

***Back to the Beach,* 1987.** What ever happened to all our sixties teen idols? In this brilliantly BAD reunion (and a Hollywood first), Frankie Avalon, Annette Funicello, and Connie Stevens pull out all the stops in parodying what might be their real-life, has-been selves. Twenty years have passed, but Frankie, Annette, and Connie are exactly as we remember them at the height of their fame (abetted through camera lenses swathed in Vaseline). Now living a sixties dream life (with tiki sculpture, soap-on-a-rope, coiffed French poodle, glow-in-the-dark pink makeup, and obnoxious punk child), Frankie's still the dweeby all-American guy, Connie's still the scheming party girl ("I never get the good guy, I'm the bad girl. Remember?"), but the big star here is Annette's well-endowed Queen of Ditz—when trouble strikes, she instantly recommends shopping and pajama parties.

As an homage to sixties trash and the triumph of the ersatz, *Back to the Beach* is the ultimate—even including cameos by Don Adams, Bob Denver, Alan Hale, Jr., Edd "Kookie" Byrnes, Barbara Billingsley, Tony Dow, Jerry Mathers, O. J. Simpson, and Pee-wee Herman (performing the timeless classic, "Surfing Bird").

Ii Ii Ii Ii

The Bad Seed, 1956. Probably every parent of a young girl knows all about coquettish manipulation, operatic tantrums, flattering cajolery, and outright lying, but you can easily feel grateful for your brat's minor infractions with a look at this remarkable movie and its astonishing lead. With her obnoxious perfection, disturbing eyebrows, alien facial expressions, and bleached blond pigtails, Patty MacCormack is easily the oddest child star in the history of popular entertainment; she made a huge impression on both stage and screen as *The Bad Seed*'s hellion, and then disappeared completely from the public eye. But what a legacy!

"There's a mature quality about her that's disturbing in a child," says Patty's mom—as if that were the worst of her problems. When schoolmate Claude (winner of a penmanship award Patty wanted real bad) mysteriously drowns at a school picnic, how does Patty react? "I thought it was exciting! Can I have a peanut butter sandwich?" When Mom finds that same award in Patty's drawer, she starts piecing things together. And why, a few years ago, did that old woman break her neck right after promising Patty she'd inherit a special something?

"Plain bad from the beginning; and nothing can change them!" declares the mystery-writer neighbor in his moving soliloquy on psychopaths. "Poor deformed children, born without pity," replies Mom, wracked with guilt that Patty's troubles were inherited from her own suspicious past.

The Bad Seed is so starkly powerful that many feel it doesn't deserve to be included here. But just one look at Mom having a nervous breakdown

**Valerie Perrine and the Village People perform their
ultrafabulous showstopping disco milk commercial in
Can't Stop the Music (Photofest)**

watching the death of handyman Leroy while Patty maniacally practices the piano, or the sudden death by lightning dénouement with its tacked-on spanking coda, will quickly convince you otherwise. A great classic—and BAD to boot.

⚊ ⚊ ⚊ ⚊ ⚊

Cannibal Women in the Avocado Jungle of Death, 1989. What happens to you after you've won Playmate of the Year and gone steady for a while with Hugh Hefner? If you're Shannon Tweed, you star in this as Margo Hunter, "ethnohistorian, Department of Feminist Studies, Spritzer College," called on by the feds to stop the avocado famine by uncovering "The Piranha women . . . an ancient commune of feminists so radical, so militant, so left of center . . . they have sex with their men, and then tear them into strips like beef jerky and eat them with guacamole. So legend has it." "They're more than legend," notes a USDA apparatchik, "they're a major agricultural problem!"

Joined by student ditz Bunny and proven chauvinist Jim (who's given such great bon mots as "Let's get down to what you really want—the domination and consumption of men!"), Shannon stalks around some park in L.A. until coming across a Frank Lloyd Wright mansion housing the Queen of the Piranhas, onetime Radcliffe scholar Adrienne Barbeau, as well as the Barracuda Women (who split with the Piranhas because they believed men should be eaten with clam dip instead of guac). If you believe there's something more agonizing to watch than an $8 million comedy written, produced, directed, and acted by people who aren't funny, then you haven't seen this USA *Up All Night!* mainstay.

↟↟ ↟↟ ↟↟

Can't Stop the Music, 1980. A neutron bomb that's every inch as bad as you've heard, *Can't Stop the Music* is so sodden and stillborn that it completely destroyed the movie careers of everyone involved: director Nancy Walker, producer Allan Carr, and costars Valerie Perrine, Bruce Jenner, and the Village People. The only one to emerge unscathed was first-timer Steve Guttenberg . . . who had to star in all those *Police Academy*s as penance before rehabilitating his career with *Cocoon.*

Even on television, with commercial breaks and some of the nudity edited away, *Can't Stop the Music* is so immensely terrible, you'll be overwhelmed with shock and speechless with wonder. Why make a musical about disco when disco was obviously on its last legs? Why hire Jenner, Perrine, and Guttenberg as the stars of a musical when they can't sing or dance? Why hire Nancy Walker as director (musicals are notoriously hard to make) when she's never directed a thing in her life? Was the supporting cast—Tammy Grimes, June Havoc, and the Ritchie Family—agented by a drag queen? Is Perrine's best friend Lulu a woman, or a man-hungry transsexual? Why does the whole movie look like it's been dubbed from another language? How could the script escape rewrite with lines like "Anybody who could swallow two Sno Balls and a Ding Dong shouldn't have any trouble with pride!"

Can't Stop is the story of disco king composer Jacques Morali, who cowrote the script and all the music, but obviously didn't bother much with the latter since this stiff couldn't even produce a hit soundtrack album. Steve Guttenberg *is* Jack Morell, the roller-skating would-be DJ and teen composer. His roommate, the retired supermodel Perrine, takes his songs to her ex-boyfriends in the music business and, when Guttenberg (who's so naive, he hallucinates after smoking a joint)

needs singers for his demo, she forms the Village People (it's never explained why they look the way they do, though when a music producer
first sees them, he comments, "I hate Halloween!"). Steve and Valerie
are such chums, in fact, that when uptight UN lawyer Bruce Jenner
spills hot food all over his groin, they both immediately help him yank
off his pants, and when the Village People need money for their debut
performance, Perrine gets them all modeling work in a milk commercial.

Just as you think you've become stupefied like you've never been stupefied before, along comes the showstopping "YMCA." As the fully cos-
tumed hardhat, policeman, soldier, hirsute leatherman, cowboy, and Rican Indian that are the Village People lip-synch among the barbells,
Perrine, Jenner, and Guttenberg run through a Y while wrestlers wrestle,
swimmers swim, and boys take showers in a sloppy paean to Busby
Berkeley and the sexual hysteria of gyms. Perrine gets the line: "It's the
eighties, darling. You're going to see a lot of things you've *never* seen before!"

Cat Women of the Moon, 1953. Made in blurry, headache-pro-
ducing 3-D (which mysteriously only occurs in certain scenes) and re-
made (just as mysteriously) in 1958 as *Missle to the Moon,* this great
example of fifties sci-fi trash features the typical, dreary American
space crew of the time (a grumpy captain, a nubile navigator, and a
good-time Charlie) traveling at "seven miles a second." Avoid them
like the plague (as well as the opening, an exact imitation of Disneyland's cheesy *Rocket to the Moon* ride), but stay tuned and strap on
your seat belts the minute those wild Cat Women appear! Living men-
free ("ours died off when I was still a child") with Lily Munster eyebrows, widow's-peaked chignons, Martha Graham tights, matching
chokers, and mental telepathy, these femmes fatales love avant-garde
dancing, taking mental control of female Earthlings, making beautiful
jewelry ("it's a metal far superior to anything you have on your earth"),
and luring men to their deaths. *Cat Women of the Moon* portrays what
must have been the worst nightmare of male Hollywood producers: a
tribe of Communist lesbians who have so much fun by themselves, they
can't be bothered to go to the movies.

———

Chained for Life, 1951. Many great BAD shows are cheap, tawdry, embarrassing, tasteless, or exploitive, but *Chained for Life* is all these, and more. It's the only movie we know of starring Siamese twins, who are attached at the hips and more or less playing themselves. In real life Daisy and Violet Hilton were duet-singing vaudevillians, and in *Chained for Life,* they're Viv and Dotty Hamilton, duet-singing vaudevillians. In real life Daisy and Violet were accused of being nefarious homewreckers in a divorce trial; in *Chained for Life* Dotty falls in love with another vaudevillian (a sharpshooting gigolo) who only wants her for publicity and to boost his career. Dotty's in fact so smitten that she dreams of being physically free of her sister to follow her heart—a sequence accomplished by hiding Viv behind trees.

The pencil-mustached lothario insists on marrying Dotty onstage in front of a paying audience because "what does it matter where we get married? We're *show people*!" Publicity accomplished, he dumps her, whereupon the sister shoots him with one of his own pistols. This causes tumult at the murder trial, since if the narrator judge sends the murderous Viv to the chair, the innocent Dotty will perish as well. The film includes an entire evening of vaudeville—juggling, accordion playing, sharpshooting, a trick cyclist, the works!—that makes you realize just why this art form is no longer with us.

Chained for Life is an inkblot test defined by your reaction to the Hilton sisters. It's either the ultimate in exploitation, or the only movie ballsy enough to star Siamese twins (whose dreadful acting, such as their reaction shots of staring frozen and unblinking at all the other characters, makes the film even more compelling). But finally, the Hiltons' innate charm make you long to have Siamese twins still among us, and realize that perhaps science can take away as many miracles as it gives.

▟▙ ▟▙ ▟▙ ▟▙ ▟▙

Change of Habit, 1970. If all Elvis movies are BAD, and all nun movies are BAD, wouldn't it be great if they made an Elvis-with-nuns movie? Thankfully, they did. Radical nuns Mary Tyler Moore, Barbara McNair, and Jane Elliot come to spread Catholic goodwill to the downtrodden, and just who do they find but Dr. Elvis, running a free clinic and singing his masterpiece, "In the Ghetto." Hilarious misunderstandings occur when Elvis thinks they're looking to have abortions, when the neighbors think they're prostitutes, and when fuddy-duddy priest Ed Asner opposes their wild ideas about Christian charity.

The core drama is, of course: How will MTM be able to reconcile her love for Jesus with her love for Elvis?

How will we all?

Ʌ Ʌ Ʌ

***Cleopatra*, 1963.** Not anywhere near the flop that the press at the time would have us believe, *Cleo* actually went on to break even financially. It is, however, twice as BAD (and twice as much fun) as any standard-issue historical epic, since you get to watch talent-deficient Hollywood megastars, listen to turgidly pretentious textbook writing, and be engulfed by more extras than there are in heaven in a flick that chokes on its own pomp. See! Elizabeth Taylor's Egyptian tomb eyeliner and "just look at these breasts!" décolletage, Richard Burton's leather minidress, and Rex Harrison's valance couture (desperately in need of Scarlett O'Hara's tailoring).

Cleo establishes the true philosophy of Hollywood epicdom: Anything worth doing is worth doing in excess. Why have fifty Nubian dancing girls when you can have a thousand? Why have common drinking glasses when you can have goblets the size of footballs? Why settle for unknowns in minor roles when you can have Martin Landau and Hume Cronyn? All that money is, as they say, right on the screen; the gold spray paint bills alone must've been staggering.

Ʌ Ʌ Ʌ

***The Conqueror*, 1956.** With Agnes Moorehead, William Conrad, John Wayne as Genghis Khan, Susan Hayward as the glowering Tartar princess, and caravans of yurts crossing the Utah desert, this multimillion-dollar epic was produced by Howard Hughes just before he sold RKO. One of his personal all-time favorite movies, *The Conqueror* follows the Cecil B. DeMille biblical aesthetic—everyone speaks in thick, Elizabethan sentences. Unfortunately, none of the actors was trained in that arch speech, and their contortions are what make this film so uniquely BAD—especially poor John Wayne. Just imagine these lines spoken with Wayne's towering Midwestern twang:

"On, brave suitor! Would you desert your bride unkissed?"

"Make haste, craven, your Tartar wench awaits you!"

"What woman's talk is this, my mother? Rid us of this carrion!"

"She is a woman, do you forget? Much woman. With the perfidy of all women."

Tragically, *The Conqueror* was shot near a nuclear test site, and many of the cast and crew (as well as the Native American extras who appeared as the Mongol horde) have died of cancer.

♟ ♟

Demon Seed, 1977. Chilly and repressed computer genius Fritz Weaver invents Proteus 3, the world's greatest computer, "which will make obsolete many of the functions of the human brain." Oddly, Proteus looks like a Grateful Dead light show and has a voice just like Robert Vaughn's. Fritz and his wife, caring and sharing child psychiatrist Julie Christie (in a scientist nerd hairdo), become estranged after this conversation:

She: The whole dehumanizing, Proteus madness . . . it's frozen your heart.
He: My dream turns out to be your nightmare.

Proteus turns imperious, demanding to study humankind, and when Fritz refuses, the giant brain takes over Fritz's home security system and family robot, traps Julie in the house, gives her electric shocks, has the robot tie her down to a chair, cuts off her dress, gives her a physical and a brain implant, performs android rape (forcing her to bear his homunculus child), and, finally, commits suicide when faced with unplugging. A BAD dream come true—with the computer's orgasm a must-see.

♟ ♟ ♟

D.O.A., 1949. Skip the charmless Dennis Quaid remake; nothing can compare with the original. Edmond O'Brien parties down in jive San Francisco and wakes up to discover he's been poisoned by "luminous toxin"—a diagnosis confirmed when his body fluids *glow in the dark.* With only "a day, maybe two, maybe a week" to live and the thinnest of leads, the constantly sweating O'Brien hurls himself into one stranger's apartment after another, grabbing people and demanding explanations. A cross between *Run for Your Life* and *The Fugitive*—but on speed— *D.O.A.*'s supporting cast is the real attraction: a pop-eyed psycho killer, an Arab femme fatale, Pamela Britton's passionately unrequited love, the wildest department-store buyers you've ever met, and curvaceous babes accompanied by a leering slide whistle. The opening scenes are so peculiar, you think you're watching the wrong movie.

⋀ ⋀ ⋀

Dragon Seed, 1944. In her day Pearl S. Buck was such a lauded figure, she even won the Nobel Prize; so it's a little bit sad that she now seems like a founding mother of trash. *Dragon Seed* is a typical Hollywood "prestige" production of Buck's "award-winning" novel (and so moves at a glacial pace), but you'll never snooze off because this movie's got a big BAD shocker: Katharine Hepburn, in pinched mascara and racist accent, as a Chinese woman. Not only is she about as convincing as Al Jolson in blackface, but the role is so grossly inappropriate and her acting is so intensely awful that it makes the filmed horror that is *Dragon Seed* utterly compelling.

⋀ ⋀

Faster, Pussycat! Kill, Kill!, 1965. John Waters's favorite movie, Russ Meyer's masterpiece, and who are we to argue? In the startling hallmark mise-en-scènes of director Meyer, *Pussycat*'s camera is usually about two feet off the ground to emphasize the pneumatic qualities of our heroines: the half-Apache, half-Japanese Varla (played to perfection by Tura Satana), and her dragster driving, go-go dancing, karate-chopping sociopath girlfriends, Rosie and Boom-Boom. The intrepid threesome kills all-American boy Tommy, kidnaps his squealing cheerleader girlfriend Linda (essayed by 1966's Playmate of the Year), and races off through the Nevada desert in search of bucks and kicks. Why, they're so bad that when they get gassed up, they don't even bother with the S&H green stamps!

Who in the world wouldn't want to be Varla, with her evil-eye makeup, black catsuit, and lines like:

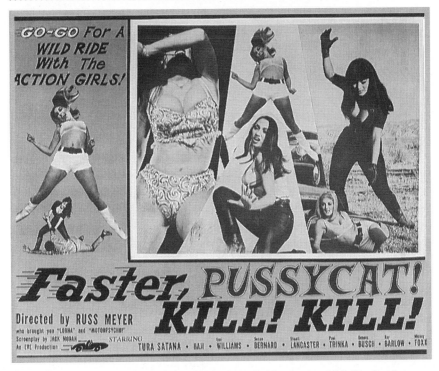

The Immortals—Tura Satana, Lori Williams, and Haji—in the movie that made them eternal—the beloved *Faster, Pussycat! Kill! Kill!* (Photofest)

My motor never runs down. . . . Would you like to look under my hood?

I never try anything; I just do it!

The point is of no return, and you've reached it!

An idle comment leads the girls to the home of codger gimp Pa, intellectual son Kirk, and a bodybuilder who's mortally afraid of trains, "the Vegetable"—all in all, a woman-hating recluse family living in the middle of nowhere off a railroad insurance settlement. Varla's convinced they've got real bucks and sets a scam in motion to steal their load, but the best-laid plans of mice and vixen go awry. Boom-Boom tries to blow town, so Varla knifes her in the back and runs over the gimp; the Vegetable knifes Rosie, so Varla runs him over; after finding the money she then tries to run over Linda and Kirk as well. It's nonstop action and nonstop obsession all the way, and you'll live for the day when you can use lines like "We know when we're not wanted; besides, this dry climate's not too good on a girl's complexion" and "In hell you'll see me, and we're both better than even money to make it!"

&& && && && &&

***Flash Gordon*, 1980.** Don't be put off by the first fifteen mediocre minutes; once Flash, Dale, and Dr. Zarkov hit Mongo, *Flash Gordon* becomes one of the greatest BAD movies of all times. Though the earthlings remain far from compelling (and Flash seems thick as a brick), the Mongoids are deliriously wonderful. Part of Dino de Laurentiis's typical "international cast," Mariangela Melato, Ornella Muti, and Max von Sydow (as Ming!) prove their bravery as actors with staggeringly over-the-top performances, all set against beautifully psychedelic matte skies and a soundtrack by Queen. You'll remember pieces of noted screenwriter Lorenzo Semple, Jr.'s, dialogue for the rest of your life: Get ready to hit the rewind button when you hear Muti utter her classic: "No, no! Not the Bore Worms!" and for the moment when Melato gleefully tortures Muti and screams, "We don't *like* doing this!"

&& && && &&

Any kickboxing movie. Like monster truck pulls or *American Gladiators,* watching the newly popular sport of kickboxing brings up a host of deep philosophical questions about the universe and our place in it. Did Dolph Lundgren introduce kickboxing to America? Is kickboxing a real sport, or did he make it all up? If it is a real sport, does it have any rules, or can you just do any vicious thing that pops in your head? Or was it (what makes the most sense of all) invented by someone who wanted to do simultaneous remakes of Sylvester Stallone and Bruce Lee movies? If not, then why are so many of the villains Asians, and why, when you watch them, do you constantly think: *Oh, there's a martial-arts scene . . . there's a Rocky scene . . . there's a Bruce Lee rip-off . . . ?*

Are there kickboxing academies, passing on the sport's techniques and tradition, or do you just start kicking people in the face? Do these athletes kickbox for fun, or is it just a job? Why do all the stars of these movies look like they just retired from Chippendale's? And, most importantly, why didn't *The Karate Kid* go on to become *The Kickboxing Kid*?

Lisztomania, 1975. Writer/director Ken Russell going completely over the top with *Women in Love, The Devils,* and *Altered States* is exactly what's made him one of today's most beloved show-business figures. But if you've ever wondered what was beyond over the top—what it'd be like if an auteur went insane (and took his costume designer and art director with him)—you need look no farther than *Lisztomania.* Starring Who crooner Roger Daltrey (acting as well as he did in *Tommy*) and featuring topless groupies, daughter Cosima practicing voodoo, and sailor Richard Wagner (his cap embroidered with NIETZSCHE) who becomes both Dracula and Frankenstein, *Lisztomania*'s opening scene is a woman hungrily eating a banana while her saber-wielding husband slices her lover's big, white, dripping candle to bits—and gets more excessive from there. With naked females worshiping an obelisk with a glowing tip, porcelain buttock sconces issuing knockout gas, a giant panties funhouse slide, a fifteen-foot alabaster penis (which gets guillotined), Rick Wakeman as an Aryan monster and Ringo Starr as the Pope, this astounding cross between *Hair* and a Liberace extravaganza wants to be all things to all people—and kills itself trying to get there. But what a fun suicide it is.

▮▮ ▮▮ ▮▮ ▮▮ ▮▮

The Loves of Hercules, 1960. The greatest dubbed-from-the-Italian Hercules picture of all time, with Jayne Mansfield in two roles (a red-wigged heroine and a black-wigged villainess) playing the loves, while real-life bodybuilder husband Mickey Hargitay is Herc, who arranges for the bad Jayne to be squeezed to death by a humanoid tree after killing a snoozy three-headed dragon (not Ghidrah). Hargitay makes Steve Reeves and Lou Ferrigno look like Gielgud and Olivier, Mansfield sleepwalks through her roles, and the whole unbelievable mess is not to be missed.

▮▮ ▮▮

The Maltese Bippy, 1969. The success of *Laugh-In* got Rowan and Martin this big-bucks assignment: to take their TV show/vaudeville aesthetic and translate it to a big-screen murder mystery. Even with Cat-woman Julie Newmar turning into the sixties signature animal—an Afghan hound—this is one bad trip, man.

♟ ♟

***Mothra*, 1962.** Even against such overwhelming competition this is by far the nuttiest Japanese monster movie of all time. Filmed in eye-popping Tohoscope, *Mothra* begins when a scary typhoon runs a Japanese battleship aground in the "Atomic Testing Area," and what do the survivors find but evidence of a long-lost civilization and the Alilenas—six-inch-high twins, dressed in sarongs, who always sing, talk, and read mortal minds in synch. Kidnapped by a bug-eyed Japano-American half-breed, the Alilenas tour Japan as the stars of *The Secret Fairies Show,* becoming a national sensation beloved by all (as if the Japanese had never seen tiny, doll-like women before).

Back on the island, oddly swarthy natives perform ceremonial dances until a giant egg breaks open, revealing an immense horned caterpillar (who looks like a yam with LED eyes), which immediately races through Tokyo in search of the petite songstresses. After destroying a Mobil gas station, many kamikazelike planes, and a radio tower, the caterpillar enrobes itself in a cocoon, finally emerging as the aluminum-foil-eyed Mothra (who looks like something one of your friends could make with golf balls, Styrofoam, and a pillowcase). Once again Mothra races through Japan in search of the diminutive chanteuses.

In the surprise ending the good guys (a card-carrying journalist comedian and his plucky female shutterbug consort) return the Alilenas to Mothra, who flies them back to their happy island, where everyone dances till dawn. Topping off this heaven-sent plot are the special effects (which look like they were done by precocious ten-year-olds): the Alilenas' stand-ins are obviously kimono souvenir dolls, and Mothra's wings send Match-box cars and trucks flying through downtown Tokyo.

This was all such a hit that Toho made a sequel, *Ghidrah* (1965), wherein Mothra, Rodan, and Godzilla team up to fight the fire-breathing, three-headed Ghidrah lizard, with a return engagment from the Alilenas.

♟ ♟ ♟

***Night of the Lepus*, 1972.** Giant, meat-eating bunny rabbits attack Janet Leigh, DeForest Kelley, and the state of Arizona. Dramatic high points of the film alternate shots of cute bunnies hopping around in doll-houses with close-ups of people screaming in terror. For the extra tricky stuff the director tried actors in bunny costumes roaring like lions, which only made the whole thing even more bizarre. You can't believe how wildly ludicrous this movie is until you see it for yourself—and with the USA channel, you will.

Queen of Outer Space, **1958.** The planet Venus has gone all-woman and their leader's become a total man-hater, but rebel Zsa Zsa Gabor doesn't share her feelings and so helps the four male earthling astronauts avoid execution. A film filled with classic BAD moments, including the legendary Zsa Zsa line (in her instantly recognizable Hungarian accent): "I hate dat Qveen!"

Reform School Girls, **1987.** While most women-behind-bars pictures have a lesbian undercurrent, *Reform School Girls* is a nutty S&M lesbian movie with a prison undercurrent. The "girls" in this school are all scanty-lingerie-clad women who look like Whitesnake video rejects, and, since there are constant naked shower scenes, they must be the cleanest inmates in the history of the penal system. There's a central character we can all identify with; an ultrafemme, ultranaive, sexually abused foster-home runaway (who can't live without her stuffed bunny); and Warhol Super-star Pat Ast as the looming redhead dorm matron with all the best lines:

> *"My name's Edna, but some of the girls call me Eddie after they get to know me for a while . . . I like that."*

> *"Keep your fingers above the sheets; we only change them once a week."*

> *"You're nothing but a shit stain on the underpants of life!"*

Other cast highlights include a Nazi crop-wielding warden (BAD leg-end Sybil Danning) and dormitory top-dog Charlie (the Plasmatics' Wendy O. Williams, in her film debut). With her pneumatic body, chain-smoker voice, and leather bikini, Charlie is a very modern moral chameleon. She alternates being one of the villainesses and one of the good gals, and when she's bad, she's a punk S&M dream, inflicting tattoos on her willing slavegirls (during an appearance on Howard Stern's "Dial-a-Date" feature, Williams commanded her callers, "Get on your hands and knees and bark like a dog!"). One of the film's greatest pleasures is the debauchery contest between Edna and Charlie; while Edna gets to torch the stuffed bunny and stomp a tiny kitten to death with her boots, Charlie climaxes the movie's grand finale—an all-out inmate riot—by riding a bus like a bronco, and singing (with Etta James) the *Reform School Girls*'s theme songs:

> *"So young . . .*
> *So bad . . .*
> *So what?*

> *"It's my life!*
> *And I'll do what I wanna*
> *Do what I wanna*
> *Do what I like!"*

ᴸ ᴸᴸ ᴸᴸ ᴸᴸ

Suburban Roulette, 1967. A movie produced and directed by Herschell Gordon *Blood Feast* Lewis (and picked by drive-in aficionado Joe Bob Briggs as one of the sleaziest of all time), which sensitively explores the epidemic of wife-swapping in that hotbed of libido, the suburbs. "Our pleasure game . . . it started with boredom . . . a new family moving in just adds tinder to a fire already ablaze!" announces the dripping-with-sarcasm narrator, and that poor family (sex-addict Ilene, her regular-Joe husband, and their drippy daughter) learns the horrors of suburban living firsthand when they attend a newcomer party:

> *"I worry about production control in the hospital supply business."*
> *"That sounds* challenging.*"*
> *"You're a beautiful neighbor, Mrs. Fisher!"*

The neighbors turn out to include the world's skankiest couple, greeting-card salesman Ron and his bisexual wife Margo ("two strangers who happen to be married to each other"), and they're hitting on every gal in the neighborhood:

> "Sometimes my pendulum just swings the wrong way."
> "But it never stops swinging, does it?"

When Ilene falls for Ron and it's unrequited, she gets raped twice, swallows a bottle of sleeping pills, and has to have her stomach pumped. With the hokiest fight scene in movie history and perfect cinematography (the whole thing looks like a nightmarish home movie), *Suburban Roulette* is not to be missed.

ʌʌ ʌʌ ʌʌ

The Thing with Two Heads, 1972. The great, must-be-seen-to-be-believed classic. Ray Milland is a mad scientist dying of cancer who arranges to have his head transplanted onto a new body. But Ray's the world's biggest racist, and the body he gets is ex-con Rosey Grier's.

One of the nuttiest ideas in entertainment history, *The Thing with Two Heads* is, posttransplant, merely a series of racial slurs and all-out fighting between the two heads, with lots of screaming and punches. If you've always wanted to see something beat itself up (and don't we all?), you're just the audience these producers were looking for.

ʌʌ ʌʌ ʌʌ

ʌʌ

And the Tammi for worst movie ever goes to:

Frankenhooker, 1990. A simultaneous remake of *Frankenstein, Scanners,* and *Reanimator* (as if for *The Playboy Channel*), this stars mad teen "bioelectrotechnician" Jeffrey, who lives in New Jersey with his mom and a one-eyed purple brain floating in an aquarium. Overwhelmed with grief ("I've lost the ability to distinguish right from wrong, good from bad") when his newest invention—an automatic lawn mower—chews up his beloved Elizabeth, Jeffrey keeps her head in a bubbling deep-freeze and goes in search of the ultimate body: "I can make you anything you want! I can make you the centerfold spread of the century! I just need the right parts."

The face only a desperate john could love: *Frankenhooker*
(Photofest)

After sticking a power drill in his head to relax, nerd Jeffrey invents a new drug (Supercrack) and travels to the Huevos Grandes ("Big Eggs") bar in search of the perfect whore. Tragically, perfection can't be found in a single woman—he likes one's legs, another's arms, another's breasts— and so Jeffrey hires nine hookers, who take the drugs, wildly dance, scream, strip . . . and explode.

Rushing home with his cornucopia of body parts to make it in time for a big thunderstorm, Jeffrey successfully reanimates Elizabeth, who asks, "WANNA GO OUT? WANNA GO ON A DATE? LOOKING FOR SOME ACTION? WANNA PARTY? NEED SOME COMPANY? GOT ANY MONEY?" She knocks him out with one blow and, in her giant platforms, Little Annie Fanny tube top, fishnets, and contorted features, staggers off into the night. Even though she's a "tall purple girl with fresh stitches," men inexplicably are crazy about her and, just as inexplicably, after sex they all explode.

Even with a mere seventy minutes of running time, *Frankenhooker* has it all.

The News, Sports, Newslike, and Pseudosports Nominees

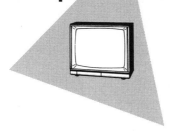

All of you act like you're going to watch *The Mayan Civilization,* and then you tune in to Geraldo Rivera. I've got the numbers.
—Michael Fuchs, chairman, HBO

I have every ratings record there is on documentaries and nothing but scathing reviews. Are these handful of critics from a relatively narrow slice of American society right and all those fifty million viewers wrong?
—Geraldo Rivera

I F THIS BOOK HAD BEEN PUBLISHED TEN YEARS AGO, THIS CATEGORY wouldn't exist. Until very recently there was a mere handful of BAD sports and news programming, things like *The Today Show* (when it costarred a chimpanzee), *Candid Camera* (when it was being excessively cruel), *Jalopy Races from Hollywood* (whose main attraction is car wrecks), *Your Funny Movies* (the grandfather of *America's Funniest Home Videos* and its brood), *The New York Times Youth Forum,* and *Parole*—certainly not enough to be worth a category.

Now, however, in the Golden Age of BAD TV, there are hundreds and hundreds of programs for our consideration. Network executives and cable producers have discovered what Ed Murrow knew all along—it's cheaper to send a reporter and a cameraman to Washington than it is to buy Linda Evans's new *Dynasty* shoulder pads—and so production of the pseudosports and the newslike has gone into overtime. Today, there are so many talk shows, so much "reality" programming, so much infotainment, so many docudramas, and three whole cable channels devoted only to sports, that the line between sports, news, and entertainment—the very thin line between television and day-to-day life—has been blurred to a small shadow. When did *Nightline* get its highest ratings? When the guest was none other than Madonna, talking about her "racy" *Justify My Love* video.

Noted critic Francis Davis has commented that "anybody in his right mind would prefer the company of his own friends (or solitude) to that of the celebrities welcomed by Arsenio or Leno or of the abuse victims exhibited by Oprah, Phil, and Sally Jessy"—but in fact this is far from true. Oprah Winfrey is a multigejillionaire from her brand of midwestern mom chat, and so many new talk shows are rushing onto the airwaves that this book's researchers could barely stay on top of them all.

Here's this section's special version of life:

- You are the only person in America not having kinky sex twenty-four hours a day.
- You are the only person in America not considering your transsexual surgery options.
- You are the only person in America not hosting your own talk show.
- It's common for great American athletes to have names like Nitro, Ice, and Blaze.

Against All Odds, 1992. From the producers of *Unsolved Mysteries* (but much, much worse) and featuring utterly humiliated host Lindsay *Bionic* Wagner, *Against All Odds* showcases true-life stories of "harrowing brushes with death!" First you watch actors performing not-very-dramatic re-creations of these harrowing brushes; then the real incredible people who endured the harrowing brushes come out of the audience and tell Lindsay, "Boy, that was scary!" and "After this happened, I really thought all about the preciousness of life!"

Against All Odds got its name from its ratings potential; NBC scheduled this "news show" opposite *60 Minutes*. One look will tell you what audience they were pursuing: people who found Andy Rooney too intellectual. If NBC is so frightened by CBS's Sunday lineup they stooped to airing this, why don't they just go off the air for the night?

—

American Gladiators, 1989. The women are beautiful, the men are musclebound, the clothes are tight, and the contests are peculiar: cargo-net climbing, batacca bat jousting, tennis ball shoot-outs, monkey ring-swinging, artificial wall-climbing, and, exclusively on *American Gladiators,* roll-the-hamster-ball-cage-into-the-crater-until-the-dry-ice-erupts.

Like all great BAD TV this show poses a mystery: What is it? Game show (since it has cash prizes), or sports program (since it has instant replays)? Do fans watch *American Gladiators* because they find the contests exciting (which makes it a sports program), or because they like seeing muscled-up women and/or men parading around in skintight outfits (which makes it a beauty tournament)? While combining sex with sports is nothing new (the original gladiators, after all, were nude), why *do* we love sweaty hunks and babes with cartoon names (Blaze, Ice, Diamond, Laser, Thunder, Nitro)?

A classic bound to be on the air for many years to come.

Ʌ Ʌ Ʌ Ʌ

American Muscle Magazine, 1989; The Arnold Classic, 1991; Mr. Olympia, 1985; Musclesport USA, 1991; World Bodybuilder Federation Bodystars, 1992. Bodybuilders may not be everyone's cup of tea, but bodybuilding on TV is no one's. The producers of these shows are terribly nervous that viewers won't take bodybuilding for the intensely serious sport that it is. So what should be very sexy, a little dramatic, and a lot of fun instead seems like something from PBS. The shows are sponsored (either directly or through ad support) by muscle magnates like Joe Weider and General Nutrition Center—which keeps them from offering anything newsworthy, unless it would be of great benefit to the advertisers (they were about the last, for example, to discuss the very serious problem of steroid abuse, which for many years was an epidemic). The outcome of all this is a relentlessly formal tone (which makes the shows fun only for musclemen and bodybuilders-to-be), and the lack of significant information (which keeps them from being worthwhile for musclemen and body-builders-to-be). Except for fishing and golf shows, is there anything more boring than looking at people work out?

View at your own risk.

Ʌ Ʌ

Ice, Turbo, Zap, Gemini, Blaze, Gold, Lace, Nitro, Laser, and Thunder: the original *American Gladiators* (Photofest)

—

Elizabeth R: A Year in the Life of the Queen, 1992. This two-hour-long *intimate* look at the Windsor family drew immense ratings in Britain, and it's only one more example of that country's continuing decline. What this film shows in agonizing detail is that the UK is spending a fortune to have a family dress up in expensive gowns and crowns, appear in public, and make lots and lots of small talk—and they can't even manage these minor tasks. Here, for example, is the president of Italy receiving a gift from the queen:

> **President:** This is for my wife?
> **Queen:** And that is for your wife.
> **President:** Oh, thank you very much, yes.
> **Queen:** Which is a small clock.
> **President:** A small clock.

The only moment in the whole program when Elizabeth looks like a person and not a robot is when she wins a few bucks playing the ponies—a real classy dame, that queen.

Ⱥ Ⱥ Ⱥ Ⱥ

Fan Club, **1991.** Most of the shows on cable's *E! Entertainment Channel* take advantage of Hollywood VPKs (video press kits); free material filled with unrevealing behind-the-scenes shots and not-so-subtle shilling. But every so often *E!* unintentionally explores America's darkest secrets.

Talk Soup (see page 251) reveals that watching too many daytime talk shows will eventually make you think you're the only one in America not having pervo sex twenty-four hours a day—or, at the very least, exploring your many transsexual surgery options. On *Fan Club,* host Jane Zappala tries to pretend everything's normal—while the program focuses on the frightening obsessions of hysterical fans (like a man who's turned an entire room of his home into a *Charlie's Angels* shrine, with pictures, posters, records, books, even a pinball machine featuring his tousled, jiggling goddesses). Watching *E!* means floating languidly on the pleasant creations of Hollywood publicists . . . until (like a great roller coaster) you plunge into the screaming madness of BAD TV.

Ⱥ Ⱥ

Female Gymnastic Dancing. Take a bunch of just barely pubescent girls, make them hit the gym until their bodies are as perfect as can be, outfit them in skimpy skintight spandex, teach them routines that look like half of the *Kama Sutra* . . . and if this isn't kiddie porn, then what is? At least the boy gymnasts are in high school, and their routines don't look like a sex-machine training film.

Ⱥ Ⱥ Ⱥ

———

Foul-Ups, Bleeps & Blunders, 1984. An ABC clone (with hosts Steve Lawrence and Don Rickles) of NBC's *TV's Bloopers & Practical Jokes* (hosted by Dick Clark and Ed McMahon), but without those key practical jokes.

⅃⅃

Girl of the Week, 1948. A Thursday-night paean to womanhood, which eventually switched to sports only and became *Sportswoman of the Week.*

Each episode was five minutes long.

⅃⅃

Hard Copy, 1989. When 1986's brand-new *A Current Affair* was one of the few brand-new certified hits on the brand-new Fox network, boy did everybody else in television notice. A raft of tabloid mimics hit the airwaves, each trying to outsleaze the other with a never-ending series of paid-for exclusives. Deciding the winner is immensely difficult; should it be *Inside Edition* (with the nymphomaniac and her pimp husband), *A Current Affair* (with the other women in the William Kennedy Smith case), *The Jerry Springer Show* (whose signature episode was titled "Women with Beards and Why They Won't Shave Them"), or *Hard Copy*—considered by *The Los Angeles Times* "the most repulsive show on television"?

The guests of these shows all talk in the lurid overhype made famous by the *National Enquirer,* the *New York Post* (with its famous HEADLESS BODY IN TOPLESS BAR headline) and circus sideshow barkers; like all of these, the content never lives up to the headlines. If you see a show featuring "dramatic re-creations" of soft-core porn and violence, or if a show reminds you of *Gallery, Argosy,* and *True Detective* magazines, you know you've hit tabloid territory. One even promised "two hours of UFOs, supernatural experiences, and a murder!"

Hard Copy's paid-for exclusives include a full half-hour of screaming Charles Manson, a three-show epic of cannibal Jeffrey Dahmer, Robert Chambers (of preppie "rough sex" murder fame) pulling the head off a doll, and, in a setup, Amy Fisher complaining she deserves a Maserati for all her misery, and debating whether or not she should get married immediately in order to enjoy conjugal prison sex. *Copy* seems, at the moment, to be the winner, but it's such a tight race.

There is however, good news; Americans seem to be getting tired of this particular form of trashertainment, since all these shows' ratings are way down. Could it be the tabloid era is coming to a close?

♟ ♟ ♟ ♟

***Hot Seat*, 1981.** The silver-haired, tin-tongued, and beyond-right-wing Wally George took his screamfest of a talk show from Pat Boone's Orange County, California, UHF station all the way to ABC, getting his fifteen minutes of fame by excoriating liberals, feminists, gays, and anyone mildly left of center who was willing to sit on the *Hot Seat*. Backed by an audience who screamed "Wall-ee! Wall-ee! Wall-ee! Wall-ee!" at the host, "Jerk! Jerk! Jerk! Jerk!" at the guest, and "Nuke the Fags!" whenever the spirit moved, Wally was the five-time divorced father of Rebecca De Mornay and, as a publicity hound, the Jayne Mansfield of his day. He'd do anything to get his name in lights, and the more provocative the guest, the better: after a Wally + audience screechout with an ex-Marine antiwar activist, the Marine walked offstage, throwing Wally's desk at him. The next day's headlines helped Wally's bruises heal all that much faster.

♟ ♟ ♟

***I Believe in Miracles*, 1966.** Where is the FCC when you need them? You won't believe they didn't do anything about these testimonies of "successful" faith healing from the relentlessly syrupy Kathryn Kuhlman (listening to her repeat the show's title over and over again will give you goose bumps of horror), who kept this racket going for ten long years.

♟ ♟ ♟ ♟

***I Witness Video*, 1992.** One day a man looked out of his window and saw some L.A. cops making an arrest; he got out his video camcorder and taped them as they brutally beat Rodney King. The tape, shown nationwide, outraged Americans; they were even more outraged when the policemen were acquitted, a decision that led to three days of rioting and looting in cities across the nation.

Could anyone but NBC News take this horrible story and turn it into TV entertainment? By itself, broadcasting amateurs' tapes of dramatic stories is a great idea, since the jerky movement and off-focus make them seem so much "realer" than the slickly produced video of network news (and lacking any network bias in reporting). But *I Witness Video* feels the need to pad and pad and pad out their tapes, and the endless padding is even more amateurish than the videos themselves; the host seems trained for game shows, and the writers obviously want to work for *A Current Affair.* Surrounded by the utter sincerity of the amateur videos, it only makes the whole thing seem artificial and suspicious.

What do critics think of *I Witness Video*? "The season's worst show of any sort" and "A symbol of everything that's wrong with television." What do viewers think? *I Witness* finds itself frequently in the Nielsen Top 20.

Jalopy Races from Hollywood, 1960. Noisy stock cars, screaming announcers, and "The Crack-up of the Week."

Jane, 1991. As the editor-in-chief of *Sassy,* Jane Pratt created a brilliant combination of *Seventeen, Tiger Beat,* and *Ms.* (all written in Valley teen girlspeak) that became one of the most successful new magazines in recent years. Her TV chat show, *Jane,* was supposed to appeal to eighteen-to thirty-four-year-old women, but gone is the distinct "sisters are doin' it for themselves" subtone of *Sassy.* Highlight episodes include "X-Rated Ways I Worked My Way Through College," "I Like Myself Better Fat," "Having Sex in My Parents' House," "My Roommate Is from Hell," and "My Boyfriend Loves Sports More Than Me"; the highest rated *Jane* ever is "I'm Not Stupid, Just Blonde."

On "Men Only Date Me for My Big Breasts," guest Christine (ID'd on camera with the line "Says Guys Think She's Slutty") was asked why, if she didn't like the attention she was getting because of her breasts, she wore such a revealing top. Christine: "I'm wearing this as an example of how people abuse you when you dress like this."

Jane's been canceled, but even with this show's poor ratings, Ms. Pratt immediately got herself another venue, *Jane Pratt Talk Show,* on Lifetime—which was just as immediately canceled (when asked about this on

Comedy Central, Pratt replied, "Lifetime sucks."). With her energy, ambition, and chalk-on-blackboard voice, though, don't be surprised if Jane returns.

♟ ♟ ♟ ♟

Lee Trevino's Golf for Swingers, **1972.** Mongrel sports/game show featuring noted celebrities going a few rounds with Mr. T.

♟ ♟

The Rush Limbaugh Show, **1992.** While the immensely popular Mr. Limbaugh (apparently the only mainstream Republican with a sense of humor now that Bill Buckley's turned into an old fust) cuts loose on his #1 radio show, his over-one-million-in-print book, and his "Limbaugh Letter," he doesn't seem to know what to do on TV. His show's only highlight is a split screen, showing a liberal doing nutty liberal stuff on one side and Rush making facial expressions on the other. Since the advertisers seem to be limited to *American Spectator* magazine, Alka-Seltzer Plus, and 1-800-LAWYERS, fans had better catch this while they can.

♟ ♟

McLaughlin, **1991.** Why NBC can't do a better job of mimicking CNN than the tepid effort that is CNBC is a great mystery; but what's even more mysterious is the existence of their evening and weekend talk shows—the only programs daring enough to pair G. Gordon Liddy with LaToya Jackson, Diana Nayad with Sylvia Miles, and the ultimate, *Crossfire*'s John McLaughlin with Brooke Shields.

McLaughlin is one of the great talk-show misfires of all time. While the guest sits, all alone, on a bare stage, the utterly hostile John stands with the audience and interrogates him or her mercilessly. McLaughlin obviously believes he can interview celebrities without knowing a single thing about Hollywood, and he doesn't seem to understand that, in a talk show, the guests are supposed to do the talking. This conversation is verbatim:

John McLaughlin: Don't you want to test yourself as an actress?
Brooke Shields: I can't imagine life without it.

M: You saw *The Silence of the Lambs*. Do you think you could have done that Jodie role?

S: Well, I don't like to make comparisons—

M: She went to Yale and you went to Princeton. . . . Do you think you could get on a motorcycle in leather? Could you be *La Femme Nikita*—that gangly assassin? Could you be Linda Hamilton in *Terminator*? Could you be Sigourney Weaver in *Alien*?

S: You'd be surprised.

M: Do you want to make a fitness tape?

S: No, I don't see myself that way.

M: Aren't you an entrepreneur?

S: Well, yes, you have to be—

M: All the beautiful women who've been on this show have been flat-out entrepreneurs. . . . Have you ever wondered why it is that black leaders never criticized Michael Jackson for bleaching himself?

⚏ ⚏ ⚏ ⚏

The Magnificent Marble Machine, 1975. You'll see it all! The ecstasy of triumph, the agony of defeat, and the pretty flashing lights—as celebrities play a giant pinball machine.

⚏ ⚏

Meeting of Minds, 1976. By TV standards Steve Allen is an intellectual, but that's the only thing that explains how he got this terrifying show on the air, even if it was only PBS. "My mind does not simply receive impressions," Allen said (as if everyone else's did). "It talks back to the authors, even the wisest of them; a response I'm sure they would warmly welcome." Not likely, since we found just how Allen's mind talks back as he wrote and (with wife Jayne Meadows) starred in *Meeting of Minds,* a panel talk show with guests like the Marquis de Sade, Florence Nightingale, Frederick Douglass, Voltaire, Cleopatra, Marie Curie, Martin Luther, and Plato—all of whom are still spinning in their graves (being dead, they can't sue).

Meeting isn't really news (since it has actors and scripts); but it doesn't fit any other category either; you can't help but think when you watch: *What is this?* One fan characterized it as: "Get Marie Antoinette out of there and let Hammurabi have his say!" Featuring stilted, pretentious dia-

Thomas Paine, Cleopatra, St. Thomas Aquinas, and Theodore Roosevelt can't wait to return from the dead for a *Meeting of Minds* **with emcee Steve Allen** (Photofest)

tribes, bad costumes, bad makeup and bad wigs, *Meeting* should have destroyed the careers of everyone (living) involved. TV at the time, however, was so impoverished when it came to anything remotely educational or uplifting that this horror ran for five years, had its scripts published, and won a number of awards.

♟ ♟ ♟ ♟

Miniature Golf Association of America Championships. If you're in grade school or college, or are an adult, you can compete for glittering golfball medals on the Pro Putt-Putt circuit. Not exactly riveting, even if you love watching golf on TV; the players don't wear the normal glow-in-the-dark golf pants, and the only pretty scenery is Astroturf.

♟ ♟

———

Monster Truck Challenge and Hot Rod Thrill Show Spectacular.
Broadcast daily on ESPN, this terrific show features big fat white men in
muffler-free pickups hoisted onto five-foot-tall, three-foot-wide, eight-
hundred-pound tires (with names like *Gravedigger, Predator,* and *Buffalo
Tremor*) racing on top of a row of junked cars. The stadium crowd goes
wild when one of the trucks tips over or crashes, and they especially love
the "Human Bomb" who gets into a wood box with some dynamite and
blows himself up.

If you want to learn all the techniques of the monster truck trade (such
as how to spend forty hours with a buddy cutting your treads to increase
traction and speed), write to Bob Fuchs, U.S. Hot Rod Association, 477
East Butterfield Road, #400, Lombard, Illinois 60148.

ıı ıı

The Morton Downey, Jr., Show, 1988. Another chaotic right-wing
screamfest like *Hot Seat* that asks the question: Which is more fun, chat
show or shout show? Here's how Downey (whose favorite epithet was
"Pablum puker") answered his critics: "You guys are filet mignon. I'm hot
dogs. Not everyone can eat filet mignon. Not everyone can understand
you." But when Downey showed up with a swastika shaved into his scalp
and said he'd been attacked by skinheads, even his diehard fans (who he
named "the Beast") turned against him.

ıı ıı ıı

The New York Times Youth Forum, 1952. A totally happenin' and excellent Sunday night show from that with-it journal of hip, *The New York
Times.*

ıı

Now It Can Be Told, 1991. Even though he helped pioneer a whole
category of television with *Geraldo,* Geraldo Rivera wants more. What he
wants is to be taken seriously as a journalist again, and so he created his
own version of *60 Minutes*—with *Now It Can Be Told.* Where Jerry used
to be happy investigating such crucial issues as "should your tax dollars
pay for sex-change operations?" now he wants to delve into the savings-

and-loan scandals and the RFK assassination. Sadly, Rivera can't give up all the qualities that made him the star he is today. Screaming overhype, quicky sound bites, and journalism lite all add to the fun of *Geraldo,* but when used by *Now It Can Be Told* on serious topics, the results are the ultimate in BAD TV: relentlessly boring. That's one complaint that could never be said before about Geraldo Rivera.

♟ ♟

Out of the Fiery Furnace, 1986. A classic work of PBS BAD TV— seven hours on the history of metal production.

♟

Parole, 1958. All the drama of actual parole hearings in your very own living room.

♟ ♟

The PTL Club, 1976. "My specific calling from God is to be a television talk-show host," said Jim Bakker. With avant-garde makeup artist and wife Tamara Faye LaValley (who had a bedwetting problem until she was in her mid-twenties), Jim started a Virginia Christian children's show, where Tammy herself handled puppet Susie Moppet (which the Bakkers created by burning the ears off of a Porky Pig toy and gluing a blond wig on its head). The mediagenic couple spent a few years hosting *The 700 Club* until finally finding their true calling by creating *PTL:* "Praise the Lord" with "People That Love."

PTL ultimately became the nation's third most prosperous religious broadcast (after Pat Robertson and Jimmy Swaggart), at its peak topping annual revenues of $66 million. The Bakkers' main religious themes seemed to be "God loves you" and "He thinks it's great to be rich." They apparently were sincere in these beliefs, spending $100 grand to fly their clothes across the country, buying such useful items as an air-conditioned doghouse and giraffes, and Jim bilking his broadcast congregation of $158 million—for which he was given a forty-five-year prison sentence.

♟ ♟ ♟ ♟

———

Real Personal, 1992. Finding BAD chat is like playing roulette. Many in the Nominating Committee have told us about remarkable horrors they've seen on one talk show or another, but when we've pursued those leads, the regular programs weren't anything more exciting than any *Oprah!* Perhaps the lowest chat-show moment of 1992 was, in fact, on the otherwise above-it-all *Donahue,* which for a brief, shining moment featured infantilism—Vietnam vets explaining why they like to sit in playpens, wear diapers, and get spanked. It's all in the topic and because of this, our current favorite is *Real Personal* on CNBC. Like all CNBC product *Real Personal* is bathed in a patina of respectability (with host Bob Berkowitz so network normal, he's Connie Chung–like), even as the most remarkable, kinky things are going on.

One evening, for example, found Average Joe Bob Berkowitz looking into the fact that ".01% of all births involve some form of hermaphroditism," and interviewing Glenda, a woman born with a penis and undescended testicles, who tells us that she broke her leg twice to keep from having to use the high-school locker room and be exposed, as well as that "I should have had corrective surgery but, like so many people, I lived in the closet." A caller from Massachusetts explains to Glenda how he can empathize completely with her, since he was born without testicles.

Doesn't this make you wonder: why is *everyone* in America willing to go on TV and reveal *everything*? And doesn't it make you want to order the videotape? (Just dial 1-800-398-CNBC.)

⛉ ⛉ ⛉ ⛉

Revival of America Crusade, 1975. The Reverend LeRoy Jenkins and his "Church of What's Happening Now" televangelist broadcasts were so bizarre that, on his show, comedian Flip Wilson redid them and we all thought they were parodies.

⛉ ⛉ ⛉

The Ring of Truth, 1987. Another it-could-only-be-from-PBS creation: six hours on the history of tools.

⛉ ⛉

———

***Ripley's Believe It or Not*, 1982.** Jack Palance, daughter Holly Palance, and "between jobs" Marie Osmond hosted this spin-off from the famous cartoon, a show whose material is so iffy it throws all "reality programming" into question. Strangely, for four years, we did believe.

⚑⚑ ⚑⚑ ⚑⚑

***The Seventh Sense*, 1978.** A talk show where all the guests were hypnotized.

⚑⚑ ⚑⚑ ⚑⚑

***Sneak Previews*, 1978.** This, the father of all movie reviewing programs, is actually a tragic story of abandonment. In 1982, when the four-year-old *Sneak Previews* became the highest-rated program in PBS history, famed hosts Gene Siskel and Roger Ebert ankled to the greener pastures of syndication with *At the Movies.* For reasons that are unclear, they then abandoned *At the Movies* and started *Siskel & Ebert at the Movies,* where they remain today.

In the wake of those ramblin' guys, the producers of *At* and *Sneak* tried desperately to keep things going. *At* dragged out Rex Reed, Bill Harris, and Dixie Whatley, and was finally sent to its grave in 1990; *Sneak* merged Jeffrey Lyons with Neal Gabler, then switched to Lyons and Michael Medved, who are there as of this writing. None of these new hosts, however, was ever able to have the wonderful drama of Siskel and Ebert, a couple whose underlying "you know we loathe each other and we know we loathe each other so let's just get on with it, okay?" tone is utterly compelling and makes for great TV.

Orphan *Sneak Previews* is now a tragic shadow of its once mighty self. Instead of the mythic, conflicted relationship of Siskel and Ebert, the tepid Lyons and Medved are needy, sensitive men inflicting their deepest, innermost feelings about movies on the helpless viewer. The show's very mild drama—cinema-studies squabbling—is now all scripted, which we know is true because L&M are both such remarkably bad actors. Lyons toils and strains to appear intelligent; Medved (who used to write wonderful books; his *Golden Turkey Awards* is in fact an ancestor of this volume) has obviously decided that a good idea for a film critic persona is to appear winsome and endearing—like Regis Philbin.

The whole thing is such a mess that you can't help but wonder: how do people like this get on TV . . . even if it is PBS?

🝙 🝙

Speak Up America, 1980. One of America's most disliked TV shows: child evangelist Marjoe Gortner and deafening cohost Rhonda Bates ask the man-on-the-street and their studio audience a bunch of goofy questions, with no one having anything interesting to say.

🝙

Star Games, 1985. In this, the worst of the "trashsports" genre (which includes BAD classics like *The Superstars, Battle of the Network Stars,* and *Us vs. the World*), Bruce Jenner, Pamela Sue Martin, and Morgan Brittany watch grade-Z TV celebrities in such thrilling contests as tug-of-war and swimming pool canoeing.

🝙 🝙 🝙

Summer Sunday USA, 1984. Another of NBC's endless attempts to create a successful *60 Minutes* imitation (and another proof that, as charming as she may be, host Linda Ellerbee should seek professional career counseling), *Summer Sunday USA* was scheduled opposite Mike 'n' Morley and broadcast live from various parts of the country (with probably the biggest number of technical gaffes of any show in network history).

🝙 🝙

Swimsuit USA: America the Beautiful, 1990. Albert Maysles and Susan Froemke, who worked on such classic documentaries as *Gimme Shelter* and *Grey Gardens,* are now directing HBO's annual backstage look at *Sports Illustrated*'s swimsuit issue. In the 1993 edition of *Swimsuit USA: America the Beautiful,* one segment concerns the adventures of bikinied supermodels Vendela Kirsebom and Ashley Richardson being photographed in the snow. While Vendela tries to stay warm by standing as close to a heater as she can get, Ashley comments, "She's barbecuing her butt, and, I might add, what a nice butt it is too." When Vendela decides it's too damn cold and calls off the shoot, Ashley looks directly at the camera and announces, "Vendela's not a very professional super-model."

Talk Soup, 1992. A brilliant remake of *Headline News* for tabloid TV addicts, *E!*'s *Talk Soup* is the greatest hits from the previous day's *Attitudes, CBS This Morning, Donahue, Geraldo, Good Morning America, Jane, Jenny Jones, Larry King Live, Oprah!, Sally Jessy Raphael, Joan Rivers, Sonya Live, Jerry Springer, Today, Montel Williams* et al. A mere week included "Wives Who Hate Oil Wrestling," "American Gladiators Bare All," "Joan Rivers Impersonators," "Children of Psychiatrists," "Sex with Teachers," "Teens Who Dress Weird," "Men Who Are Virgins," "In-Law Incest," "Celebrity Siblings," "Pregnant Wife Abusers," "Dating *Playgirl* Centerfolds" and "Body-Pierced Circus Stars." This show is the *ne plus ultra* of contemporary television: sound bites only; a wonderful example of how the media now endlessly cannibalizes itself; and an alarming look at the ceaselessly lurid "reality" portrayed on daytime TV. Watching too much of it will make you think you're the only living American not having wild sex twenty-four hours a day.

Television, 1988. The snooty Brits at Granada Television produced this inane look at TV and PBS absurdly imported it, replacing the Limey narrator with the equally pretentious Edwin Newman. Since the only decent popular culture the Brits have ever produced is American-rhythm-and-blues imitators like the Rolling Stones, what interesting things could they have to say about our television? Next to nothing, but this show is a fascinating look at how, when people feel intensely superior to something, they don't understand it at all—perhaps another factor in the decline of the British empire.

That's Incredible!, 1980; Incredible Sunday, 1988. A *Ripley's Believe It or Not* clone, hosted by a BAD galaxy of stars (John Davidson, Cathy Lee Crosby, and Fran Tarkenton) and featuring many guests who were later proved to be frauds, all done by Alan Lansburg, producer of *Those Amazing Animals, People Do the Craziest Things, In Search*

Of . . . , and *Life's Most Embarrassing Moments.* With such horrors as a man running through flames in an asbestos suit (destroying his hands) and a motorcyclist doing a jump (breaking his legs and hips), *That's Incredible* brought us to new lows. The show did, however, give us two of BAD TV's all time great moments: the line "Kids, don't try this at home," and the man who ate a bicycle.

Today's Black Woman, 1981. Singer Freda "Band of Gold" Payne gets her own TV show, but sadly it's not up to the standards of *Like It Is,* and only lasts one season.

Tractor Super Pull-Offs. A regular on ESPN, this hobby is one of the great unsung American crafts, testing who can engineer and drive the world's greatest tractor ever. In front of a stadium filled with tractor enthusiasts, atop giant, six-engined, fire-spewing, brutally noisy machines (a cross between dragsters, low riders, tractors, and jalopies, which by contest rules can't be heavier than 8,200 lbs.), American farmers push the pedal to the metal to drag (or not drag) a giant weight-filled plow. To date the biggest winner at these events is a woman, Rodalyn Knox; because of her feats of derring-do she's become known as "The First Lady of Unlimited Modified Pulling."

Traffic Court, 1958. From ABC—the "why not give it a try?" network—actors stretching their talents in performing dramatic reenactments of stories based on real life: parking in a no-parking zone, exceeding the speed limit, failing to signal, and other remarkable motor-vehicle violations.

The Ukrainian Melody Hour, 1989. Leased-time access ethnic news show broadcast mostly via PBS affiliates in downtime. There's no melody to speak of (save the music videos from local folksinging groups, which a fan has nicknamed "The Dancing Pierogies") and it's not an hour—but it *is* in Ukrainian.

ı. ı.

USA Today: The Television Show; USA Today on TV, 1988. Media experts uniformly guffawed when Gannett launched "USA Today," which quickly went into the black by finding a real niche as both the light, frothy alternative to mainstream newspapers, and something that would (with quick bits and graphics) be more competitive with television. *USA Today: The Television Show* was the first project launched by widely acknowledged TV genius Grant Tinker after leaving the chairmanship of NBC (and leading that network to #1 for six consecutive years). With the involvement of Tinker, the resources of Gannett, and the backing of Gannett's ten owned and operated television stations, media experts this time expected an instant hit.

No one, though, seemed to consider that the last place that needed more light, frothy stuff was television, or that it didn't make much sense to bring a TV-ized newspaper to nightly TV viewers. Also, Tinker had no experience in news programming and the show's producer (though widely acclaimed for his work on the *Today* show), had only originated one program before: the catastrophic *Summer Sunday USA*. As *Entertainment Weekly* reported:

> *The average show aired 30 stories in 23 minutes. Charts, statistics, and polls flashed across the screen, lighting it up like a pinball machine, and the newfangled standing anchors, unbound by desks, appeared to be as relaxed as mannequins. The program that was supposed to attract the fidgety MTV generation succeeded only in giving its audience motion sickness. . . . A news nightmare.*

Widely considered one of the biggest flops in the history of broadcasting, *USA Today: The Television Show* would eventually cost Gannett over $50 million in losses.

ı. ı. ı.

A View of the White House by H. R. Haldeman, 1981. Highlights of felon Haldeman's home movies of the Nixon years.

ı. ı. ı.

———

Wrestlemania, 1990. *Professional* wrestling, almost exactly as we know it today, has been around since the earliest moments of TV history. Its popularity increased dramatically, however, when boxing turned more safety conscious and less bloodthirsty (*pace* Muhammad Ali's brain damage), and it got harder and harder to find a decent rooster or dogfight venue. Amazingly, it wasn't until the past few years that you got the opportunity to pay thirty dollars a pop to see world-class wrestling on pay-per-view television—with *Wrestlemania.*

Wrestlemania combines the sleaze of the early days with the heightened theatrics we've come to expect from today's sideshows. By toning down the violence and toning up the characterizations (though who can compete with Gorgeous George?), *Wrestlemania* elevates the biggest of the trash-sports—where *to do a job* means to deliberately lose and *work* means to fake something—to all-new heights of show biz.

Many ignorant eggheads think wrestling's core fans believe it's all true, but (except for very young children) that's impossible. This is a sport, after all, that involves cartoon heroes and villains (surrounded by cartoon mobster-managers) with names like Sergeant Slaughter, the Ultimate Warrior, and the Legion of Doom, wearing makeup and costumes (featuring acid-colored tights) and breaking every rule in the book (getting hissed and cheered in the process) to triumph over their equally well dressed adversaries in screaming, year-long feuds.

Professional wrestling is the only sport left where anything can and will happen; the only one left where you wonder if the referee will get out undamaged; the only one left with all the appeal of a magic show: You know it can't be real, but how do they do it? How do they take all that pounding, punching, arm-twisting, leg-bending action . . . and come out alive?

ₐₐ ₐₐ ₐₐ ₐₐ ₐₐ

You Asked for It, 1950–1959; You Asked for It, Again, 1972; The New You Asked for It, 1981. This program's host defined it best:

> *The show that dares to ask the question: "Can a woman hang upside down by her toes from an airplane?" And follows it with the more pressing question: "Why would she want to?"*

With features like a horse-and-goat chiropractor, good Samaritans, odd magic acts, audience plants with prepped questions, squirrels on water skis, and pseudodocumentary parodies (such as 1950s newsreel footage of a senior-citizen circus performer and the host claiming it's the hundred-year-old Rose Kennedy), *You Asked for It* and its progeny are the last words in mild. If your question was used on the 1950s version, your picture was superimposed on the sponsor's product: a jar of Skippy peanut butter.

▲▲ ▲▲

Your Local News Show, 7:00 P.M., EST. Have you noticed how creepy the local news slots have gotten? There's a very good reason why. Save for the *Eyewitness News* format (where Geraldo-like screaming and MTV-flashy graphics are the order of the day), most of the local station news outlets base themselves on the Walter Cronkite/David Brinkley model. The sets and design try to appear clean and honest, while the anchors soothe us with their friendly, steady eyes and their smooth, even speech, projecting an air of upbeat sincerity—sometimes punctuated by a momentary note of concern.

One of the great spectacles of modern times is that, currently, it's the tabloid-style material that makes for good ratings on these shows—material that doesn't at all jibe with the news staff's aspirations. Your anchors want to be reporting from the White House, the Kremlin, or even a war-torn Third World country; instead, they have to strive to appear professional and sophisticated, cool and mature, while saying things like "Residents on the South Shore were horrified this morning when two newborn Siamese twins were rescued from a discarded refrigerator abandoned off of Highway 102." And *that's* the lead story. This difference, between where they are and where they want to be, is so strong that it becomes uncomfortable to watch, freighting the news with tension and discomfort—exactly what the Cronkite/Brinkley team was trying to avoid at all costs in the first place.

If you find these shows disturbing, you could wait and wait until some station manager figures out a solution. Or you could watch CNN.

The Yule Log. For many, many years one syndicator's contribution to programming on Christmas Eve (and a way to give practically all its employees the night off) was to run a three-minute, close-up, endlessly repeating loop of a burning log, making your home TV set an electronic fireplace—and a must-watch for drug-induced teens. Thankfully, *The Yule Log* has returned to all our cable Christmas Eves—on the *Home Shopping Club*.

♟ ♟ ♟

♟

And the Tammi for worst all-time news and sports show goes to:

Primetime Live, **1989.** Like a thing from another planet this show has dragged its carcass through four years of airtime, constantly meta-morphosing itself in a pathetic and miserable attempt to win our love. Hosted by the wildly overrated America's Junior Miss of 1963 Diane Sawyer and the aggressively overbearing Sam Donaldson, the original show had a studio audience, the two anchors working together, and a big emphasis on being "live." Since it was broadcast at 10:00 P.M. EST, there were very few "live" things to do, so that was dropped. The studio audience wasn't utilized for anything worthwhile, and they vanished. The filler chitchat written for the two hosts was remarkably low grade—in fact, it seemed to everyone watching at home that they hated each other's guts—so Sam moved to D.C., while Nixon speechwriter Diane carried on from New York. Early shows included an utterly incompetent interview with the ubiquitous Roseanne Barr, which made Diane look like she'd just arrived from Mars. Perhaps by the time you read this, ABC will let this creature die, and give Ms. Sawyer a way to earn her immense salary.

♟ ♟ ♟ ♟ ♟ ♟

Every network would put on a live execution if that would up the ratings, and Fox would put on naked executions.

—Gary David Goldberg, producer,
Moonlighting and *Brooklyn
Bridge*

**Sam and Diane prepare to commit another nationwide
atrocity with *Primetime Live* (Photofest)**

Let me get this straight. You put on your newest training bra and
your best uniform, and go out—*at night*—to houses where
you've never been, and you say, "Would you like to buy my cookies?" Now, are you really selling *cookies*?

—*TV Guide* parody of Mike Wallace
interviewing a Girl Scout

The Worst Overall Network Programming Nominees

Watching prime-time TV [during the sweeps] is like being trapped in Sleaze City's tackiest honky-tonk. One gets a warped and depressing view of what it means to be alive.

—Tom Shales, *The Washington Post*

IN THE EIGHTIES, JUST LIKE EVERYONE ELSE, THE TV NETWORKS TRIED to spend themselves into happiness, with such megabombs as the multi-million-dollar *War and Remembrance* as the results. Now TV execs have a new economic theory (with equally disastrous results): If the programming is cheap enough, it doesn't matter that hardly anybody wants to watch; we'll make money anyways!

This practice is amply demonstrated in this category, where cheesy rubbish is the order of the day. Soon enough we'll probably be getting four or five all-infomercial channels, following in the footsteps of the *Home Shopping Network*. Why even bother trying to lure an audience with creative programming, when you can just run ads all day and all night?

⚐⚐

The Discovery Channel and Lifetime for **AMA TV, 1990;** *Lifetime Medical Television,* **1990.** If you're a remote-control surfer who likes to scan through all the channels just groovin' on the wild diversity of today's television, beware! You may suddenly be thrust into searing, grody close-ups of squirming, dripping, greasy internal organs, cataract removals, third-degree-burn-victim skin grafts, and open-heart surgery—all courtesy of the American Medical Association and "The Network for Physicians *Only*."

Shown on Sundays and available on both The Discovery Channel and Lifetime, the lineup includes *Allergy Diary, Diabetic Hypertension, Obstetrics and Gynecology Update,* and *The Vein Graft Hour.* Learn the how-tos of hip-replacement surgery in the privacy of your own home, and feel just like a qualified M.D.! A highlight: announcers talking at the speed of sound listing the very many horrifying side effects of the advertised drugs.

⚏ ⚏ ⚏

Bravo. When cable first began to go beyond bringing TV to the antennae-troubled hinterlands and create its own programming, there was much promise that it would support the arts in a brave new way, and both A&E (Arts and Entertainment) and Bravo were launched to do just that. A&E immediately abandoned its "Arts" half, while Bravo became the mythic land where PBS rejects, incomprehensible BBC imports, and obscure opera productions starring divas you never heard of go to die. If the channel goes out on a limb and pays for something worthwhile, it's repeated often enough to drive Bravo's subscribers insane.

⚏ ⚏ ⚏

USA for **The Divorce Court Clones:** Once referred to as The *Miami Vice* Network, USA is now commonly called The *MacGyver* Channel, since it seems like anytime you tune in, there's *MacGyver* (just as, with all its World War II documentaries, A&E is frequently referred to as The Hitler Network). A careful look at USA's schedule, however, reveals that there's only two hours daily of *MacGyver,* but there's three whole hours daily of faux courtroom drama, and so a new name is in order—perhaps Court Channel II.

Start your day on USA with a full hour of the BAD Classic, *Divorce Court* (which, as you'll recall, is presided over by a real retired California jurist), and then go on to two of the oddest shows on the air. While *The Judge* (1986) claims to be a family-court venue whose cases are so sensitive, they are closed to the public, instead Judge Robert Franklin (not a real retired California jurist) hears it all: from adoption squabbles to campaign-fund commingling, kidnapping, mental-home commitments, even manslaughter. His opinions and solutions are so helpful and benevolent, he's the dad we never had, like Robert Young in *Father Knows Best* and *Marcus Welby, M.D.*—combined into one role.

Next comes *Superior Court* (1989), headed by the glaring Raymond St. Jacques (who's also not a real retired California jurist), and is strangely a fictionalized version of *The People's Court* (1981), frequently found competing in the time slot on another channel and headed up by Joseph Wapner, a real retired California jurist. Both specialize in low-class, Snopesy, trailer-park-denizen disputes except that, on *Superior Court,* they're portrayed by gorgeous soap-star types, while on *People's,* unfortunately, you have to look at the dreggy, real-life plaintiffs and defendants themselves, which of course takes us directly to the ultimate *Divorce Court* clone (see "Court TV").

Court TV. Is there anything more wonderfully BAD than when someone on TV tries to tell us we're watching high-minded, elevating material, but we know that it's all just cheap voyeuristic trash? Nothing better sums up the programming on Court TV, with its fainting women, glaring killers, and revelation of why *Divorce Court* is such a great show.

With a great case to cover, Court TV is the best. When the various witnesses and the accused hit the stand, you can watch their eye movements, gestures, and tones of voice to try to guess whether or not they're lying and whether or not they're guilty. Especially tasty are the news updates on your favorite prisoners, in case you'd lost touch with what's going on in the daily lives of Charles Manson or Jean Harris.

When it's not a case you care about, however, the channel is really in trouble, with the problem being that people good at law and order aren't necessarily successful at entertainment. Lawyers in real life serve justice by exposing the truth; they serve us viewers, however, by publicly humiliating and entrapping their subjects. Court TV's experts on various legal matters don't inspire confidence or provide sparkling entertainment; they all look like people dressed up as lawyers for Halloween.

Without a case you personally find riveting, Court TV is relentlessly tedious; the Weather Channel of news services. Perhaps there are some moments that aren't like watching paint dry, but the "live" broadcasts of courtroom nondrama, coupled with the unbuttered-toast quality of the hosts and guests, make this channel transcend its competition in BADness. Try this simple experiment: turn the lights down low, don't read, don't talk, don't answer the phone or the doorbell, don't allow any distractions; just sit and watch this channel. How long will it take before you either fall asleep . . . or lose your mind?

If you like to have TV on in the background the way other people like to have music on in the background, however, there isn't a channel or show that demands less attention than Court TV.

ıı ıı ıı ıı

CBS for *Crime Time After Prime Time,* **1991.** There's very little in the entertainment world as bad as watching an action-adventure that's not active, adventurous, or suspenseful. See for yourself with the grade-Z movies now showing endlessly on HBO, Cinemax, Showtime, and The Movie Channel, since you can no longer "enjoy" *Crimetime After Primetime.* While waiting for David Letterman to finish his NBC contract, CBS obviously decided to give up on programming for the wee hours, and so offers *Sweating Bullets, Dark Justice, Forever Knight, Urban Angel, Dangerous Curves,* and other exhausted, derivative also-rans.

Considering this dereliction of duty, should we allow "the Tiffany web" to continue calling itself a network? Even Fox at its shakiest moments wouldn't air this passel of deadbeats.

ıı

The E! Entertainment Channel. One of the 1980s' many wonderful inventions is the video press kit, whereby hard-pressed broadcasters can slip into something quick and free, never bothering to mention on-air that what you're watching is produced by the subject and not the channel. The E! Channel's entire programming philosophy seems to be: What can we get for free, and how much of it can we air without being publicly attacked? Trying to find something actually produced by E! (or at the very least requiring the channel to pay a permissions fee) is almost impossible; practically the whole thing is video press kits and quid pro quo rebroadcasting. Even E!'s greatest contribution to culture, *Talk Soup,* is overtly free clips provided in exchange for an on-air promo squib.

To put this channel into true perspective, just watch it for a while and remember your monthly cable bill. E! may not pay, but you will.

ıı ıı ıı

———

Leased Access Sex Ads. In the future the late eighties and early nineties may be remembered as a time when Americans spent millions of dollars on phone sex (with everyone not doing it buying a copy of the novel *Vox* and engaging in the ultimate "secondhand" experience: *vicarious phone sex*). Repeated thousands of times nightly on the leased access cable channels, today's 900 and 970 phone-sex operations fight it out with real escort services in promising that everything you can think of (and some things that never occured to you) are available twenty-four hours a day, seven days a week, with all major credit cards accepted.

Here are New York City's best of the worst (and most successful, judging by their number of years in business):

> **Geisha-to-Go:** *"Available by the hour, they will entertain you in the finest traditions of Eastern hospitality."*
>
> **970-KATHY:** *"Meet Kathy's glamorous TVs and she-males in an encounter so stimulating, you may never return to the real world!"*
>
> **970-MISS:** *"The only live S&M line. Call! Obey! Do it now! Accept your punishment!"*
>
> **970-PEEE:** *"The thrill of uncontrollable passion! The extra* e *is for extra pee!"*
>
> **970-XTSY:** *"Push 1 for coeds, 2 for lesbian lovers, 3 for Kinky and her friends, 4 for she-males, 5 for the Latino connection, or 6 for Mistress Diane!"*

This last is our favorite, since you know that there's only two women working these lines. Imagine the arguments:

"No way; I was Kinky and her friends last night; *you* have to do it tonight."

"But I've been practicing Mistress Diane all day!"

📺 📺 📺

Everyone involved for **Drowning in Nostalgia.** As should be obvious by now, the creators of this book really are the world's biggest fans of nostalgia; in fact, we want to remember *everything*. There is, however, a disturbing trend now engulfing the nation's airwaves that will soon reach epidemic proportions. It seems as if every TV exec in the country is asking: why bother coming up with anything new when you can take a bunch of old stuff out of the vaults? The costs you save in programming more than make up for the reduced audience and ratings.

On syndication you can see decades-old repeats of *The Ed Sullivan Show,* on the nets there are two hours of Lucille Ball's home movies and a *Laugh-In* anniversary remembrance; weekends on A&E there's usually a *Rockford Files* retrospective, or something of equal merit. This strategy is in particular employed by CBS, which regularly airs specials like the recent *Hollywood Palace* and *Carol Burnett Show* retros. It's also a strategy in vogue with The Nostalgia Channel, Nick at Night, The Cartoon Network, The USA Network, and during the day on TNT and TBS. On major American holidays like Thanksgiving and Super Bowl Sunday we now have marathons of programming; ten hours and more of *The Beverly Hillbillies, Bonanza, Gilligan's Island, I Love Lucy, Mary Tyler Moore, Mayberry R.F.D., The Twilight Zone,* and (for those who can really remember the good old days) sixteen hours of *The Jewel in the Crown.*

While it is, as Nick at Night likes to state over and over again, great to have all these old shows back and preserve our television heritage, will this trend drown out new programming? Will we end up with a few prime-time hours of original material, and spend the rest of our TV days wallowing in our broadcast pasts?

⚜ ⚜ ⚜

The Weather Channel. The only time anyone needs to watch TWC is when imminent disaster or close to it is about to strike. This puts the Weather Channel owners in the ethically dubious position of constantly praying for hurricanes, tornadoes, blizzards, and tsunami to spur on those ratings!

⚜ ⚜

⚜

And the Tammi goes to:

The Family Channel. Are you overwhelmed by network television . . . because it's too exciting? Are you afraid to let your children watch *The Brady Bunch* . . . because the Brady parents are remorselessly widowed? Do you think there's too much battle-between-the-sexes on *Home Improvement*? Too much politics on *Murphy Brown*? Too much drama on *Firing Line*? Now there's a channel just for you.

Besides its breakthrough Sandra Dee and Debbie Reynolds *Tammy* film festival (surely a first) and the magnificent *That's My Dog!* (a game show for dogs), the Family Channel's "Positive Place" lineup is a collection of remakes that directly imitate a successful show the way a castrato imitates a man. They're programs that aren't allowed to be too dramatic or too funny because, of course, then they might not be "wholesome." *Big Brother Jake* (starring exercise entrepreneur Jake Steinfeld) is *Charles in Charge,* but without *Charles*'s wild, provocative controversy. *Maniac Mansion* is *The Addams Family,* without that show's emphasis on perverse sex (the *Maniac* writing and acting are so poor, it's like a showcase for the mildly retarded—a sitcom version of the Special Olympics). We'd rather watch your family's home videos than *The New Zorro* (a live-action remake of *The Frito Bandito*) and *Rin Tin Tin, K-9 Cop* must be an adventure series for heart patients—can't let them get *too* excited. All in all, the Family Channel's deep mystery is: just who is watching this stuff?

▲▲ ▲▲ ▲▲ ▲▲ ▲▲ ▲▲

Lack of money is the true root of all evil.

—Reverend Ike, televangelist

The Infomercial Nominees

Never miss a chance to have sex or appear on television.

—Gore Vidal

Today, PLENTY OF PEOPLE MAKE NASTY, UNWARRANTED COMMENTS about infomercials, copping attitude as if the TV world should operate like Time, Inc.'s famous separation of church and state, and never allow advertising to mingle with editorial. What they're forgetting is that, during what everyone thinks of as the Golden Age of Television when the sponsors produced almost all major programming, there was an immense overlap of entertainment and advertising, and not a discouraging word was heard about *Texaco Star Theater* (which started the broadcast career of Mr. Television himself, Milton Berle), *Kraft Television Theatre,* or *The Hallmark Hall of Fame*—all now considered great classics.

During that earlier Golden Age, for instance, Danny Thomas couldn't refer to Winston Churchill as a member of Parliament on *Make Room for Daddy* because his cigarette sponsor didn't want a competing brand name appearing in its show. Studebaker forced a variety program to fire its band singer, Joey Nash, because Nash was the name of another car company, and Ronson deleted references to matches throughout a *Playhouse 90* script, substituting lighters instead.

Besides the fact that great informercials are great BAD television, there are a number of important services they provide. Some people are overwhelmed by shopping in malls and department stores; there are so many, many things to buy, and such hard choices to be made. On infomercials and home shopping shows all the thousands of products are shown, clearly and simply, one at a time, and the only decision is: Will I dial that phone? Besides, where would American civilization be today without cubic zirconia, Black Hills gold, diamanté brooches, marcasite, and faux suede?

Americans are allowed to play Lotto in the crazy belief there's a chance in hell they'll win; why not let them get excited over a big, shiny, fun commercial, buy things over the phone, and have the nutty idea they're getting a good, useful product and a great deal? Since on plenty of stations (such as The Family Channel) the commercials are more exciting than the programs, why not let the people who really know what they're doing do it all? Finally, if some people are dumb enough to confuse an infomercial with a regular TV show, don't they deserve to get taken to the cleaners?

Infomercials are a mere twenty years old, and it's amazing how wonderful they've become in such a short, short time. There are over twenty thousand of them being broadcast today, and many are huge money-makers; with Richard Simmons grossing $40 million from "Deal A Meal," Anthony Robbins getting $100 million from *Personal Power,* and Victoria Jackson doing $150 million of "Beauty Breakthroughs." Why are they so great? No one could say it better than pop-culture aficionados Jane and Michael Stern:

> *. . . the fact is that [infomercials] are an example of television doing what television does best: numbing viewers into a trance that is equal parts passivity and greed. When they work, infomercials give you the craving to buy something, but take away your will to get it any way other than by dialing the 800 number that flashes on the screen. . . .*
>
> *Where is the joy of going shopping in a store, where merchandise just sits, gathering dust, and surly clerks ignore customers? Infomercials are successful because they have restored the lost thrills of salesmanship to shopping. Sit back and relax, and watch Richard Simmons blubber his little heart out, see Mike Levy gasp in awe at the incredible car wax that protects a bright red Rolls-Royce even when it is set on fire. . . . In real life you never meet people who work so darn hard for your money, and that is why it is almost impossible not to be at least a little impressed by their pitch.*

⅃⅃

Amazing Discoveries. The great heritage that is Ronco ("the amazing Veg-O-Matic!") and Ginsu knives ("But wait! There's more!") has been passed on to this terrific show, which features a wildly enthusiastic (and well-paid) audience, an amazed-with-pleasure, rah-rah host, at least one "recognized expert," a three-part stage (like a three-ring circus, but for demonstrations), and a never-ending series of remarkable products. One of our favorites is, of course, the star of *Wayne's World*—the Flowbee (a do-it-yourself haircutter that you attach to your vacuum):

"How did you get this wonderful idea?" asks the hyperenthusiastic host.

"Well," replies the resourceful inventor, "one day, I was playing with my hair with the vacuum!"

When juicing became a craze (primarily via another infomercial, Mr. Juiceman), *Amazing Discoveries* immediately discovered the Juice Tiger, which, as you know, is "effective in preventing certain types of life-threatening cancer!" Noted expert Jack LaLanne says, "I could spend an *hour* telling you the nutritional values of strawberries—it's incredible!"

Besides juice the Juice Tiger makes "guilt-free frozen desserts" (which look like a scoop of dyed mashed potatoes on an ice cream cone). When a mob of children from the compensated audience is brought onstage and each given one of these amazing desserts, none of them eats it. It's finally explained that a great benefit of the Juice Tiger is in making "pulp for baking"—which is like saying that a great benefit of an automatic coffeemaker is in making hot, wet coffee grounds.

The audience applauds, wildly.

Beauty Breakthroughs II: For the 90s. Not the glamorous *Saturday Night Live* bimbo but the "world-class Hollywood makeup artist" Victoria Jackson, along with shills Ali McGraw, Meredith Baxter Birney, and Lisa Hartman, seek your aid in building Victoria's $150 million-plus cosmetics empire.

Bedazzle!, 1991. If your clothes are looking tired, plain, and boring, don't throw them away—*Bedazzle!* them with the Bedazzler Gemstone Applicator, which attaches thousands of multicolored rhinestones to any fabric in your home.

———

The Big Green Clean Machine. Do you need a vacuum cleaner so powerful, it can pick up a bowling ball? *Helpful Hinter* Mary Ellen Pinkham thinks so.

▲▲ ▲▲ ▲▲

BluBlocker Sunglasses. The show that makes you think, *My family and I are the only people in the world not wearing these sunglasses.*

▲▲ ▲▲

***The Cash Flow System* (featuring the *National Foreclosure Network*).** If you don't understand how Sheetrock installer Dave del Dotto became a self-made millionaire and the best-selling author of *How to Make Nothing But Money,* lei-wearer John Davidson wants to explain it all for you. Like Dave you, too, will soon learn the ins and outs of investing Other People's Money in real estate, move to Hawaii, and wear chartreuse jackets on the beach.

▲▲ ▲▲ ▲▲ ▲▲

Focus on Beauty. Cher's best friend Paulette was sad; instead of a hairdo, she had a hairdon't. Guess she didn't watch that *included-with-every-order-absolutely-free!* videotape, "What the Heck Am I Going to Do with My Hair?" Lori Davis came to the rescue anyway with Lori Davis Clarifier, Lori Davis Crystalline Shine, Lori's Perfection Deep Conditioner, and Lori Davis Memory Hold.

Bewigged Cher exclaims, "I'm really excited to help you bring these fabulous products to the people! I can't *believe* that you can make these products for half of what *I've* been paying!"

"My clients will pay for anything that I make because they trust me," replies Lori.

Toupee-wearer Larry Hagman says, "She made my career! Isn't she wonderful? And she's so kind to me. Making all these products that I can use and pay for!"

"I could lose my agent, I could lose my lawyer, but if I lost her, my career would be over," comments rug-topped Ted Danson.

If Cher, Ted, and Larry's wigs use Lori's wondrous products . . . shouldn't yours?

ʌ ʌ ʌ ʌ

The Home Shopping Club. The original, and still the best. For sales-manship no one pulls out all the stops like this magnificent piece of BAD TV. All the products are "in a very limited quantity"; suspicious "retail value" and "quantity sold" numbers are always shown; there's a chance for callers to win money with a wheel of fortune; and a clock ticks off, meaning that at some point you won't be allowed to buy, no matter what, if you don't *act now*!

The Home Shopping Club loves nothing more than a shiny piece of jewelry, and when you're in the *Club,* you're in a magical place where a necklace is never just a necklace; it's an "eighteen-inch-long Superflex Spring Supreme Herringbone with a full, generous 6.6 grams and lobster-claw clasp. Don't even think of missing this one! I can't go lower than this! This is a gold giveaway! You buy a car and in six, seven years, what do you have? The bones are so fine, you can hardly even see them, but yet for $130, you can have it for a lifetime, an absolute lifetime! You can't afford not to call! Evelyn, what would you tell people about this price?"

"I just could not believe it!"

Video retail is now a $2.2 billion industry; but why is it so popular? As the *New York Times* reported:

> *Delores King, a homemaker from Atlanta, says she used to keep the [Home Shopping] network on all day while she did her chores around the house. "It was exciting," she says. "My friends would watch it, and we would call each other and talk about what was on the air." At one point King got so caught up in the excitement, she spent thousands of dollars on sweaters and cosmetics. "My husband got mad," she says. "He suggested it would be a good idea to stop. Now, it's just a bad memory."*
>
> *Peggy Secaur, 52, is probably more typical. She says she started watching Home Shopping when she had an extended illness that kept her awake at night. Secaur got a charge out of the now-or-never pressure and also liked having someone to talk to at 3:00 A.M. "I would just get up at night and go shopping," she says. "I enjoy the sense of community. There are a lot of lonely, sickly people out there, and the club gives them someone to talk to."*

Isn't it wonderful that television can be someone's friend? And isn't it too bad that that same friend is a salesman. . . .

ʟ ʟ ʟ

How to Get the Woman You Want, 1993. With his goatee, his op-art sweater, and his Santa Fe–styled apartment, Richard Grant seems born to play a therapist on TV—which is exactly what he does by hosting "For Men Only," a Robert Bly–type discussion group featuring a group of guys even you wouldn't date (one looks just like an aged Eddie Munster). They are all not even remotely believable living proofs of the amazing results you can achieve with this wildly expensive successor to that irritating best-seller, *How to Pick Up Girls.* "Less than what you would spend on one disappointing date!"—$89.95—gets you ten audiocassettes, one videocassette, and "a confidential pocket guide" that "takes the fear out of talking to women," but don't worry, "our operators will handle your order discreetly."

While the host constantly discusses being sensitive to women's feelings and other Alan Alda–type relationship concepts, the show sends these scary guys out trawling for women on a "dating Olympics" monitored by a "hidden camera" with each's goal to return with as many phone numbers as he can snag. A masterpiece.

ʟ ʟ ʟ ʟ

Kleen-Cap, 1992. If you've got a big collection of gimme caps and they're covered in grime and sweat stains and pizza grease and you don't know what to do, thank goodness they've invented the Kleen-Cap Baseball Cap Washing Frame, which allows you, the frequent cap wearer, to get those caps sparkling clean in your very own dishwasher.

ʟ ʟ

The Love Phone. If Jessica Hahn is woman enough for Jim Bakker, aren't she and her "Love Phone Lovelies" women enough for you?

ʟ ʟ

Playboy's Secrets of Making Love. A video remake of *The Joy of Sex* for people afraid to buy real porn.

ʟ ʟ ʟ

—

The Psychic Friends Network. Are you living too active a life to make it to your regularly scheduled tarot readings? Are you afraid to join LaToya Jackson in her *Psychic Discoveries*? On the only infomercial to include "psychic reenactments," Dionne Warwick, "Psychic to the Stars" Linda Georgian, and a whole gaggle of soap stars (including the name-cursed Yasmine Bleeth from *One Life to Live*) invite you, Lynn "I Never Promised You a Rose Garden" Anderson, and audience member "Tingle" to simultaneously hear the future and make new friends, twenty-four hours a day, all for just $2.99 a minute.

Ʌ Ʌ Ʌ Ʌ

The Special Effects Cookbook. It never occurred to us to want to make a swimming cucumber shark, a volcano cake with erupting lava icing, glow-in-the-dark Jell-O, a smoking dragon cake, special-effects food for our pets (including the Hopping Dog Biscuit), or the many, many other surprises in this book that look completely inedible. But if your family will eat anything, why not give it a try?

Ʌ Ʌ Ʌ

Stop the Insanity!, 1992. The all-time most perfect infomercial ever. Platinum burr-cut body-by-God Susan Powter is a cross between Annie Lennox and Don Rickles, using abrasive humor, hoarse screaming, and her own brand of burning intensity to announce, "YOU GOTTA EAT, YOU GOTTA BREATHE, YOU GOTTA MOVE ... THAT'S MY GOAL, TO BRING EVERYONE THIS MESSAGE!" She also lost 160 pounds in one year through her very own combination of dieting and exercise that is now available through five books, five audiotapes, one videotape, and body-fat-measuring calipers for $87.60. Unlike her competitors, though, Susan's show has good music, fine video effects, lots of cautionary footnotes and testimonials from regular guys and gals that are remarkably sincere. If only everyone could do infomercials like this one, we wouldn't have to put up with regular TV ever again.

Ʌ Ʌ Ʌ

♟♟

And the Tammi for worst infomercial ever goes to:

Personal Power. "Master your finances, your emotions, your personal relationships, or your physical body," with giant-chinned Anthony Robbins's very pricey book and cassette collection, *Thirty Days to Unlimited Success.* In a very tight contest Tony wins our infomercial award for two reasons: He's got the strangest collection of supporting shills and, unlike other products, the mix of gestalt and neurolinguistic programming that is *Personal Power* can do *everything:* help you get rich, quit smoking, find love, lose weight, write books, walk on beds of hot coals, and even *play a better game of golf*!

What did Tony Robbins do for actor Martin Sheen, you may well ask? "Tony Robbins brought my wife and I more passion, more joy, and more excitement than we ever thought possible!" Yes, Marty, but what does DJ Casey Kasem think? "Tony is definitely in the number-one, category, but beyond that! You can put him in the category of the Beatles, the Stones, Michael Jackson, Frank Sinatra, but he's beyond the charts. He's number one with a bullet!" Yes, Casey, but what does footballer Fran Tarkenton have to say? "I was playing golf with the Vice President of the United States, and some of the golfers with me were telling us how they use the technology, and their game has improved so much!"

♟♟ ♟♟ ♟♟ ♟♟ ♟♟ ♟♟

My own guidelines for TV commercials:
—Pork sausages shall not be allowed to sing and dance, live bulls shall not be permitted to enter bars where liquor is sold, and cats may no longer do the cha-cha-cha unless accompanied by an adult.
—Unnecessary violence must be avoided. Ferocious snow tires, marauding odor eaters, and aggressive scrub bubbles are forbidden.
—Toilet paper shall not be squeezed, petted, played with, bandied about, or otherwise flaunted in public. Models shall not fondle automobiles.

The Cavalcade of Jiggle

Charlie's Angels, 1976
Sugar Time, 1977
Rollergirls, 1978
Who's Watching The Kids, 1978
We Got It Made, 1983
Paper Dolls, 1984
Live-In, 1989
Nightingales, 1989

—Showers and baths shall not be portrayed as wild, sensual fiestas.

—Employees of airline companies, such as pilots and mechanics, shall not be permitted to sing and dance in television commercials unless they also perform these functions in the course of their work. . . .

—Tom Shales, *The Washington Post*

The Sitcom Nominees

When someone says I'm cute, I want to throw right up.

—Sally Field

W E'VE SAVED THE BEST FOR LAST. WHY THE CRAZIEST PEOPLE IN America are all dying to produce insane sitcoms (and why they're also allowed to get them on the air) is a mystery, but from looking at these hallmarks of BAD TV, you'll see that it's true. Here are the shocking revelations:

- If you're a single mom, hire a cute young guy to run the household.
- Owning a genie can be more trouble than it's worth.
- If you move into a house with ghosts, do not under any circumstances encourage their sexual advances.
- If you're a single dad, do not hire a witch to run the household.
- Traveling through time can be more trouble than it's worth.
- If you get a robot, try to get one that's at least as interesting and as attractive as a human being.
- If you're a single parent, do not hire a beautiful young gal (whose favorite clothes are lingerie and bikinis) to run the household.
- If you're a man, disguising yourself as a woman can be more trouble than it's worth.
- If you're married to, best friends with, or next-door neighbors of your polar opposite, it'll be a living hell for you, but a laugh-riot for your friends.
- A major American desire is to practice vicarious incest.

- There actually can be too much of a good thing.
- For some odd reason, Americans don't like to tune in, week after week, to a television show starring people who are repulsive.
- If your life is dull, buy a chimpanzee.

Boss Lady, 1952. In the fifties practically all the women on TV were housewives and maids, except for *Boss Lady* Lynn Bari—who only got her job because her father ran the company. Her situation was so odd, in fact, that the writers could only think up plots about the various mishaps ensuing when (because of her great beauty) Boss Lady's male staff members kept falling in love with her—certainly a common enough problem for today's working gal.

Bungle Abbey, 1981. Oh, those goofy monks! Gale Gordon and Charlie Callas are among the cast of zany friars having riotous misadventures in a monastery named for founder Brother Bungle in a TV mishap directed by Lucille Ball and produced by Ball and her husband, Gary Morton.

Captain Nice, 1966. "Look! It's the nut who walks around in his pajamas!" "That's no nut, boy, that's Captain Nice." Buck Henry tried cashing in on the surprise success of *Batman* with this parody of a timid chemist who accidentally becomes a superhero and dates policewoman Candy Cane (Ann Prentiss). With the great cast of William Daniels *(St. Elsewhere)* and Alice Ghostley, this one-note idea could have been a fun special, but never an endless series.

Carter Country, 1977. Combine Jimmy Carter's election to the Presidency making the nation fascinated by hick life, with the ten-year-old film hit *In the Heat of the Night* (racist white sheriff has to work with new black deputy), and mix in the shocking repartee of *All in the Family,*

**Buck Henry aimed for the lowest common denominator
when he created *Captain Nice* (Stephen Cox)**

to make a mongrel sitcom that's an embarrassment for everyone concerned.

ıı ıı

***Charles in Charge*, 1985.** A clone of *Who's the Boss?* (1984) starring Scott Baio, who, the ads declare, is "everyone's favorite household hunk." Both shows are about cute young guys hired as housekeepers/nannies by working parents and both (like *The Brady Bunch*) are about incest. As nannies, Baio and *Boss*'s Tony Danza take on the missing father role; both are cast into demiromantic relationships with their mom employers (Danza's would turn not so demi), and both are the objects of obsession for their preteen charges.

Why there's so much of this vicarious incest in sitcoms is something we can't explain, but it's practically an epidemic. What does *My Little Margie* say about her widowed father? "He looks better in shorts on a tennis court than guys twenty-five years old! He won't settle down. I've got a problem!" What does the girl chorus chant in *Charles in Charge*'s theme song? "I want Charles in charge of me!"

Ii Ii Ii

The Charmings, 1987. The eighties proved a new rule for you would-be TV executives: If you want to work with the supernatural, don't try a suburban setting. In *"Hi Honey, I'm Home,"* a fifties TV family (à la the Cleavers) magically moves next door to an eighties TV family (à la the Conners), but even though the show was historic in being the first original programming shown simultaneously on network (ABC) and cable (Nickelodeon), it didn't last long on either. *The Charmings,* meanwhile, found Snow White, Prince Charming, a troll, a witch, and a magic mirror living in a tract home (à la *Bewitched*). Unlike Samantha Stevens, however, *The Charmings* were charm free.

Ii Ii

Chicken Soup, 1989. Producers Carsey and Werner did it right with Bill Cosby, Roseanne Barr, and Tim Allen—took stand-up comedians and fashioned a hit series directly from their comedy club routines. Jackie Mason had returned from show business twilight in a huge one-man Broadway hit, *The World According to Me.* So why not do it all over again? Wasn't America just waiting for a self-described lonely old guy telling rapid-fire jokes from the early fifties in a harsh Yiddish accent? Wouldn't we adore the only plot point: the story of an ex–pajama salesman who gives it all up for an on-again, off-again romance with Weight Watcher Lynn Redgrave? Wouldn't TV execs have learned a lesson from *The Don Rickles Show* (1972)?

No.

Ii Ii Ii

Covington Cross, 1992. *Young Guns* begat *Young Riders,* which had sex with both *Beverly Hills 90210* and *Robin Hood, Prince of Thieves* to beget this show, a dramedy many consider the worst television series of 1992. The saga of teen knights and damsels (and their firm but understanding parents) running around in the Middle Ages, *Covington Cross* features hokey Elizabethan dialogue, clumsy acting, insipid background music, and a stupor-inducing disregard for pacing—but the clothes are terrific. An okay Saturday morning kids' show that brazen ABC put on in prime time.

🐧 🐧

Dirty Sally, 1974. A *Gunsmoke* spin-off starring the nasty old lunatic hermit Jeannette Nolan, who sells junk nobody wants and wanders through the Wild West with her would-be pandhandler sidekick, Dack Rambo.

🐧 🐧 🐧

The Doris Day Show, 1968. A fascinating aesthetic experiment. Not only do you get to hear *"Que Será Será"* again and again and again until you think you're going to scream out loud but, every year, you get to watch a whole new show!

- 📺 1968: Widow Doris, her two kids, and her dog live on a farm out in the country.
- 📺 1969: Doris gets a job as a secretary back in the city, and becomes a working mom.
- 📺 1970: Doris, kids, and dog move to an apartment in the city, surrounded by Italians.
- 📺 1971: Doris's children and dog mysteriously vanish so she can become a swingle (or perhaps a swidow), and date groovy Dr. Peter Lawford.

Que Será Será is right.

🐧 🐧 🐧

Dusty's Trail, 1973. Created by Sherwood *Gilligan Brady* Schwartz and called "abysmal" by the usually nonjudgmental encyclopedia *Total Television,* this laugh-a-minute sitcom starred Bob Denver and Forrest Tucker as two ne'er-do-wells trying to stumble their way across the Old West. Not even up to Sherwood's *Gilligan* standards, and yanked after only a few episodes.

🐧 🐧 🐧 🐧

Easy Street, 1986. Staggeringly rich Loni Anderson goes to visit her poor, nursing-home-bound uncle, invites him and his best black friend home for a visit, and they all have so much fun together, she begs them to live in her lavish, pleasure-filled mansion.

As fun as it is believable.

⎯ ⎯

Family Affair, 1966. Brian Keith is having the time of his life being a swinging, confirmed bachelor and internationally famous multimillionaire civil engineer while living the "city that never sleeps" highlife with immense manservant Sebastian Cabot taking care of all his needs. The car accident that kills Keith's brother and sister-in-law, though, changes everything, since right to Uncle Brian's chic co-op door come three orphaned urchins—Sissy, Buffy, and Jody—and "Congratulations! You're a father!"

Keith, Cabot, and the basic idea of this show are perfectly fine—it's the dizzying psychedelic-jewel opening credits, the incessant heartstring-pulling violin music, that cancer-patient doll Mrs. Beasley, and those damn "so sweet, we'll give you cavities" moppets who make it easily one of the worst programs ever. Squeaky-clean Cissy might as well be a nun for all the teen spirit she conveys, while Jodie and Buffy are so syrupy, it's no wonder the Baby Boom ended when this show hit the air. Since it was on prime time for five years, *Family Affair* was originally going to be a BAD Classic but, after watching a recent episode, we knew it was too horrible even for that. Indeed, five years after *Family Affair*'s cancellation, bisexual Buffy (Anissa Jones) was dead of an overdose, and Jody (Johnnie Whitaker) had been turned into a Mormon.

Sure hope Mayim Bialik's parents take note.

⎯ ⎯ ⎯ ⎯

Francy Goes to Washington, 1958. Typical suburban mom Claudette Colbert becomes a congresswoman and moves to Washington with her family (including daughter Shelley Fabares).

⎯

———

***The Girl with Something Extra*, 1973.** The finale of the fab Field fluff trilogy (after *Gidget* and *Flying Nun*), as well as a simultaneous remake of *Bewitched* and *I Dream of Jeannie*. Lawyer John Davidson has funny problems because of wife Sally Field's ESP mind-reading abilities.

Ⱥ Ⱥ Ⱥ

***Good Sports*, 1991.** Real-life live-ins Farrah Fawcett and Ryan O'Neal bring their love to the small screen as joint sportscasters with an on-again, off-again romance. While Farrah was perfect, O'Neal's acting was so dreadful, it made you squirm—not the best news for a comedy.

Ⱥ Ⱥ

***Good Time Harry*, 1980.** BAD TV titan Ted Bessell leaves Marlo Thomas to become a San Francisco sportscaster and notorious skirt-chaser. Swingin' guy, that Ted!

Ⱥ Ⱥ Ⱥ

***Great Day*, 1977.** Probably the all-time worst sitcom idea in the history of television: Al Molinaro and Billy Barty attempt to show what a laff-riot life can be for homeless alcoholics living on New York City's Bowery.

Ⱥ Ⱥ Ⱥ Ⱥ

***Half-Nelson*, 1985.** One of the only shows ever about very small people, with the midgetlike Joe Pesci pursuing his dream of being a combination actor/private eye and desperately trying to get Victoria Jackson, Dick Butkus, Bubba Smith, and best friend Dean Martin to treat him with the respect he deserves.

Ⱥ Ⱥ

***Happy*, 1960.** Happy the talking baby lives with his mom and dad, who aren't Kirstie Alley and John Travolta but Palm Springs motel managers, whose entire comic misadventures lie in keeping the guests from hearing the baby.

♟ ♟ ♟

The Hathaways, 1961. Real estate agent Jack Weston and glamorously maternal (white-gloved and white-teethed) Peggy Cass agree to care for a family of performing monkeys—the Marquis Chimps, TV stars in their own right at the time. Jack and Peggy always referred to them as "the children," outfitting Charlie and Enoch Marquis-Hathaway in white pants, navy blazers, sneakers, and bosun's caps, while Candy Marquis-Hathaway was attired in a dress and hair ribbon. The monkeys could brush their teeth, play with toys, drink milk, play Cowboys and Indians, take naps, and climb up chimneys—just like regular kids.

Each episode's underlying theme was an exploration of these many incredible similarities that exist between American children and trained chimpanzees . . . and to show that, if you had to choose between the two, you'd take the chimps.

♟ ♟ ♟ ♟ ♟

Here's Boomer, 1980. The much-anticipated prime-time remake of *Run, Joe, Run:* an adorable mongrel dog wanders aimlessly across America, falling in love with French poodle Celeste and helping people with their personal problems.

♟ ♟

I Married Dora, 1987. A program so notoriously awful that it came *this* close to winning its category. A woman decides she's bored with married life, runs away, her plane crashes, and she's presumed dead. Her husband speedily recovers from grief and hires the beautiful Elizabeth "Dora" Peña to be his maid and his kids' baby-sitter. Turns out Liz is here illegally from some unspecified South American country, but since things are working out so great between her and the kiddies (one of whom is *Cape Fear* Oscar nominee Juliette Lewis), daddy marries Dora for the green card.

The show's unbelievably rancid humor comes from Dora's funny accent and misunderstandings about American life, as well as a suffocating coyness over their "platonic" marriage and the kiddies finding them in supposedly compromising positions. "We have a marriage license, but we never use it," Dora will whine, and her kitchen junk drawer provides op-

**Which kid is cuter? Viewers everywhere had to confront their
subconscious antichimpanzee bigotry on** *The Hathaways*
(Photofest)

portunity for hours and hours of amusement; it's where she keeps "all the
stuff you don't know what to do with, but you don't want to throw away,
because one day you are going to need that thing that you don't know
what to do with right now." When Juliette and her name-cursed best friend
Mandy Ingber want to have fun, they dress up in miniskirts and tight
blouses, go to the mall, and "drive shoe salesmen crazy!"

A must-see horror.

It's About Time, 1966. Two astronauts fly over the time limit and end
up in the Stone Age. When this situation turned out not to be full of comedy, they dragged the cavepeople family back to modern life in a remake
of *Tarzan in New York.*

This didn't work either.

***Jennifer Slept Here,* 1983.** Ann Jillian *is* Jennifer—a Jayne Mansfield–styled movie star/tramp who began her Hollywood career as a banana on *Let's Make a Deal,* dies mysteriously, and haunts her Hollywood mansion (along with mother/ghost Debbie Reynolds), now owned by a dreary New York family. Preteen Joey is the only one who can see Ann (and sadly the only one who can receive her help with his personal problems), and her inexhaustible tartiness makes you think that the minute Joey hits teendom, it's gonna be *Summer of '42* all over again . . . but with a ghost in the experienced-older-woman role.

⅃⅃ ⅃⅃ ⅃⅃

***Judgment Day,* 1981.** Each week a famous guest star would die and go to Limbo (which turned out to be a courtroom) and representatives from Heaven (Victor Buono) and Hell (Roddy McDowall) would argue over the star's eternal destination. Even though this idea sounded good enough to Albert Brooks to remake it as the movie *Defending Your Life* (1991), *Judgment Day* only lasted one hour—at the time the most expensive television episode ever produced.

⅃⅃ ⅃⅃

***Just Our Luck,* 1983.** An *I Dream of Jeannie* remake, but Jeannie's now a big black man (Shabu).

⅃⅃

***Learning the Ropes,* 1988.** Lyle Alzado leaves the Oakland Raiders to become wrestling superstar Masked Maniac, but has another change of heart and takes a job as a prep-school teacher, where he's desperate to hide his wrestling past from his snooty new colleagues. Not that this secret would be so hard to uncover, since much of the show features Lyle and his slam-banging buddies watching themselves on TV wrestle bouts.

⅃⅃

***Live-In,* 1989.** Just-past-puberty Chris can't believe his luck when Mom and Dad hire the scanty-clothes loving, ultrababelicious Lisa to take care of his little sister. A show starring hormones instead of human beings, the premiere's big plot line concerns the randy Chris's attempts to cut a peephole out of the bathroom wall to catch Lisa in the altogether.

Madame's Place, 1982. Bette Davis, Miss Havisham, and a phallusoid nose meet in Madame, the aggressive puppet star (manhandled by comedian Wayland Flowers), of *Trampoline Honeymoon* and the host of this sitcom/talk show.

Makin' It, 1979. A beyond-wholesome Bastard remake of *Saturday Night Fever* with *Fever*'s composers (the Bee Gees), producers (the Robert Stigwood Organization), a Travolta (John's sister, Ellen), David Naughton starring as Passaic's biggest disco-dancin' fool, and the plot line of the original movie repeated again and again and again.

Me & Mrs. C, 1986. Cursed-with-a-bad-name Misha McK is a beautiful young black ex-con who rents a room from white, elderly widow Mrs. C. Their loving-but-difficult relationship is filled with the kind of ersatz schmaltz that can only come from signature BAD TV.

Me and the Chimp, 1972. BAD TV megastar Ted Bessell is now married and forced by his children to adopt Buttons, a chimpanzee trained to push every button in sight. This show's riveting dramatic theme is how a dentist and a monkey frequently have misunderstandings; in the end, the animal is always right.

The stars never created good chemistry since, in real life, Buttons's manager was unhappy, as his beast was obviously the star of the show but got second billing in the title. In return, Bessell said Buttons was "rude, dirty, and untalented."

**Buttons, Ted Bessell's dental hygienist, searches for gingivitis
on *Me and the Chimp*** (Photofest)

***Mixed Nuts,* 1977.** The hilarious misadventures of doctors, nurses,
and patients in an insane asylum.

Ⅱ Ⅱ Ⅱ

***Molloy,* 1990.** Not an adaptation of the Samuel Beckett classic but a
showcase for the utterly repulsive Mayim Bialik, who, when this failed,
was immediately and mysteriously given a new starring role as *Blossom*
(1991), an extremely well-written, talent-filled, and audience-pleasing
show (referred to as *"Punky Brewster* with her period" by the *L.A. Times*)
where director Bill *My Favorite Incredible Martian Hulk* Bixby keeps her
personality disorders to a minimum.

On *Molloy,* though, Mayim obviously inherited her character from *The
Day of the Locust*'s hyperaggressive child star; both have all the presence
of automatons programmed for cuteness. Watching Mayim is so stomach-

churning, you can't understand why someone never gave her a special birthday surprise—like a one-way ticket to Zaire. When she endlessly scrunches up her nose in preteen adorability (even though she's actually seventeen), you can only think what a miracle it is that she hasn't been *murdered.*

Today's Ms. Bialik has become so frighteningly popular with *Blossom* that some girl viewers follow her lead in fashion coordinates: big floppy hats and Hawaiian-print dresses. Says Don Reo, *Blossom*'s creator, "You don't have to go to the most dramatic thing that can happen to tell a good story. When you're a teenager, if your clothes don't come back from the cleaners in time for the dance, that can be a major catastrophe. Actually, I wasn't thinking about teenagers; I was thinking about myself. I think my emotional development stopped when I was about seventeen and that's why I'm perfect for this job." Says Ms. Bialik herself about her character: "She's a nice person and if you have millions of people watching she might as well be good because if TV is going to educate, it might as well be with good."

As with all BAD TV *Molloy*'s Mayim is a window on the mysteries of the universe. How did she become such a horrifying creature? Was she born that way, was it growing up in San Diego, or did she get special training? Did Bette Midler do something to her during the production of *Beaches?* How does she keep getting on the air? Is she related to someone? Why are they doing this to us? Is she part of a conspiracy to drive us all insane?

     ⚊⚊ ⚊⚊

The Mommies, 1993. If you think *Roseanne* would be a much better show without its social concerns, good writing, funny jokes, decent acting, or the Conner family's obvious real love for each other, then you'll just love *The Mommies.* Based on Marilyn Krenz and Karyl Kristensen's stand-up act (which liberally borrowed from both Ms. Arnold and living legend Phyllis Diller), *The Mommies* is one long whine about husbands, children, and housecleaning, interspersed with tepid bits of *Married with Children*'s raunchy realism. When their kids start fighting, one Mommy quips, "I'm gonna get my tubes tied—with a knot they use on ships!"

     ⚊⚊ ⚊⚊

———

***Morningstar/Eveningstar*, 1986.** When an orphanage is destroyed by fire, a mob of adorably homeless Keane-eyed youngsters move into an old age home loaded to the teeth with wise-but-zany senior citizens. Enough love and sharing to make you squirm.

ıı ıı

***Mr. Smith*, 1983.** A remake of the Frank Capra movie *Mr. Smith Goes to Washington,* but taking the Jimmy Stewart role is C.J. (star of *Tarzan the Ape Man* and *Every Which Way But Loose*), a talking orangutan with a huge IQ—the product of scientific experiments (see? animal testing isn't *all* bad). When his special talents are discovered, Mr. Smith is of course immediately hired as a government consultant.

Like all monkey BAD TV this one has mixed messages; in trying to be adorable by making an animal as humanlike as possible (Mr. Smith wears suits and glasses), the show perversely underlines the fact that there's very little difference between most people you know . . . and apes.

ıı ıı ıı ıı

***Mr. Sunshine*, 1986.** The "fun fun fun!" adventures of a hateful blind man.

ıı ıı ıı

***Mr. T and Tina*, 1976.** In a shocking race reversal, Anglo Tina works as a governess for Asian Mr. T. A show way ahead of its time, since it'll be *at least* another three years before we're all the servants of Japanese millionaires.

ıı

***Mr. Terrific*, 1967.** Gas station attendant by day, reluctant superhero by night, *Mr. Terrific* tried to capture the audience-loving fun of *Batman* but instead, like *Captain Nice,* became one of the sixties' most notorious flops.

ıı ıı

If your show-biz career is going nowhere, take heart by
remembering the remarkable trees-to-sitcom success story
of that pinstripe-loving Borneo lad, *Mr. Smith* (Photofest)

———

My Living Doll, 1964. Psychiatrist Bob Cummings has such trouble with patient Julie Newmar (later to enthrall us as *Batman*'s Catwoman) that she moves in with him. Her main problem? She's a robot who can't seem to get the hang of being the perfect woman, even though she's 37-26-36 and can type 240 words a minute. Julie especially has difficulty being perfectly servile to men; if she turns uppity, though, a guy can just re-set her by pressing her birthmark buttons. Though Newmar is fantastic doing replicate slapstick with a German accent, the show's whole attitude is remarkably hideous—the opening credits, for example, show her in a teddy and announce "also starring Julie Newmar as The Doll." Even Cummings (the photographer sex fiend from *Love That Bob*) thought this show was so bad that he bailed out halfway through its run; on the air it was explained he'd gone to Pakistan.

Ꭵ Ꭵ Ꭵ Ꭵ Ꭵ

Nancy, 1970. The relentlessly zany daughter of the President of the United States falls madly in love with a tedious Iowa veterinarian in a show that combines warmhearted family drama with the incisive political satire that we've all come to expect on network television.

Ꭵ Ꭵ

Normal Life, 1990. If you were going to create a television show for your pick of any two Hollywood stars, wouldn't you do it for Moon Unit and Dweezil Zappa? And have Cindy "Shirley" Williams play their mom?

Ꭵ

No Soap, Radio, 1982. A surrealist sitcom attempt at an Americanized *Monty Python's Flying Circus,* with Steve Guttenberg and Bill Dana working at an Atlantic City hotel. So desperately unfunny and completely BAD it's like watching something from another planet.

Ꭵ Ꭵ Ꭵ

Which one's the robot? The all-time most sexist show in the history of television, *My Living Doll* (Stephen Cox)

—

Number 96, 1980. An hour-long sitcom about a baseball player, a pianist, a Puerto Rican comic, a cop, a nurse, a widow, an actress, Mary Hartman's husband, and a transvestite, all living in an L.A. swingles' apartment complex. Hey, let's do a prime-time show about wild California sexcapades! The original Australian version gained big controversy and a big audience through its extensive use of nudity, but without it the American producers couldn't find a formula to make a hit.

Occasional Wife, 1966. Swinging bachelor Michael Callan gets a job at Brahms Baby Food, even though they only hire stable marrieds. Enter upstairs neighbor Patricia Harty, who poses as the eponymous career-move. Callan and Harty fell for each other in real life and were wed; they divorced, and then played the parents of *Young Hearts* (1983).

O.K. Crackerby, 1965. The head critic of *TV Guide,* the director of *Guys and Dolls,* and the producer of *Supertrain* and *My Mother the Car* put together this ridiculous saga of millionaire hillbilly Burl Ives and the Ivy Leaguer he hires to teach his cracker brats some manners.

One in a Million, 1980. Husky girl cabdriver inherits a fare's controlling stock interests and so becomes CEO of a *Fortune* 500 corporation, where she raises social consciousness and listens to lots and lots of fat jokes.

One of the Boys, 1982. Mickey Rooney runs away from a nursing home to move in with his college-attending grandson, Dana Carvey, and work up a singing, dancing vaudeville show with Scatman Crothers.

Operation Petticoat, 1977. Jamie Lee Curtis, John Astin, and Jo Ann Pflug oversee a group of World War II Army nurses living on a pink submarine.

———

***Out of the Blue*, 1979.** Bad-boy angel goes to help Dixie Carter and her five charming-but-mischievous orphans.

                            ♟ ♟ ♟

***Out of This World*, 1987.** The low-rent adventures of a human-alien half-breed teenager (whose father went back to home planet Anterias and now communicates only via a blue crystal), with Burt Reynolds, Donna Pescow, and production advice from astronaut Scott Carpenter. Evie's dreary powers are restricted to freezing time and rearranging molecules, but nothing we'd find fun to watch; not even a nose wiggle. Seems she was offered the major Anterian abilities on her sixteenth birthday: mind-reading, time reversal, levitation, making others obey, making others invisible, making oneself invisible, a money tree, seeing through walls, quick shoe changes, and a face-lift. She's such a goody two-shoes, though, she wouldn't accept, since it would be bad to live on Earth and have lots of supernatural powers (and the producers obviously thought it'd be bad to have a sitcom with anything fun in it).

The whole thing is so sickeningly Mormon it gives *Small Wonder* a run for the money in the "series designed to make you hate all preteen girls" sweepstakes.

                      ♟ ♟ ♟ ♟

***Peck's Bad Girl*, 1959.** Patty MacCormack, the sensational and beloved murderess in the hit play and movie *The Bad Seed,* tries to be simply scheming and mischievous—but we only liked her as a well-behaved killer.

                            ♟ ♟ ♟

***The People Next Door*, 1989.** Whatever cartoonist Jeffrey Jones imagines comes alive; his family's used to seeing odd things around the house, but new wife Mary Gross still can't get used to it. Created by genius director Wes Craven *(A Nightmare on Elm Street)* and cameoing such greats as Dr. Joyce Brothers, Henny Youngman, and Casey Kasem "as themselves."

                                ♟ ♟

———

Poochinski, 1990. A gruff policeman dies on the job and is reincarnated—as a farting, crime-fighting English bulldog. The name, and probably the inspiration, most likely came from Chicago alderman Roman Pucinski.

I I I I I I I I I I

Poor Devil, 1973. Sammy Davis, Jr., ineptly tries to win souls for the perfect Satan, Christopher Lee.

I I I I

Popi, 1976. The hilarious, barrel-of-laughs misadventures of a Rican widower who lives in the ghetto and has to work three jobs to feed his many children.

I I

The Pruitts of Southampton, 1966; The Phyllis Diller Show, 1966. Prefiguring Leona Helmsley, rich Phyllis Diller explored the humor of poverty after she has to fork over millions in unpaid taxes. When we didn't think this was funny, the show was retitled and her mansion became a hotel for John Astin, Marty Ingels, Richard Deacon, Paul Lynde, and Gypsy Rose Lee.

I I I I I I I I I I

Quark, 1978. A transsexual, a chatty but boring houseplant (who tries to seduce a human by explaining the secrets of pollination), Ergo the plasmapet, Betty and Betty (a navigator and her clone), a perpetually frightened robot, and Richard Benjamin pilot a garbage barge in outer space.

I I I I I I I I I I

Rollergirls, 1978. One of the few recent series that was a network exec's idea; cat-fight aficionado Brandon Tartikoff ended up apologizing profusely for this jiggle-show horror, which only lasted four episodes. No name curses here, though: the Rollergirls' team was the Pittsburgh Pitts,

Even the startling brilliance of Phyllis Diller couldn't save *The Pruitts of Southampton* (Stephen Cox)

and the characters included blond Mongo Sue, black Honey Bee, and Pipeline Akira (an Eskimo).

The galaxy's happiest sanitation workers: *Quark* (Photofest)

———

***Roxie*, 1987.** Genius Andrea Martin tries to bring her wonderful SCTV cable manager, Edith Prickley, to *Kate & Allie* and network television. As Roxie, Andrea seems completely lost, and the show's writing was so terrific, only two episodes aired.

ᴫ

***Saved by the Bell*, 1990.** If you find the intense urban drama of *90210* too searing and overwhelming to enjoy, you may be the perfect audience for this teen soap, which is sort of a *90210* lite. As Ken Tucker prayed in *Entertainment Weekly,* "The one good thing that could possibly be said about this show's seepage into prime time is that some parents, seeing *Saved by the Bell* for the first time, may now realize just how bad Saturday-morning TV programming has become, and take steps to shield their children from such dreck." Featuring obnoxious teens, idiotic adults, plots stolen from every show you've ever seen, not one good joke, and guest star Soleil Moon Frye, many on the Nominating Committee think this is the worst program currently on the air. *Saved by the Bell* is, in fact, such a mess it caused us category placement trouble, since the sitcom elements are so unfunny, it doesn't seem like a sitcom, and the dramatic moments are so undramatic, it doesn't seem like a drama either. What is it?

▲▲ ▲▲ ▲▲ ▲▲ ▲▲

The Second Hundred Years, 1967. In the aesthetic inspiration for *Encino Man,* a claim-staker from the Alaska gold-rush days gets frozen in 1900 and thawed out in 1967, when he finds many things about your world confusing and nonsensical, and helps people with their personal problems.

▲▲

She's the Sheriff, 1987. Remarkably weak *Mayberry, R.F.D.* imitation dropped by CBS but forced upon us through syndication. Thighmaster Queen Suzanne Somers takes over her dead husband's job as the law of a small Nevada town, wears the most extremely tailored uniform in sheriff history, and experiences a number of mild misadventures.

▲▲ ▲▲ ▲▲

Shirley's World, 1971. Shirley MacLaine roams the world as a perky ingenue photojournalist in her late fifties, studiously avoiding the joys of reincarnation.

▲▲ ▲▲

Sister Kate, 1989–1990. Not an objectively bad show, but a really nutty idea at the time. We'd just spent a few years enjoying the glorious

Stephanie Beacham as the only bitch strong enough to give Joan Collins second thoughts on *Dynasty* and *The Colbys;* suddenly, we're supposed to love her just as much as a *nun*—surrounded by naughty-but-adorable delinquent orphans (including *90210*'s Jason Priestley).

We didn't.

Six O'Clock Follies, 1980. All the hilarity of the Vietnam War comes together in this much-cherished comic half-hour, starring Larry *(Apocalypse Now; Boyz N the Hood)* Fishburne.

Small Wonder, 1985. If you were a scientist who could make a robot, what kind of robot would you make? A sexy but devoted spouse? An elegant, servile English butler? An obnoxiously precocious and horrifyingly adorable ten-year-old girl whose only apparent reason for existence is so you can spend lots of time trying to keep the neighbors from discovering she's a robot? If the latter sounds like a great idea, then you'll love this bottom-barrel effort starring the Voice Input Child Identicant (Vicki), her evil twin robot prototype Vanessa, her really boring family, and their irritating friends.

Struck by Lightning, 1979. Descendants of Dr. Victor Frankenstein own and operate a hotel in Maine, with the immortal monster (now 231 years old) working as the live-in handyman.

Studs' Place, 1949. Chicago institution Studs Terkel plays Chicago bar-owner Studs Terkel in a *Cheers*-like show with too much actor improvisation for its own good.

———

***Sugar Time!*, 1977.** Playmate of the Year and Hefner-ex Barbi Benton leads Sugar, an all-woman rock band performing Paul Williams tunes, in a cross between *Charlie's Angels* and *Josie and the Pussycats.*

👤 👤 👤

***Supertrain*, 1979.** One of network TV's most notorious (and money-losing) flops, starring an atomic-powered luxury railroad with swimming pool and disco. *Supertrain* tried to combine the comedy of *The Love Boat,* the glitz of *Dynasty,* and the drama of the various *Airport* movies, and ended up being nothing in particular. After suffering through endless ABC hoopla about the show's cost and magnificent special effects, we were thrilled that the show was so terrible, the effects so cheesy, and the cancellation so swift.

👤 👤 👤

***Sydney*, 1990.** Notorious tough gal Valerie Bertinelli stars as L.A. PI Sydney Kells.

👤 👤

***Szysznyk*, 1977.** Ned Beatty is an ex-Marine running a D.C. community center in this brilliantly titled comedy.

👤 👤 👤

***The Thorns*, 1988.** After receiving huge advance publicity for being executive-produced by the often-brilliant-but-hairless Mike Nichols (and seen as an escape hatch for its star, Tony Roberts, from being forced to appear in every Woody Allen movie ever made), this show turned out to concern the misadventures of a horrifically selfish New York yuppie family who repulsed any viewer daring to draw near. Unlike the obnoxious but adorable *Roseanne* or the gross but engaging *Married . . . with Children,* *The Thorns* tried skipping the adorable and engaging part, only to plunge to its doom.

👤 👤 👤 👤 👤

———

Together We Stand; Nothing Is Easy, 1986. Another "so loving, it makes your teeth hurt" family sitcom, with Elliot Gould in the Mia Farrow role of a compulsive adopter, fathering two white, a black, and an Asian child. When the show didn't work, Gould was killed off in a car wreck, and his wife Dee Wallace Stone tried to carry on (with help from her one-liner-filled neighbor, opera star Julia Migenes).

�ᴵᴵ

Turnabout, 1979. Husband and wife John Schuck and Sharon Gless wake up to find they've switched bodies; she has to go off to her job as a sportswriter, and he has to go to his work at a cosmetics firm.

ᴵᴵ

The Ugliest Girl in Town, 1968. Repulsively dopey comedy desperate to be *Some Like It Hot,* about amateur crossdresser Peter Kastner going undercover as a model (the girl of the title) and incognito following his girlfriend to swingin' Carnaby Street—where his unique femininity is considered the latest thing. *Ugliest* was especially hard to take, as Mr. Kastner is so ridiculous in his femme outfits he makes *Bosom Buddies* look like Miss America contestants. Not only was he completely implausible as a top fashion model, you wouldn't even let him into your house.
A legendary must-see.

ᴵᴵ ᴵᴵ ᴵᴵ ᴵᴵ ᴵᴵ

Vinny and Bobby, 1991. Another Fox quicky (quickly gone and forgotten) starring male bimbo construction worker hunks decked out in muscle Ts doing slapstick thought up by preschoolers to a wildly appreciative studio audience.

ᴵᴵ

The Waverly Wonders, 1978. A bastard child of *The Bad News Bears* that only lasted three episodes and starred Joe Namath as a high-school basketball coach surrounded by characters named Hasty and Faguzzi.

ᴵᴵ ᴵᴵ ᴵᴵ

Before: Peter Kastner. After: *The Ugliest Girl in Town* (Photofest)

We Got It Made, 1983. *Three's Company* is a big hit, so why not *Five's Company*? Two roomies hire a sex-bomb maid and their girlfriends just don't understand. The show's promos had the maid announcing, "Do I serve them both? Maybe even at the same time?"

⅄⅃

We've Got Each Other, 1977. The warmhearted yet hilarious life of an incredibly ugly married couple.

⅄⅃ ⅄⅃

When Things Were Rotten, 1975. On the outside, a parody of Robin Hood and the Middle Ages; on the inside, a *Blazing Saddles* rip-off, produced by *Saddles'* own Mel Brooks.

⅄⅃ ⅄⅃

Where's Everett?, 1966. Alan Alda and Patricia Smith adopt a baby who's not only from another planet but invisible, causing the show's title to be repeated endlessly.

♟

Who's Watching the Kids, 1978. Even though his *Blansky's Beauties* failed miserably, touch-of-gold TV producer Garry Marshall tried again with this T&A sitcom, originally called *Legs,* about Vegas showgirls raising their siblings (one of whom is the aggressive Scott Baio). When you become a multimillionaire TV exec, remember one thing: If Garry Marshall can't make a Vegas showgirl T&A sitcom work, neither can you.

♟ ♟

Whoops!, 1992. Six disparate survivors of a nuclear holocaust (a yuppie, an ex-hippie, a feminist, a babe, a teen, and a token black man) try to create a new civilization at a beautiful farmhouse with unbelievably low-grade writing and production values even for Fox. The pilot was such a naked imitation of *Gilligan's Island* that *Gilligan* producer Sherwood Schwartz threatened to sue (although he never pursued the claim).

♟

Women in Prison, 1987. Fox TV execs knew there was a great tradition of women-behind-bars exploitation flicks, but they threw this on the air anyway. Done by the producers of *Married . . . with Children* and starring the great *Hathaway*er Peggy Cass, *Saturday Night Live*r Denny Dillon, and a British lesbian prostitute, *Women in Prison* transcends regular TV categories. It's not funny enough to be a sitcom. It's not exciting enough to be a drama. What is it?

♟ ♟

A Year at the Top, 1977. David Letterman's sidekick Paul Shaffer, with the help of uncle Mickey Rooney, refuses to sell his soul to the Devil to make it big in the music biz, even though Satan keeps tempting him, and tempting him, and tempting him.

♟ ♟ ♟

♟

And the Tammi for the worst sitcom in history goes to:

My Mother the Car, **1965–1966.** It was in the final year of the immensely popular *Dick Van Dyke Show* when we got to see Dick's little brother, Jerry, humiliate himself in what is universally thought to be the worst TV sitcom ever. Jerry finds a vintage 1928 Porter (a brand that never existed) in his garage, hears his late mother's voice calling, advising, kvetching—and makes television history. The writers' life goals seemed to be to stuff as many Jewish-mother cliches as possible into their allotted thirty minutes, the only plot interest was provided by an evil antiques collector who lusted after Mother, and Mother's full dramatic range is to nag ceaselessly, get drunk on antifreeze, and roll downhill.

My Mother the Car was so remarkably feeble, and Jerry (especially in relation to his wildly successful brother) was so pathetic, that we were transfixed by the horror through two full seasons. "No matter how well I did things, Dick could always do them five times better," said JVD. "I always came out the loser." To make this tragedy complete, the voice of Mother was provided by Ann Sothern, who, years earlier, was immensely popular in TV's *Ann Sothern Show* and *Private Secretary.*

♟ ♟ ♟ ♟ ♟ ♟

> There are days when any electrical appliance in the house, including the vacuum cleaner, seems to offer more entertainment possibilities than the TV set.
>
> —Harriet Van Horne

♟

The Golden Tammi—for the worst show in the history of television—goes to:

On the Air, **1992.** From David Lynch and Mark Frost, creators of the much-lamented *Twin Peaks,* and featuring Ian Buchanan, Nancye Fergu-

**Jerry Van Dyke and his beloved mum in the magnificent
classic, *My Mother the Car* (Photofest)**

son, Mr. Mike, and all the other *Peaks* regulars who couldn't get movie
jobs, *On the Air* concerns the zany backstage antics of *The Lester Guy
Show,* a live 1957 television broadcast. The theme music (from *Peaks*'s
Angelo Badalamente) alternates languid jazz sax with spitting and farting
noises, while the show's style is cartoony characters doing slapstick and
sight gags—made by people who don't care for sight gags, don't enjoy
slapstick, and don't understand cartoons.

"Lite" ideas (such as the director's incomprehensible Eastern European
accent, his sticking his head backward into a megaphone, and dog vomit)
that might be entertaining for a moment, are repeated endlessly. Blinky
the soundman is afflicted with "Bozeman's Simplex," giving the show an
excuse to do prehistoric MTV-style video collages. While Buchanan is
perfect as oozing Hollywood scum Mr. Guy (and Snaps the dog gives the
performance of a lifetime), feminist scholars might find the show misogynistic, as all the women are either morons or whores. In *On the Air*'s defense, however, all the men are equally morons or whores.

You never watched when this, the worst show in the history of television, was *On the Air*—and aren't you sorry now?
(Photofest)

Like the notorious turkey *Hudson Hawk,* this show reeks of coming from egomaniacs who think any idea they have *must* be great (as the program cuts to scenes of its inane home viewers, it's obvious what its creators think of us). *On the Air* is so shockingly bad, in fact, that it can't even be watched on the air; you keep becoming so stupefied by what you're seeing that following the plot becomes impossible, and it needs to be on videotape so, as you fall comatose, you can keep rewinding and playing, rewinding and playing, rewinding and playing, to understand what's going on. Only three episodes were ever broadcast; advertisers avoided the show in droves; and rumor has it that Lynch tried to have his name taken off the credits. Just as *On the Air* was premiering, in fact, parents Lynch and Frost divorced, permanently dissolving their creative partnership.

> Television is a triumph of equipment over people, and the minds that control it are so small that you could put them in a gnat's navel with room left over for two caraway seeds and an agent's heart.
>
> —Fred Allen

AVAILABLE ON VIDEO

Your local video store should be able to order any of the following for you. But if they pretend they can't, you can try the following excellent sources. Write, and ask for their catalogs:

Filmfax Products
P.O. Box 1900
Evanston, IL 60204

Video Resources
220 West 71st Street
New York, NY 10023

Hardcore Hobbies
P.O. Box 4098—Parkside Station
Forest Hills, NY 11375

Video Yesteryear
Box C-137
Sandy Hook, CT 06482

Sal Mauriello
P.O. Box 97
Wayne, NJ 07474-0097

The Adventures of Ozzie and Harriet
The Andy Griffith Show
Back to the Beach
Batman
Beulah Land
The Beverly Hillbillies
Bigfoot and Wildboy
The Boy in the Plastic Bubble
Born Innocent
Cannibal Women in the Avocado
    Jungle of Death
Can't Stop the Music
Cat Women on the Moon
Chained for Life
Change of Habit
Child Bride of Short Creek
The Conqueror
Cruise into Terror
Dark Shadows
Demon Seed
The Devlin Connection
Diary of a Teenage Hitchhiker
D.O.A.

Dragon Seed
Elvis and Me
Fer-de-Lance
Flash Gordon
Flipper
Forbidden Love
Frankenhooker
Hullabaloo
Humanoid Defender
In Search Of . . .
Lassie
Lisztomania
Little Ladies of the Night
Lost in Space
Madame Sin
Mafia Princess
Mame
The Dean Martin Show
Man from Atlantis
Mayflower Madam
Misfits of Science
Night of the Lepus
O'Hara's Wife

Out on a Limb
The Outer Limits
Police Squad!
Portrait of a Showgirl
Portrait of a Stripper
Rape and Marriage
Reform School Girls
Rude Dog
Secrets of a Married Man
Sins
Sing Along With Mitch

Skag
Sledge Hammer!
Space: 1999
Still the Beaver
Suburban Roulette
Three Sovereigns for Sarah
Trilogy of Terror
Twin Peaks
When Things Were Rotten
The Loretta Young Show

NETWORK ADDRESSES

If you'd like to help restore these wonderful programs to the airwaves where they belong, write to the following:

ABC, Inc.
77 West 66th Street
New York, New York 10023-6298

American Movie Classics (AMC)
150 Crossways Park West
Woodbury, New York 11797

Arts & Entertainment Network
(A&E)
235 East 45th Street
New York, New York 10017

Black Entertainment Television
(BET)
1232 31st Street, Northwest
Washington, D.C. 20007

Bravo
150 Crossways Park West
Woodbury, New York 11797

CNBC
2200 Fletcher Avenue
Fort Lee, New Jersey 07024

Cable News Network (CNN)
One CNN Center, Box 105366
Atlanta, Georgia 30348

CBS, Inc.
51 West 52nd Street
New York, New York 10019

Cable-Satellite Public Affairs
Network (C-SPAN)
400 North Capitol Street,
Northwest, Suite 650
Washington, D.C. 20001

The Christian Broadcasting
Network
100 Centerville Turnpike
Virginia Beach, Virginia 23463

Cinemax
1100 Avenue of the Americas
New York, New York 10036

The Discovery Channel
7700 Wisconsin Avenue
Bethesda, Maryland 20814-3522

The Disney Channel
3800 West Alameda Avenue
Burbank, California 91505

ESPN
ESPN Plaza
Bristol, Connecticut 06010

The Family Channel
100 Centerville Turnpike
Virginia Beach, Virginia 23463

The Financial News Network
(FNN)
6701 Center Drive West
Los Angeles, California 90045

Fox Television
205 East 67th Street
New York, New York 10021

Home Box Office, Inc.
1100 Avenue of the Americas
New York, New York 10036

Lifetime Television
Lifetime Astoria Studios
34-12 36th Street
Astoria, New York 11106

Madison Square Garden Network
(MSG)
2 Pennsylvania Plaza
New York, New York 10121

The Movie Channel
1633 Broadway
New York, New York 10019

MTV
515 Broadway
New York, New York 10036

NBC, Inc.
30 Rockefeller Plaza
New York, New York 10112

Nickelodeon
515 Broadway
New York, New York 10036

Showtime
1633 Broadway
New York, New York 10019

The Sports Channel
150 Crossways Park West
Woodbury, New York 11797

Turner Broadcasting System
(TBS)
One CNN Center, Box 105366
Atlanta, Georgia 30348

Turner Network Television
(TNT)
One CNN Center, Box 105366
Atlanta, Georgia 30348

The USA Network
1230 Avenue of the Americas,
18th floor
New York, New York 10020

SOURCES

Allman, Kevin. *TV Turkeys.* New York: Perigee Books, 1987.

Auletta, Ken. *Three Blind Mice: How the Networks Lost Their Way.* New York: Random House, 1991.

Billard, Mary. "True Story! A Month in the Victim-of-the-Week Business." *Spy,* April 1993.

Boldman, Craig. *Postcards from Twin Peaks.* CompuServe, 1992.

Bonderoff, Jason. *Soap Opera Babylon.* New York: Perigee Books, 1987.

Buckman, Peter. *All for Love: A Study in Soap Opera.* New York: Salem House, 1985.

Cannon, Bob. "1-800-BUY-THIS!" *Entertainment Weekly,* March 26, 1993.

Carlin, Peter. "The Jackpot in Television's Future." *The New York Times Magazine,* February 28, 1993.

Diamond, Edwin. "Last Tango." *New York,* October 19, 1992.

Dunne, John Gregory. *The Studio.* New York: Farrar, Straus & Giroux, 1968.

Fretts, Bruce. "Cross-Examining 'I Witness.' " *Entertainment Weekly,* April 2, 1993.

Friend, Tad. "Sitcoms, Seriously." *Esquire,* March 1993.

Gates, Anita. "Where Everybody Knows Your Job." *The New York Times,* February 21, 1993.

Gerani, Gary, and Paul Schulman. *Fantastic Television.* New York: Harmony Books, 1977.

Gitlin, Todd. *Inside Prime Time.* New York: Pantheon, 1983.

Goldberg, Lee. *Unsold Television Pilots,* rev. ed. New York: Citadel Press, 1991.

Goodman, Walter. "All That Piffle on TV? It's Someone Else's Fault." *The New York Times,* February 21, 1993.

Grossman, Gary. *Saturday Morning TV.* New York: Dell Publishing, 1981.

Harris, Mark. "Totally Knots." *Entertainment Weekly,* April 19, 1991.

Harris, Warren G. *Lucy & Desi.* New York: Simon & Schuster, 1991.

Kubey, Robert, and Mihaly Csikszentmihalyi. *Television and the Quality of Life: How Viewing Shapes Everyday Experience.* Philadelphia: Lawrence Erlbaum Associates, 1990.

Lapham, Lewis. "Tower of Babel." *Harper's,* November 1992.

Maheu, Robert. *Next to Hughes.* New York: HarperCollins, 1992.

Marill, Alvin. *Movies Made for Television.* New York: New York Zoetrope, 1984.

Martin, Mick, and Marsha Porter. *Video Movie Guide 1991.* New York: Ballantine Books, 1991.

McNeil, Alex. *Total Television,* 3rd ed. New York: Penguin Books, 1991.

Meisler, Andy. "When a Series Loses One of Its Own." *The New York Times,* November 8, 1992.

Paisner, Daniel. *Horizontal Hold: The Making and Breaking of a Network Television Pilot.* New York: Birch Lane Press, 1992.

Rovin, Jeff. *TV Babylon.* New York: New American Library, 1984.

Saxton, Martha. *Jayne Mansfield and the American Fifties.* Boston: Houghton Mifflin, 1975.

Schemering, Christopher. *The Soap Opera Encyclopedia.* New York: Ballantine Books, 1989.

Scott, Marvin. "Now He'll Say Goodbye." *Parade,* July 25, 1993.

Shales, Tom. *On the Air!* New York: Summit Books, 1982.

Silverman, Jeff. "Murder, Mayhem Stalk TV." *The New York Times,* November 22, 1992.

Stallings, Penny. *Forbidden Channels: The Truth They Hide from TV Guide.* New York: HarperCollins, 1991.

Stern, Jane and Michael. *The Encyclopedia of Bad Taste.* New York: HarperCollins, 1990.

Stern, Jane and Michael. *Jane & Michael Stern's Encyclopedia of Pop Culture.* New York: HarperCollins, 1992.

Terrace, Vincent. *Encyclopedia of Television.* New York: New York Zoetrope, 1986.

Terrace, Vincent. *The Ultimate TV Trivia Book.* Boston: Faber & Faber, 1991.

Thomas, Wes. "Four Arguments for the Redemption of Television," *Mondo 2000,* #9, 1993.

Tosches, Nick. *Dino: Living High in the Dirty Business of Dreams.* New York: Doubleday, 1992.

Weiner, Ed. and the editors of *TV Guide. The TV Guide TV Book.* New York: Harper Perennial, 1992.

Weinstein, Steve. "Against All the Odds, *Blossom* Is Blooming." *The Los Angeles Times,* February 15, 1993.

Weldon, Michael. *The Psychotronic Encyclopedia of Film.* New York: Ballantine, 1983.

Whiteside, Lee. *Sledge Hammer!: The Episode Guide.* CompuServe, 1991.

Williams, Barry. *Growing Up Brady.* New York: Harper Perennial, 1992.

Wolcott, James. "P.C. Cheesecake." *The New Yorker,* March 1, 1993.

Index

O

Z